REGIONAL INTERESTS IN EUROPE

THE CASS SERIES IN REGIONAL AND FEDERAL STUDIES
ISSN 1363-5670
General Editor: John Loughlin

This series brings together some of the foremost academics and theorists to examine the timely subject of regional and federal studies, which since the mid-1980s have become key questions in political analysis and practice.

1. *The Political Economy of Regionalism*
   edited by Michael Keating and John Loughlin

2. *The Regional Dimension of the European Union: Towards a Third Level in Europe?*
   edited by Charlie Jeffery

3. *Remaking the Union: Devolution and British Politics in the 1990s*
   edited by Howard Elcock and Michael Keating

4. *Paradiplomacy in Action: The Foreign Relations of Subnational Governments*
   edited by Francisco Aldecoa and Michael Keating

5. *The Federalization of Spain*
   Luis Moreno

6. *Local Power, Territory and Institutions in European Metropolitan Regions*
   edited by Bernard Jouve and Christian Lefevre

Regional Interests in Europe

Wales and Saxony as
Modern Regions

Jörg Mathias
Aston University

FRANK CASS
LONDON • PORTLAND, OR

First Published in 2004 in Great Britain by
FRANK CASS PUBLISHERS
Crown House 47 Chase Side, Southgate
London N14 5BP

and in the United States of America by
FRANK CASS PUBLISHERS
c/o ISBS, 920 58th Avenue, Suite 300
Portland, Oregon, 97213-3786

Website http://www.frankcass.com

Copyright © 2004 Jörg Mathias

British Library Cataloging in Publication Data:

Mathias, Jörg
   Regional interests in Europe: Wales and Saxony as modern regions
   1. European Union – Wales 2. European Union – Germany – Saxony
   3. Wales – Economic conditions 4. Wales – Economic policy 5. Saxony (Germany) –
   Economic conditions 6. Saxony (Germany) – Economic policy
   I. Title
   338.9'429

ISBN 0-7146-5583-X

Library of Congress Cataloging-in-Publication Data:

Mathias, Jörg
   Regional interests in Europe: Wales and Saxony as modern regions/Jörg Mathias.
      p. cm.
   Includes bibliographical references and index.
   ISBN 0-7146-5583-X (cloth) – ISBN 0-7146-8467-8 (pbk.)
   1. Regional planning–Wales. 2. Regional planning–Germany–Saxony.
   3. Regional planning–European Union countries. I. Title.

HT395.G72W325 2003
307.1'2'09429–dc22

2003055416

*Typeset in 10/12.5pt Palatino by FiSH Books, London
Printed in Great Britain by MPG Books Ltd, Victoria Square, Bodmin, Cornwall*

Contents

Preface by John Loughlin   vii

List of Tables   ix

Acknowledgements   xi

List of Abbreviations   xiii

Introduction   xvii

1   Regions and Regional Development in the
Competitive Environment of the European Union   1

2   Regional Socio-economic Conditions, Interests and Strategies:
Wales and Saxony   30

3   Public Actors in Regional Development   79

4   New Forms of Public–Private Interaction in Wales and Saxony   110

5   Conclusions: What Makes a Modern Region?   136

Appendices

A. The REGE Wales Project   163
   A1.   The International Framework of the Project, and European
        Comparison   163
   A2.   Return Ratios and Composition of the Welsh Panel of
        Respondents   169
   A3.   Text of the REGE Wales Questionnaire   171

B. Overview of Interviews   191
   B1.   Interview Methodology   191
   B2.   Standard Interview Structure   192
   B3.   Institutions Interviewed in Wales   193
   B4.   Institutions Interviewed in Saxony   193

Bibliography   197

Index   211

Preface

Jörg Mathias is part of the second generation of scholars who have pushed forward the analysis of the regional question from a political science perspective. The great merit of these scholars' work is that it has an important empirical focus, while it is also grounded in the theoretical debate on territorial politics which has developed over the last fifteen years or so. One part of the research presented here by Mathias has its origins in one of the few broadly based empirical regional research programmes (REGE), led by Beate Kohler-Koch of Mannheim and including the present author, that have been conducted in Western Europe. Mathias, working in collaboration with myself, was responsible for much of the evidence collection in the Welsh case. However, Mathias's research project led him to expand on this initial research by also studying the region of Saxony. The outcome has been a highly impressive comparison of the two regions. As a native of that region but also with a near perfect command of English and an impressive knowledge of the Welsh scene, the author was particularly well-placed to carry out this comparison.

The emphasis in this work, as in the original REGE project, was on regional 'actors'. Mathias places these in the context of considerable change in both Saxony and Wales over the past fifteen or twenty years. Among his most important insights is the emergence of 'Europe' as a factor structuring new forms of public–private interaction in both Wales and Saxony. In the case of Wales, this restructuring has received a further boost following the devolution reforms and the setting up of the Welsh Assembly in 1998. Although the Welsh empirical research was carried out before devolution and, indeed, devolution was still only a twinkle in the eye of some parts of the Opposition, it demonstrates that the ground was already being laid for this. Finally, Mathias offers some valuable and interesting reflections on the meaning of what is a 'modern region', which will provide further stimulus to this increasingly important debate.

John Loughlin
Cardiff
October 2003

List of Tables

2.1	Distribution of Employment in Wales, 1989–94	39
2.2	Regional Development Funding Available in the Industrial South Wales (Objective 2) Area, 1994–96	41
2.3	Gross Domestic Product in Saxony, 1991–99	44
2.4	Employment in Saxony, by Sector, 1991–99	46
2.5	Use of ERDF Funds in Saxony, 1991–93	48
2.6	Regional Development Funding Available in Saxony, 1994–99	49
2.7	Welsh Local Government Reform: Territorial Changes, 1996	55
2.8	Distribution of Welsh Westminster Seats among the Parties in the 1992, 1997 and 2001 General Elections	62
2.9	Membership of Parties in Saxony, 1990–99, and Distribution of Saxon *Landtag* and Bundestag Seats in the 1990, 1994 and 1998/99 Elections	70
3.1	Regional Development Funding for the New *Länder*, 1991–93	102
4.1	Public Accountability of Quangos in the UK, 1995	116
4.2	REGE Panel Perceptions of Relative Overall and Networking Importance of Actors in Regional Development in Wales, 1996	124
4.3	REGE Panel Perceptions of Relative Influence of Actors on Various Stages of Regional Development Projects in Wales, 1996	126
4.4	Volume of Saxon Foreign Trade with Selected Countries, 1995 and 1999	130
A1.1	Composition of the European Panel	164
A1.2	The Importance of Regional Government in General, and with Regard to Regional Development Policy and R&D Policy in Particular	165
A1.3	Should Regions have a Greater Influence Within the EU in General, and Should Regions have More Direct Say in the Shaping of EU R&D Policy?	165
A1.4	Expected Features of a 'Europe of the Regions'	166
A1.5	Views on the Economic Impact of Establishing the Single European Market, in Particular Whether it Would be Useful to	

        Follow the Market-oriented Trend within the Single Market,
        and Whether EU Competition Regulations have Harmful
        Effects on the Regional Economy   166
A1.6 How are Structural Funds from the EU Reaching the Region
        Perceived by Those Whom They are Destined For?   167
A1.7 General Perceptions of the Political Climate in the Region 167
A1.8 The Role of Public Actors in Public–Private Relationships: Does
        the Regional Government Usually Set the Right Priorities?
        Is the Regional Government the Primary Source of Initiatives?
        Are Public Servants Usually Open to Outside Suggestions?
        Are the Interests of Important Groups Usually Disregarded in
        the Process of Public Policy-making?   168
A1.9 Which Campaigning private Interest Groups Should have
        More Influence in the Future?   168
A2.1 Questionnaires Sent Out per Area and Actor Category   169
A2.2 Returns per Area and Actor Category   170
A2.3 Return Ratio per Area   170
A2.4 Return Ratio per Actor Category   170

Acknowledgements

To a very large extent, this book is the result of my research for a Ph.D. degree at the University of Wales, Cardiff, conducted between 1995 and 2000. Naturally, I am particularly indebted to my supervisor there, Professor John Loughlin, for his invaluable advice and support throughout all stages of the work. Also, I would like to express my gratitude to the members of the team working on the international research project, REGE, co-ordinated by Professor Beate Kohler-Koch, University of Mannheim, Germany, whose invaluable work on the REGE methodology contributed significantly to the design and conduct of the empirical part of this book. Similar thanks are due to the numerous representatives of institutions and organisations interviewed in Wales and Saxony who gave their time and expert knowledge so freely. I am also grateful to my German friends and colleagues Anett Pförtner, Thomas Kuzias, Karsten Neumann, Jens Posselt and Uwe Steinmetz, who, over the years, have consistently helped me to gather up-to-date data on Saxony and provided considerable support during my fieldwork in the region. Finally, a special acknowledgement is due to Professors Jeremy Richardson and Jim Bulpitt (†), then of the University of Warwick, Coventry, without whose support in the early stages this book would probably not have been written.

List of Abbreviations

ABM	*Arbeitsbeschaffungsmaßnahme(n)*
ADC	Association of [Welsh] District Councils
AEBR	Association of European Border Regions
AER	Assembly of European Regions
AM	Member of the Welsh Assembly
AWC	Association of Welsh Counties
BGB	Bürgerliches Gesetzbuch
BZfPB	*Bundeszentrale für Politische Bildung*
CBC	County Borough Council
CBI	Confederation of British Industry
CCT	compulsory competitive tendering
CDU	Christlich-Demokratische Union (GDR and FRG)
CEDRE	European Centre for Regional Development
Commission	Commission of the European Communities
CoR	Committee of the Regions of the European Union
CPMR	Conference of Peripheral Maritime Regions
DBD	Demokratische Bauernpartei Deutschlands (GDR)
DBRW	Development Board for Rural Wales
DDR	see 'GDR'
EAGGF	European Agricultural Guidance and Guarantee Fund
EEC	European Economic Community
EP	European Parliament
ERDF	European Regional Development Fund
ESF	European Social Fund
EU	European Union
FDGB	Freier Deutscher Gewerkschaftsbund (GDR)
FDP	Freie Demokratische Partei
FRG	Federal Republic of Germany
FSB	Federation of Small Businesses (Wales)
FUW	Farmers' Union of Wales
GA	Gemeinschaftsaufgabe [Verbesserung der regionalen Wirtschaftsstruktur]

GBl.	*Gesetzblatt* (GDR)
GDP	gross domestic product
GDR	German Democratic Republic
GG	Grundgesetz [für die Bundesrepublik Deutschland]
Grüne	Bündnis 90/Die Grünen
IGC	Intergovernmental Conference
HoL	House of Lords
KAB	Bundesverband der Katholischen Arbeitnehmerbewegung
KPD	Kommunistische Partei Deutschlands (GDR, 1945–46)
LDPD	Liberaldemokratische Partei Deutschlands (GDR)
LVZ	Leipziger Volkszeitung
MdB	Mitglied des [Deutschen] Bundestags
MEP	Member of the European Parliament
MLG	multi-level governance
MP	Member of Parliament
NAW	National Assembly for Wales
NDPB	non-departmental public body
NDPD	Nationaldemokratische Partei Deutschlands (GDR)
NF	Neues Forum
NFU	National Farmers' Union
PDS	Partei des Demokratischen Sozialismus
PFI	Private Funding Initiative
quango	quasi-non-governmental organisation
R&D	research and development
REGE	*Regionales Regieren in Europa: Regionen als Handlungseinheiten in der europäischen Politik*
RETI	Association of European Regions of Industrial Technology
RTP	Regional Technology Plan
Sächs.	*Sächsisch (-er; -e; -es)*
SächsPolG	Polizeigesetz des Freistaates Sachsen
SALZfPB	Sachsen-Anhaltinische Landeszentrale für Politische Bildung
SDA	Scottish Development Agency
SEA	Single European Act
SED	Sozialistische Einheitspartei Deutschlands (GDR)
SLA	Statistisches Landesamt [des Freistaates Sachsen]
SME	small and medium-sized enterprise
SMWA	Sächsisches Staatsministerium für Wirtschaft und Arbeit
SNP	Scottish National Party
SP	Scottish Parliament
SPD	Sozialdemokratische Partei Deutschlands
TEC	Training and Education Council
TEU	Treaty [of Maastricht] on European Union

THA	*Treuhandanstalt*
TUC	Trades Union Congress
UK	United Kingdom
US	United States
WDA	Welsh Development Agency
WEC	Wales European Centre [Brussels]
WLGA	Welsh Local Government Association
WO	Welsh Office

Introduction

The problem of how to organise and manage the process of sustainable regional development has recently come to the fore in many places across the industrialised countries of Central and Western Europe, and especially within the European Union (EU). Numerous empirical studies on European regions have indicated that now is the time to conceive and implement innovative courses of action required to face new economic, social and cultural challenges while dealing with the legacy of the past in an appropriate way (Bullmann, 1994; Keating, 1995; Keating and Loughlin, 1997; Jeffery, 1996; Kohler-Koch, 1996; Lynch, 1996). This process, however, does not occur in a vacuum. Regions face various natural, economic, social, socio-cultural, political and administrative conditions when embarking on a development process. There are also a number of influences from the outside world reaching a region, whether these are welcomed by regional actors or not. To begin with, three obvious factors can be distinguished: the activities of states to which regions belong, and of neighbouring regions either within or outside the borders of the same state; the activities of the EU and its member states, and subsidiary agencies acting on behalf of the union; and processes of economic and social integration on an even larger, possibly global scale, mainly brought about by multinational corporations, internationally operating non-governmental organisations and international agreements entered into by the region's home state or the EU. This situation suggests that regional development is a complex and multi-faceted task, comprising socio-economic, political and socio-cultural elements.

The aim of this book is to investigate ways and means by which political actors in EU regions that are not marginalised but are nevertheless less well-developed try to create and implement strategies of regional development in the context of globalisation processes and regional policy-making by EU institutions and national governments. The book further seeks to investigate to what extent some regions, ostensibly developing into socio-economic policy-makers in their own right, influence processes of policy-making in some policy areas at the national and EU levels of government.

These questions are embedded in the more general debate on the nature of the EU integration process, and the means by which further integration may be achieved. Regional actors could potentially develop into major European actors insofar as readjustments of the EU polity are concerned, which in turn might lend itself to a reshaping of the EU's policy-making if not its governmental system; i.e. its system of governance, not its system of government (Rhodes, 1993; Kohler-Koch; 1996). Therefore, an investigation is called for concerning the various configurations, characteristics and political behaviour of present-day EU regions, with particular reference to their policy-making processes and interest representation activities. The main focus here will be on the activities and interests of key political actors in the regions, and their political behaviour in pursuit of these interests. These questions will be looked at in turn.

Chapter 1 surveys the state of debate in the current literature on regions and regional development in the EU. The main focus here is on the treatment of the regional question in European integration, with further reference to external circumstances, such as globalisation. Utilising the concept of multi-level governance and other, to some extent related, models of analysing the changing nature of governance in the EU (e.g. Keating, 1992; Loughlin, 1994, 1996; Kohler-Koch, 1996, 1998), the state of the theoretical debate on regions and their activities is summarised. The empirical part of this book consists of a comparative analysis of regional interest formation, and the behaviour of regional political actors in the pursuit of these interests. Thus, Chapter 2 introduces Wales and Saxony by way of mapping the socio-economic background of their two polities, and charting the structure of the relevant political actors in these regions. Chapter 3 takes a closer look at the changing nature, and the new roles, of the public actors in Wales and Saxony; and Chapter 4 explores the developing landscape of semi-public and private actors, and investigates new forms of public–private partnerships and related forms of co-operation.

Most of the empirical data presented in the Welsh part of the empirical analysis derive from the Regional Development and its European Dimension in Wales research project (see Appendix A), conducted by Professor John Loughlin and myself at the School of European Studies, University of Wales, Cardiff, between April 1995 and January 1997. This project consisted of a questionnaire survey of 123 public, semi-public and private institutions and organisations in Wales, on various themes associated with the structure of the Welsh actor landscape, the nature of politics in Wales, the development of regional interests and means of interest representation, and the impact of the European Research and Development Fund (ERDF) and of other EU funds received by Welsh actors. Particular reference was made to the processes of regional development policy and research and development policy. The data of the questionnaire survey were supplemented by the study of relevant policy documents published by Welsh actors, and a series of interviews with some key representatives of Welsh organisations between 1996 and 1999.

The Welsh project was part of a larger international research project, *Regionales Regieren in Europa: Regionen als Handlungseinheiten in der europäischen Politik* (Regions as Political Actors in Europe, an integration better known by its German acronym REGE, which was devised and co-ordinated by Professor Beate Kohler-Koch and her team at the Mannheim Centre for European Social Research, University of Mannheim, Germany, and included copartner institutions in Barcelona, Lyon and Montpellier.[1] The project compared nine EU regions along the lines indicated above. Key findings regarding the European comparison have already been published (Kohler-Koch u.a., 1998; Negrier, 1998).

As Saxony was not one of the regions investigated in the REGE project, the Saxon data have been obtained by searching the available government and other official documents, and policy statements by non-public actors.[2] The main source of information, however, was a series of interviews with representatives of Saxon institutions and organisations, conducted by myself at different periods between 1995 and 1999[3]

The final chapter summarises the empirical findings, and conclusions are drawn concerning the present and potential future roles of regions within the EU system of governance.

NOTES

1. A full list of these copartners and the individuals who worked for them on the REGE project is given in Appendix A1.
2. The academic literature on post-1990 Saxony is still rather thin.
3. All interviews took place under strict assurances of confidentiality, commonly known as Chatham House Rules.

1

Regions and Regional Development in the Competitive Environment of the European Union

THE REGIONAL QUESTION IN THEORIES OF INTEGRATION

A remarkable phenomenon presents itself right at the start of the investigation: the absence of a distinguished regional question from much of the European integration debate right up to the late 1980s. The belonging of regions to states as the key actor in European politics for the best part of the last two centuries has brought the regions and 'stateless nations' (Nagel, 1994) right into the maze of European power politics, but usually as objects rather than subjects acting on their own accord. Until the 1960s, the EU followed this trend as many member states regarded the 'regional question' as one of only domestic concern (Loughlin, 1996), to be dealt with as seen fit by the member states' individual governments. The result of this was the absence of a distinct EU regional policy beyond some general provisions designed to facilitate economic cohesion, as planned and implemented by the member states' governments. It was not until the 1970s that the EU 'discovered' its regions – and then only in an economic sense, as having different problems and needs (Loughlin, 1995).

It took another 20 years or so, and three major reforms of EU regional policy, until the regions were eventually recognised as political actors, with the establishment of the Committee of the Regions of the European Union (CoR), and the ERDF demand to consult with sub-national decision-makers – a practical implication of the 'principle of partnership', inviting regions to participate in the construction of that elusive 'ever closer union' set out in the Treaty on European Union (TEU). Nevertheless, the present EU system seems to focus on economic cohesion by all means, including political integration. This may be one reason why seemingly quite different regions with regard to identity, political and economic history and political culture nevertheless appear to produce some surprisingly similar policy outputs in terms of regional development practices, patterns of political behaviour and community development. However, the drive to bring about integration 'from above' has, on the other hand, given rise to suspicions among a considerable number of regional actors from different national backgrounds that in a European 'super-state' regional interest representation might be more difficult to achieve than within the nation-states of old. Therefore, it is essential to investigate what the current ideas on European integration hold in store for the regions.

Neofunctionalism versus Liberal Intergovernmentalism

The two main models on European integration that have emerged over the last few years are known as neofunctionalism and liberal inter-governmentalism. Both are rooted in similar concepts developed earlier, such as pan-Europeanism and federalism, and mutual security concepts derived from international relations theory. The two approaches started to emerge in the 1950s, and reached their first peak in the late 1960s. At that time, major steps towards European integration had just been completed, but limited ideas were available as to the direction and speed, or even desirability, of further progress. Modern versions of the two approaches add a number of specific features to the respective models, in an effort to understand why, how, and with what intentions in the minds of the key actors such major developments as the Single European Act (SEA) and the TEU came into being.

Neofunctionalist approaches, such as the one taken by the model's 'founding father' E. Haas (Haas, 1958, 1964, 1970), and later efforts by W. Sandholz and J. Zysman (Sandholz and Zysman, 1989; Sandholz, 1994), have presented us with a view of the process of European integration that focuses on the claim that certain policy problems are best dealt with on the European level – for instance, because a considerable amount of international co-operation is already going on in that particular field, or because it is perceived by specific interest groups concerned that in order to enhance competition certain market regulations need to be harmonised. Placing those issues in the hands of supranational institutions is an idea that derives not from national governments, but rather from specific interest groups such as business communities or other internationally operating associations, who may form pressure groups or lobbying organisations to force the thinking and action of political decision-makers into the desired directions. Once supranational decision-making is established in one field (for example, the European Coal and Steel Community), there will be a growing interest and hence growing pressures to proceed along similar lines in other policy areas as well. This line of thinking became known as 'spill-over' theory (Cram, 1997). The concept of spill-overs was later refined into a system of cross-interference among various policy areas due to a growing mutual interdependence of decision-making in these areas, before finally ending up in J. J. Richardson's 'garbage cans of primeval soup' (Richardson, 1996), where free-floating ideas gain buoyancy through sufficient backing by certain interest groups employing scientific expertise, in an otherwise uncertain world of political chance. In addition, already established supranational institutions will be able to exercise their influence with a view to broadening supranational decision-making and hence gaining more influence for themselves and their political allies.

Faced with these pressures, national governments would be forced to go along with this and to set up the necessary legislation, even though that includes some transfer of sovereignty. The motivation for these governments would be that it could be shown either that such a supranational approach is indeed in the best interest of the participating nations, or that non-participation would in the long run leave the reluctant government concerned with competitive disadvantages and a correspondingly hostile domestic business community. Either way, the bandwagon would be rolling relentlessly. The main job for a political analysis of the integration process would therefore be to focus on the roles of internationally operating interest groups, and the workings of supranational organisations. Indeed, a number of analyses following this approach were published in the late 1990s (see, for example Wincott, 1995; Richardson, 1996; Cram, 1997). However, it is worthwhile bearing in mind Cram's observation that 'the focus of study for neofunctionalists was the process of political integration itself' (Cram, 1997: 13); apparently the contents of policies and the external circumstances in which they occurred were to be investigated only to the extent necessary to highlight their existence as the rationale for altering the processes and procedures of integration. But even when sticking to a more or less 'pure' investigation of the processes, it is probably unjustified to dismiss national governments as no longer really relevant. Indeed, why would they be the target of such massive lobbying and other pressures if the alliances of international interests, together with their friends in the supranational institutions, could go all the way just by themselves? Despite the growing influence of the European Parliament (EP), the still very important role of the Council of Ministers as a decision-maker is a valid indicator of the influence of national governments. However, it has to be conceded that the function of policy initiation is now almost exclusively outside the Council's sphere of activities, their legal rights in that respect notwithstanding.

On the other hand, liberal intergovernmentalist approaches focus on the activities of states and their governments when analysing European integration. Central to this approach is the view that integration happens only if and when there is a mutuality of national interests as perceived by the respective governments. The governments then set up the necessary regulatory agencies, empowered to act on behalf of all the participating governments. Supranational institutions therefore would be little more than the extended arm of the governments of the member states, though a fairly strong one, drawing on the collective muscle of all the participants. There can be little doubt that this view was shared by most member states' governments in the early days of the European Economic Community.

It is still possible to find strong arguments for the view that national governments remain, for the time being, the decisive actors in the process of European integration. Indeed, the analyses presented between 1991 and 1995 by the leading present-day liberal intergovernmentalist Andrew Moravcsik are persuasive. The point that distinguishes his approach from traditional analyses of relations between states fostering their national interest is that he assumes an openness and flexibility in the formation of national interests. This allows for major shifts of policy – and hence bargaining positions in international negotiations – under the influence of pressure groups demanding further integration, and for suddenly 'available issue linkages' (Moravcsik, 1993: 482). Therefore, he claims, 'liberal intergovernmentalism integrates within a single framework two types of general international relations theory often seen as contradictory: a liberal theory of national preference formation and an inter-governmentalist analysis of interstate bargaining and institutional creation' (Moravcsik, 1993: 482).

He further claims that the institutions created in the process of European integration could not automatically be regarded as supranational. Their very existence and ability to act would be wholly dependent on the agreement of the national governments. In his view, 'intergovernmental institutionalism is based on three principles: intergovernmentalism, lowest-common-denominator-bargaining, and strict limits on future transfers of sovereignty' (Moravcsik, 1991: 25).

One can hardly escape the impression that this approach is influenced by concepts developed to describe processes in domestic politics in the United States (US). The supposed openness of decision-makers and their keen eye for issue linkages are a virtual mirror-image of the 'wheeling and dealing' by which the decision-making process in Congress is usually characterised. By the same token, the dependence of the powers of the institutions on the agreement, or at least acquiescence, of the national governments, which are then bound by the institutions' decisions, bear more than a faint resemblance to the 'consent of the governed' outlined in the preamble of the US constitution, although member state governments today would probably find it hard to 'alter or abolish' the institutions already created.[1] However, while in principle there is nothing wrong with comparing the processes in Europe with the American case, one should be careful to avoid a strictly structuralist view on the integration process. This question arose in the debate on the US political system too, and it was pointed out as early as 1908 by no less an authority than Woodrow Wilson that government 'is not a machine but a living thing ... shaped to its functions by the sheer pressures of life. ... No living thing can have its organs offset against each other as checks, and live' (Wilson, 1908: 56–7).

What is remarkable about both neofunctionalism and liberal intergovernmentalism is the fact that neither comes up with a detailed argument on the question of regional policy. This apparent omission might be justified insofar as the regional question captured the attention of key political actors on the European level rather late in the integration process. However, the problem had been around long enough, and was important enough, even at the time of the SEA debate, to merit a somewhat larger amount of consideration than it actually did receive by proponents of the two schools. This gives rise to the suspicion that it is the nature of the regional question itself that makes it unsuitable as a 'pet example' for either side. However, if the reason for the omission were indeed to be found in the nature, i.e. the *contents* of regional policy, we would also have a strong indication of the insufficiency of neofunctionalist attempts to stick to an investigation of the *process* of integration.

One has to be grateful to Sandholz (1994) for reminding us of the twin character of the EU as comprising both supranational and intergovernmental constituent elements, and that 'the intergovernmentalist-institutionalist dichotomy ... neglects important aspects of community politics that fit neither category' (Sandholz 1994: 259). The politics of regional policy seems to be an obvious candidate for being regarded as not fitting easily into either side of that divide, thus creating the need for a different, more flexible theoretical approach (see Kohler-Koch 1997; Knodt 1998).

From an intergovernmentalist point of view, problems associated with regional development can be regarded as essentially domestic issues, which then are, or are not – as governments of the respective member states see fit – brought to the attention of EU institutions. Loughlin (1996) accepts this view as essentially sound for the period leading up to the early 1970s. Indeed, up to then, and to a lesser extent even up to now, governments of various member states were and are actively engaged in national efforts designed to overcome regional socio-economic disadvantages. Early examples of these efforts include the neo-Keynsian approach taken by Prime Minister Harold Wilson's government in the 1960s to create a 'level playing field' in the UK economy. While the city of Milton Keynes is a lasting legacy to this era, Thatcherism brought a swift and sharp end to these concepts. In Germany, regional development is first and foremost an issue in the competence of the *Länder*. However, in order to achieve the desired *Angleichung der Lebensverhältnisse* (cohesion of living conditions), national steering mechanisms for overcoming regional disparities are in place, the *Länderfinanzausgleich* (system of equalisation payments among the Länder). Originally devised to overcome the economic disparities between the relatively better-off West German *Länder* and those that were less developed, the system came close to breaking point when the East German *Länder* joined the Federal Republic. The southern European member states, in particular Italy and France, have their own set of regional disparities, and domestic histories of addressing them. Up to the early 1970s, those domestic efforts were only loosely connected to any policy-making by or through the EEC. From the mid-1970s onwards, member states basically agreed to make the question of regional development partially a European issue in order to ease the burden of domestic regional development programmes by distributing it across the other partners. The ERDF was created in 1975 in response to the 1973 enlargement, but regional policy as such remained a national competence. With the exception of the German *Länder*, therefore, the regions themselves were treated as objects of policy-making, with no voice of their own at the key negotiation tables in Europe. This strictly intergovernmentalist argument holds until 1988 – but events since then require reconsideration.

A neofunctionalist approach, however, would have to assume the existence of non-governmental interest groups that lobby EU institutions in order to bring about a shift in EU policies towards a recognition of regional representatives as political actors, and subsequently the embarkation of the EU on a course that suits the regional interest. This approach merits some consideration because a series of events which have taken place from the late 1980s onwards lends substance to this view. Representatives of regional interests appeared in strength in the European policy arena, and even set up agencies in Brussels. Some of them were representatives of regional and local governments, others represented regional business interests (Jeffery, 1996b). The 1988 reform of the Structural Funds can be seen as their first success: the EU institutions assessed regions independently of national governments' views according to socio-economic criteria for the purpose of determining their eligibility to receive EU funds. Formal and organisational developments, such as the creation of the CoR as part of the TEU can be seen as further steps along this road. The other main indicator in a neofunctionalist argument, the strengthening of supranational institutions, also took place in the same period.

Yet the appearance of representatives of regional interests was not the starting point for EU institutions to place a greater emphasis on the regional question. Almost the opposite seems to be the case: as the governments of the member states had already placed regional development on the European agenda, it suddenly made sense for regional actors to become interested in European questions too – hence their appearance. This new opportunity encouraged those regions which for one reason or another were dissatisfied with regional development policies run by the governments of their home countries. However, their idea to 'bypass' their national governments by approaching EU institutions directly has so far been blessed with limited success. Indeed, the limits to that neofunctionalist view on regional interest representation are best clarified by what was not done: the CoR was not endowed with significant powers to deal with regional or any other questions on behalf of the EU – indeed, what was particularly bemoaned by regional representatives was the fact that the CoR did not even get the right to sue other EU institutions before the European Court of Justice (Hrbek and Weyand, 1994). Most importantly, the final say on financial decisions that affect regional policy was not given away by the Council of Ministers. Within the present format of Structural Funds management, the influence of member-state governments is being felt distinctively at every turn in the process, from national vetting procedures for applications via decision-making in the Council to the actual handling – and possible 'pocket veto' – of the funds in the implementation phase.

A 'Europe of the Regions' versus Globalisation

As we have seen, neither neofunctionalism nor liberal intergovern-mentalism provide us with a sufficient model for understanding the role and political behaviour of regional actors, and regions as actors, in the EU. So how, then, do they fit into the picture of modern EU governance? More importantly still, to what extent, and how, do they contribute to any changes to that picture?

In some of the member states the regional level is by definition part of the system of governance: there are regional or groups of local governments possessing legal rights and powers granted to them by the respective states' constitutions or other acts of empowering legislation. Representatives of these regional governments are therefore not just another interest group, but limited holders of sovereignty. This not only gives them legitimacy when speaking for their area, but also makes them the envy of minority nationalists, and regionalists in territories where insufficient or no such arrangements are in place. When both groups of representatives come together, such as in the CoR or in the various inter-regional associations that have blossomed all over Europe over the last few years, there is always a chance that envy turns into active learning from each other – phenomena known as 'demonstration effects' (Lynch, 1996: 18). This holds not only in the field of mutual socio-economic interests but also in the form of nourishing political demands for more rights, influences and freedoms as enjoyed by the more fortunate regions. For many of these regions such policy learning from other European examples constitutes a natural extension of the fight for greater recognition that formerly had been played out predominantly on the domestic scene – in some cases, such as Catalonia and Wales, for centuries rather than decades.

Moreover, as Lynch (1996) has shown, the interest groups of regions and of stateless nations with regard to Europe may be intermingled to such an extent that it does not really matter whether an element of nationhood, or rather the deprivation of the recognition of such nationhood, comes into the equation. Regions which are not stateless nations can be just as vociferous when it comes to safeguarding their interests in Europe – and just as successful, or even more so than stateless nations, in the process: the German *Länder*, as opposed to the constituent parts of the UK, are a good example here. The key point is whether an element of statehood – as in the German and Austrian cases – is present in the constitutional arrangements.

With regard to the regions having a significant say in EU governance, however, what they have achieved in the TEU seems to be the limit of what can be accomplished for the time being, at least as far as institutionalised interest representation is concerned. There appears to be no real political will among the other significant actors in the EU policy arena to experiment with a possible further federalisation beyond the provisions of the TEU and the Amsterdam treaty, let alone thinking about a replacement of the 15 member states as the constituent elements of the union for a much larger number of regions taking on this role. This is not to say that some optimistic – and very ambitious – leaders of regional and nationalist parties would not like to see this happen. Among them, there seems to be a prevalent opinion that the regions, by means of inter-regional co-operation, would make a better job of developing a meaningful European integration than the present member states' governments. Lynch (1996: 135) has labelled this phenomenon 'transnational regionalism'. So far, the thrust of empirical inter-regional co-operation literature suggests that such co-operation is still in its early days. Also it is worth noting that not all the experiments in co-operation that have taken place in recent years were instant success stories.[2]

Indeed, are political activists demanding a counterbalance to the centralisation of power towards higher levels fighting a hopeless battle against the tide of history itself? Alexis de Tocqueville suspected as early as 1840 that in a democracy centralisation would be the 'natural order of government', with individual independence and local freedoms being 'the result of artificial efforts'.[3] Neither federalism – of both the continental and the Anglo-American variety (Loughlin, 1996: 142–3) – nor the concept of subsidiarity[4] have been fully able to negate the thrust for centralisation, which was usually dictated by economic, not political, progress. Nevertheless, over the last two decades or so, it has become obvious that 'economies of scale' have found their limit in the increased number of people and even entire regions excluded from socio-economic progress of that kind, and in territories whose social disadvantages of participation outweigh the benefits derived from it. So it is not surprising that regional interests in scaling down socio-economic operations emerged and found their political expression in demands for decentralisation, subsidiarity, and enhancing diversity.

What can be regarded as the latest product of that movement towards centralisation is the dual concept of globalisation, and localisation or regionalisation. Thus, on the one hand, it consists of the economic and social activities of multinational corporations and non-governmental organisations, on a truly global scale, that have little or no respect for geographical barriers, state borders or even the applicable law in certain areas of operation. This in turn leads to global competition for the attention of these multinational actors, forcing nations, regions and minor private actors to compete for investment and for orders for goods and services. On the other hand, it consists of people of the territory concerned striving for local or regional self-reliance or even self-sufficiency and for relatively closed production and distribution cycles, and having an interest in managing local problems.

Even so, however, globalisation is by no means a new phenomenon. From Alexander the Great via the crusaders, the Romans, the Mongols, the Iberian *conquistadores*, and the Dutch, French and British empire-builders of the second half of the second millennium to the development of postwar super-powers, world history is full of endeavours to expand one's sphere of influence, economic power, and wealth. Throughout history, though, globalisation has always been a rich man's prerogative. Large-scale military campaigns, great exploratory voyages, and the development of reliable communication and transport links between the far-flung corners of one's empire took time and much money, and hence were usually affordable only to states.

Today, the balance of economic power between public and private actors has changed to an extent that private actors no longer need to hunt for business opportunities. Public actors, for the supposed benefit of their region, state or continent, go out of their way to offer those opportunities to them. Generous land allotments, infrastructure facilities at little or no cost to the investor, tax incentives, workforce qualification schemes, promises of exemption from – or at least the relaxation of – environmental protection rules, and similar measures now belong to the standard repertoire of public actors and their semi-public sales agents in the international competition for inward investment. There is hardly anything that potential investors cannot demand from a prospective location. This almost complete reversal of status between private and public actors is the key – and quite possibly the only really new – characteristic of present-day globalisation.

What is important from a political perspective, however, is that in democratic societies factional interests, using their own funds, cannot be prevented from utilising their civil liberties to further their business, even if their activities are not in the best interests of the society. As long as there is no general conflict of interests threatening the stability and safety of society, this is not only acceptable but may even be desirable in order to gain advantages in the global competition. The difficulties arise when there is an imminent or potential risk to the well-being of the people – which is supposed to be sovereign – which cannot properly be dealt with, for example threats to the environment.

Here we are up against the same problem that Locke, Rousseau, and the framers of the US Constitution – and in their wake many others, right up to the negotiators in the 1996 Intergovernmental Conference (IGC) – struggled so hard to come to terms with. Traditional means of checks against the tyranny of factions, such as outvoting them by the majority, or the imposition of state regulations, can no longer be relied upon to prevent undue harm – they are easily circumvented, again using the modern technology that allowed the modern version of globalisation in the first place. So, is it that Marx's nightmare vision of an ever more effective optimising of the use of capital through 'modern colonisation' (Marx, 1987: 792–3) has come true? If one were not prepared to go quite that far, political scientists now have taken to speculating about 'the end of domestic policy' (Voigt, 1998: 3) due to governance by networks of interest groups at home and globalisation worldwide. Hence, the quest is on for a new system of governance which allows progress through public and private initiative, and indeed competition, while safeguarding against catastrophic interruptions – natural as well as man-made – of the smooth running of that progress. That inevitably involves some element of highly centralised decision-making – albeit in a slightly different sense than the one speculated upon by Tocqueville. Once that is established, the central decision-making organs in turn need protection from being taken over by factions, thus creating a need for transparency of procedures, and meaningful democratic control.

As we have seen, while private interests have already established themselves on the global scene, public interests still lag behind in this respect. Far from being a central decision-making organ, the United Nations, despite the best efforts of its employees, was and still is little more than a lowest-common-denominator organisation with limited briefs and correspondingly low funds. Useful, and occasionally – against the odds – even successful in the fields of international security, and in the distribution of aid to the most deprived areas of the globe, it is virtually hopeless in the face of well-entrenched vested economic interests both public (national) and private.

The EU, still comprising less than half the countries of the world's second-smallest continent – but very densely populated and with one of the highest economic outputs in terms of gross domestic product (GDP) – has progressed somewhat further along the lines of developing into a centralised supranational decision-maker. Even the transfer of sovereignty from the member states to the central institutions is, in principle though not always in practice, no longer an issue. Undoubtedly, from the Treaties of Rome to the present day, this organisation and its central organs have greatly contributed to the solution of many of the continent's problems in a great variety of areas, though first and foremost in the socio-economic field.

However, the ways and means of governing this organisation always have been very much under debate, with one of the greatest issues in that debate being the question of democratic control. How could state governments, themselves only temporarily having been endowed with the powers of the sovereign by the people, possibly sign away those powers without adequate democratic checks in place? This is even more pressing insofar as the central institutions seem only too open to suggestions by factional interests.[5] The member states' ratification procedures of key agreements, in some cases also involving referenda, along with the strengthened role of the EP, go a long way towards alleviating the worst fears in that direction. However, not everybody seems to be quite satisfied, as was highlighted in the debates before and during the 1996 Intergovernmental Conference (IGC) (Falkner and Nentwich, 1995). In addition, the implementation of the European Social Charter remains dependent on the goodwill of member states' administrations, and social security provisions – such as there are – for those daring to use the SEA's 'free movement of labour' are still based on legislation dating back to 1971 (Europäische Kommission, 1994). However, this is not the place to start a further investigation in that direction.

But where does this leave the regions? Clearly, they are not endowed with the easy access to the central decision-making bodies, from which the member states' governments benefit. Even regions endowed with legal powers under domestic legislation usually enjoy only a limited freedom of manoeuvre when it comes to representing external interests officially (Loughlin and Peters, 1997). Regions lacking such official status are still worse off in that respect. Given the pressures to participate in the competition for investments, as outlined above, local and regional actors wish to present themselves and their places of origin in a favourable light on the international scene as best as they can. This is their key contribution to the present-day version of globalisation. No longer does the fear of being 'conquered' dominate regional actor behaviour, indeed a reversal of this situation seems to emerge. One has to compete for attention by strong, usually private economic actors, in a world where 'conquest' becomes 'development' and the 'fire and sword' is replaced by large sums of inward investment funds. Once the investors have started to reshape the traditional socio-economic lifestyle of society, however, fresh fears about the submergence of one's regional identity may arise, with much-bemoaned losses of independent decision-making capabilities, social status and cultural distinctness. The really influential private actors, it seems, are not particularly interested in these matters, unless there is an economic benefit to be gained from utilising a region's distinctness (Lange, 1998).

However, from the point of view of state government leaders it makes little sense to have one's regions engaged in a cut-throat competition that creates domestic unrest, eats up resources, and contributes to ever deepening disparities between regions rather than harmonisation and equality of living conditions. The EU institutions are of two minds: while regional activism can potentially be utilised to achieve cohesion throughout the Union, a greater regional involvement in decision-making may contribute to the creation of procedural, administrative and logistic structures that prove to be difficult to manage – with no guarantee that the cohesion, originally aimed for, is really going to be brought any closer.

Multi-level Governance

The most viable approach to solve this socio-economic, constitutional[6] and political conundrum seems to be the concept of 'multi-level governance' (MLG), developed by Gary Marks and others, notably Lisbet Hooghe. The basic concept of multi-level governance consists of a 'structure of authoritative decision-making – that is, the sum of rules, mainly formal but also informal, concerning the locus and practice of authoritative governance in a polity' (Marks, 1996: 22).

The key feature of this structure is a set of rules organising the functional division of labour among various levels of government. The nature of government here is, according to Marks, underpinned by three key assumptions: (1) that one has to make the distinction between political institutions and political actors; (2) that the state basically consists of a set of rules structuring authoritative relations in the polity, but not being itself an actor; and (3) that the orientation of political actors towards the rules that constrain them may change according to circumstances (Marks, 1996: 22).

The first two of these assumptions are a quite radical departure from previously established – in particular, intergovernmental – approaches which saw institutions as holders of interests, albeit changeable ones, and hence could afford to treat institutions and their representatives as interchangeable entities. In the MLG approach, the concept of 'national interest' or 'state interest' changes considerably. Focusing on political actors, i.e. real persons or groups, as holders of interests, it becomes clear that the same principle is applicable to government, being an institution of the state. As different groups win political power, i.e. the right to appoint key personnel and run state institutions, they bring along their interests and acquire the means to pursue them most efficiently – as long as they maintain the necessary popular support. Those interests, however, remain private, or factional, in nature, even when backed by the expressed will of a majority, and notwithstanding the fact that politicians in office love to claim to represent each and every individual and act to pursue or honestly broker the whole spectrum of interests prevalent in their society. As established general rules, for example constitutions, grant certain political actors the temporary right to use the state and its institutions, the capture of state institutions through success in elections is seen by the actors as a worthwhile prize.

This is not to say, however, that actors always get what they bargained for. As Marks puts it in his third assumption, the attitudes of political actors towards the established rules may change. After a succession of electoral defeats, for instance, certain actors might think along the lines of wishing to reform the established rules, for example by altering the electoral system, by limiting the formal powers of offices and institutions, by demanding more decentralised decision-making (devolution), or by establishing 'independent' watchdogs – supposedly 'beyond' the political system – to observe the proper discharge of certain necessary functions of the state regardless of who is in power. Outgoing governments might wish to fill public offices with their appointees, presenting their successors with administrations which are less favourably disposed towards the new regime.

However, political actors who have just been promoted into government office, too, might find that life on the government benches is much less comfortable than they imagined when still in opposition. On the state level, Marks has identified three scenarios in which government leaders themselves instigate action to deal with the various pressures put upon them as leaders:

A. Government leaders actually prefer to wash their hands of authority: they actively seek to shift responsibility for some set of decisions to sub-national or supranational actors. ...
B. Government leaders shift authority for some set of decisions not because they want to rid themselves of responsibility; but because some other concern outweighs their resistance. ...
C. Government leaders are unable to check or reverse dispersal of authority to sub-national or supranational institutions. (Marks, 1996: 25–32)

Taken together, these three scenarios provide another possible explanation to the question asked by intergovernmentalists and neofunctionalists alike, i.e. why so much progress in the integration process is happening. Here we also find a possible indication why state government representatives are prepared to sign away parts of the domestic decision-making power they fought so hard to win in the first place. It is noteworthy that this transfer of powers can be towards both the sub-national and the supranational levels.

From a theoretical point of view, this concept ostensibly presumes to some extent an involuntary off-loading operation by overstretched political actors unable to continue conducting the business of government by traditional means. One line of enquiry into why this situation has arisen now leads us into an investigation of the changing nature of the decision-making. Using Marks's definition of the state, i.e. a very weak view of the state as an actor, it becomes fairly easy to speculate about 'the nature of the state'.

More to the point, however, would be a functional analysis of the practice of governance, as taken on by the recipients of that former state authority. With regard to the supranational recipients, i.e. the EU institutions, Marks himself, along with Lisbet Hooghe (Hooghe and Marks, 1995), and also Hrbek and Weyand (1994), Christiansen (1995), Keating (1995), Richardson (1996), Jeffery (1996, 1996a) and Kohler-Koch (1996, 1998) have contributed significantly to such an analysis. The key focus of that research rested upon the ways and means of interest representation and channels of communication and influence between the different levels of government, thus enabling governance to be conducted in a system or network of 'vertical' co-operation among the different levels. The key findings of those investigations can be summarised as follows:

1. We are still in the early days of the emergence of such a multi-level system, which is not yet fully operational. It is also likely that rather than being a new system of governance in itself, MLG might well be a means to an end, i.e. the imperfect solution for the practical problem of conducting governance in a transitional period from the traditional system based on nation-states to a new system of which we know little so far.

2. MLG is a broad concept, but in practice there are a number of widely varying sub-systems or procedures employed in different states and in different policy areas, such as asymmetrical government and different devolution models, which cannot and should not be pressed into a rigid homogeneous framework.

3. In order to succeed in the long term, MLG-style structures of governance will have to be accompanied by a thorough application of the principles of subsidiarity and partnership, preferably on all levels, in order to avoid pitfalls in the integration process mainly associated with unnecessary friction.

4. Mainly advanced by Richardson (1996) and Cram (1997), the latest development is a reminder that an actor-centred approach needs to be taken not only with regard to state governments, but also in the investigation of supranational entities, as not only state institutions but also regional and European institutions have hardly any interest *per se* but are filled with representatives of political stakeholders promoting their own interests – hence the link to neofunctionalism.

However, while the MLG approach in general has received a very warm welcome within the academic community, political practitioners have so far taken only little note of the theoretical concept. Their hesitation is understandable, in particular because the principle of subsidiarity has not been well-received among regional political actors due to its distorted application in the TEU where it deliberately excludes the regions. That is not to say, however, that those actors were not facing changes in their polity environment which can be described in terms of MLG. Moreover, a considerable number of practitioners have acted upon these challenges, and have advanced political structures and procedures in ways which can be regarded as being in the style of MLG. Therefore, the remainder of this study utilises the MLG approach for the purpose of investigating the political behaviour of regional political actors.

REGIONS AND REGIONAL POLITICAL ACTORS IN EUROPE – A CONCEPTUAL
JUNGLE

Regions as Entities

What, exactly, are regions? The answer to that question often varies widely
according to one's own association with a certain level of government. It
varies, too, according to the specific function or policy area to be
investigated on a regional level. What we are dealing with here are sub-
state regions, not the geopolitical entities, such as Western Europe, that are
on occasions also referred to as regions (e.g. Haas, 1970). However, even on
the smaller, sub-state level there is no one definition of the term 'region'
that could be called paradigmatic. Academic researchers in regional
studies tend to use functional definitions geared towards their specific
research interest.

A very comprehensive attempt to classify concepts of regions was
undertaken by Keating and Loughlin (1997: 6–8; see also Loughlin, 1996:
147–8). They distinguish between:

1. Economic regions, mainly defined by economic criteria such as
    predominant patterns of industrial and agricultural production, the size
    and distribution of populations or similarly arbitrary designations by
    state governments for economic development purposes.

2. Historical or ethnic regions, marked by the traditionality of their
    existence as recognisable territorial units, often but neither inevitably
    nor exclusively populated by specific ethnic groups, as opposed to
    other such groups within the same state, and possessing a certain
    specific cultural and/or linguistic distinctiveness.

3. Administrative or planning regions, i.e. basically lines on a map drawn
    according to criteria of administrative convenience, population size,
    travel-to-work patterns and similarly bureaucratic definitions,[7]
    frequently used in territories which lack other regional features
    distinguishing them from the surrounding areas.

4. *Political regions*, recognisable by the existence of an elected legislative
    council, and a 'domestic' executive, of varying forms and powers, i.e. a
    regional government. Large political regions, such as the larger German
    Länder or the constituent parts of the UK, often contain within their
    territory a number of economic and administrative sub-regions.

Obviously these definitions, broad as they are, cannot be utilised easily. First, two or even three of the categories may be applicable to the same region. Economic homogeneity might coincide with historical patterns of settlement, and that region might even have its own government. Such a situation, however, must be regarded as the exception rather than the rule – however hard political actors in some regions which do not really fit that description might try to prove otherwise. Cultural distinctiveness, vociferously proclaimed by one group, might not be taken seriously – or even be regarded as offensive – by another group. Insensitive state governments of the past might have created administrative regions regardless of economic and socio-cultural criteria, and their successors might be unwilling to part with that practice. On the other hand, in cases where no ethnic consideration needs to be taken into account, historical sensitivity might have its own pitfalls. Had, for instance, the Germans in the postwar reconstruction period insisted on following the traditional pattern of political regions of the eighteenth and nineteenth centuries, they would have created an instant administrative nightmare.

The result of such a rather less sharp definition of the term 'region' is to some extent unavoidable, as regional structures and political practices based upon them vary widely throughout the EU (Loughlin and Peters, 1997; Loughlin, 2000), and occasionally even within the same member state. Keating has set out to put a positive spin on the latter phenomenon. Asking the rhetorical question 'What's Wrong with Asymmetrical Government?' (Keating, 1998: 195), he argues that asymmetrical structures are already present, and often have been for a long time, in some cases even centuries (for example, in the UK). They seem to work if not well so at least satisfactorily insofar as some form of preferential treatment for those regions which want it is being allowed, while the resulting disparities in representation on the state level have – 'surprisingly' – failed to develop into a major political issue in some member states, notably the UK and Spain, and also in Canada (Keating, 1998: 196–8).[8]

However, the practical political and administrative problems associated with such regional imbalances are not always particularly helpful in establishing and running an efficient system of governance. Enshrining such asymmetries formally as part of the rules by which the polity concerned is governed has therefore to be regarded as somewhat of a stop-gap solution, pending a negotiated settlement that accommodates the conflicting interests to the best possible extent while at the same time ensuring the establishment of a flexible and efficient system of decision-making and interest representation. These problems are more pronounced in multinational states, where the interests of different national or ethnic groupings have to be accommodated but where this has been done in the past to a not entirely satisfactory degree. Recent attempts at reform in these countries have not always helped to improve this situation (Loughlin and Mathias, 1996: 169–70).

The use of one particular description for certain regions might also indicate the pursuit of a specific agenda by the user. A persistent reference to a historical or ethnic region as a 'nation' or 'stateless nation' often implies that the user is of the opinion that such nationhood still lacks adequate recognition in political and socio-economic terms. On the other hand, for instance, Whitehall's use of the 'Standard Region' system in England (HoC, 1995: xvi) until 1999 indicated that region-making according to administrative convenience was still very much on the cards in the UK despite the significant progress towards devolution in other parts of the country. Only in 1999 was the English problem tackled by introducing a 'tripartite' regional government structure involving government offices, regional development agencies, and regional chambers elected from existing local authorities in the region (Sandford and McQuail, 2001). In other countries, for example Ireland, the creation of administrative or planning regions in recent years seemed to have as its main motivation to make the most of EU-induced regional economic development opportunities (Loughlin, 1996a 2000).

For the purpose of this study we follow the definition used in the REGE project, where 'the term "regions" refers to the political units [immediately] below the national level of EC member-states' (Kohler-Koch, 1995: 2). This definition refers to political regions. For the Saxon case this poses no problem as German *Land* conforms to the criterion of having its own government. Although Wales still has to be classified as an emerging political region, recent changes in its political and administrative set-up justify the use of this definition.

Regional Actors

Using the definition of regions as political entities, i.e. part of the system of governance, and following the actor-centred approach to MLG, what was postulated for the state and supranational levels of government would also be applicable in the investigation of the sub-national level too: regional institutions are filled with representatives of political actors promoting their own interests. While the sets of rules governing actor behaviour may vary from region to region, the principle of actors as the holders of interests remains. It would be those actors making use of whatever regional tools of governance are available. The tools themselves might be modernised as appropriate in varying circumstances – in practice a surprisingly low-key process when one thinks of it in terms of 'changing the nature of the state'. However, in this theoretical framework such modernisation processes are just an indicator for, and not the key contents of, the development of a region.

The present state of the debate in the literature on regions entering the political scene in the EU (see, for example, Négrier, 1997; Kohler-Koch, 1996, 1998; Knodt, 1998; Loughlin, 2000), suggests that it is highly appropriate and timely to investigate regional actors in closer detail – not regions as actors. The aim of this exercise is to determine regional actors' capabilities and possible functions as fully developed partners in a new system of governance in Europe. As a first approach to the question of who these actors are, one can distinguish three main categories: public, semi-public and private. What the actors in all three categories have in common is that they consist of individuals who join together in a group for the pursuit of a common group interest in one or more particular fields, including the economy, politics, social issues, the environment, and culture. Although there might be occasional exceptions in which an individual ostensibly acts alone (for example, independent members of legislative bodies, UK utility regulators), in order to succeed they need to obtain the backing of at least one of the other actors – and thus have to become representatives of interests which exceed their original, personal, scope. However, what is essential here is that we have to deal with real persons, not abstract or monolithic institutions.[9]

Public actors can be defined as groups of people running political institutions during a particular period in time. The study of these actors is of particular relevance since they are in a prime position to realise their interests, which may include a change in the rules of governance under which they gained office. A further point for consideration is their supposed responsibility for a broad cluster of policy areas affecting large parts of the lifestyle of their polity. However, it is necessary to bear in mind that the civil service is not part of that definition, as it is supposed to be one of those politically inert tools of government, although it would be true to say, however, that its personnel do not always behave in a politically neutral fashion, or that senior civil servants would not wish to extend the sphere of influence held by employees of their department. As Chapman (1978) and Lane (1987) reminds us, bureaucracies have an inherent tendency to grow, accumulate purchasing power, widen their scope of activity and possibly even create an 'oversupply' of services – and thus may become inefficient and wasteful. Nevertheless, such ambitions must be classified as private interests of the bureaucrats concerned. The definition of public actors used here only comprises elected officials[10] and political appointees. It therefore follows that upon leaving office individual representatives of public actors revert to their original status as private actors. Typical examples would be the members of a German regional parliament or the National Assembly for Wales (NAW).

Semi-public actors are groups of individuals running institutions that are not part of the machinery of government but fulfil roles and functions necessary or desirable for the smooth running of governance and the enhancement of the quality of life in society. Increasingly, semi-public institutions are used to oversee the activities of both government and private organisations, to run private–public partnerships, or to manage specific economic and social development tasks. Appointment procedures for decision-making personnel in these institutions vary widely. However, while an important criterion usually is for appointees to have task-related expertise, various private interest groups are very keen to get their own people into those boardrooms. Those appointees are prone to bring into the job interests and experience based on their career to date, but in time they may rely less on this background and more on what they learn from their new environment. The lower echelon of staff in semi-public institutions is governed by the same principle of political neutrality that applies to civil servants. Examples would be the personnel of regional development agencies.

Private actors are groups of individuals who, for the purpose of pursuing common interests, have formed organisations to represent those interests to other groups, to the general public, and to government. They deal with a wide range of issues, and can be: (i) political parties; (ii) business and labour interest organisations, including larger individual companies and trusts; (iii) social and cultural interest organisations, including those operating in the voluntary sector; and (iv) single-issue campaigning organisations. The empirical part of this book focuses on (i), (ii) and (iii), with reference to the fourth type as appropriate.

REGIONAL INTERESTS AND POLITICAL ACTION IN DEVELOPING REGIONS

Virtually all EU regions are to some extent faced with certain pressures for change and adaptation during the process of transforming themselves into 'new regions'. These pressures require more urgent attention by regional actors if the regional economy lags behind current European standards and/or there is a distinct regional or national identity to be protected. Two cases in point are the Welsh nation and the German region of Saxony. However, the principal challenges, and hence both interests and meaningful basic response strategies are applicable beyond individual regions, some specific variations notwithstanding. Given the already achieved level of European integration and similarities of lifestyle throughout the EU, it is reasonable to argue that if the challenges to regions are similar, then the regional response strategies are also likely to display a corresponding degree of similarity.

Based on this consideration, the political changes in European governance we are witnessing at present are a product of socio-economic developments that have occurred over the last 20 years or so, and are here to stay, whatever further changes may take place. The way forward from a political science research angle, therefore, would be to concentrate on the investigation of two empirically recognisable and analytically distinct phenomena: actors and processual movement.

Actors are individuals and groups of individuals who hold specific interests and wish to realise them to the best possible extent. Those interests, as well as the composition and structures of actors, may vary under different circumstances, but will not cease to exist altogether as long as holders of interests are still present in the polity. Processual movement can be defined as the processes of change and adaptation that can summarily be described as 'development', which, however, does not necessarily equate to 'progress'. The hypotheses investigated below focus on these two phenomena.

Within the EU, there are a number of public, semi-public and, in particular, private actors who regard it as in their interest to instigate a series of changes in the EU system of governance which – if carried out – would allow them a better or more efficient pursuit of their other interests. This includes a growing number of regional actors. As changes are implemented, some of these actors may join or leave the group of those still (or again) interested in further changes. However, those interested in changes individually – and increasingly jointly – embark on political strategies of interest representation to ensure that further changes are made. To that end, processes of mobilisation and political exchange are instigated and, if necessary, sustained over lengthy periods of time.

Given sufficiently similar interests held by regional actors, similar strategies of mobilisation and political exchange are employed even under apparently quite different political, social and cultural circumstances. One main reason for the occurrence of these similarities can be seen in the pressure to compete in the global race for inward investment and the need to offer an adequate physical and human infrastructure to both domestic – including one's own regional[11] – and foreign investors. Another main reason can be seen in the impact of EU regional policy, 'buying' cohesion with development funding.

However, a change in the nature of the statex[12] occurs only if the political entities replacing the old rules and structures are not only in place but also capable of taking over. This poses a challenge for regional actors who regard it as in their interest to gain control over a broader range of policy areas, as they would be in charge of coming up with workable replacement solutions. Although this principle as such may not limit regional ambition, it serves as a warning to proceed with caution – and only when having secured sufficient support from other actors and the general public.

These political phenomena are inextricably linked to both the socio-economic and socio-cultural situation in the territories in which they occur. Moreover, actor behaviour is largely determined by situational influences which shape their interests at a given point in time. It is therefore essential to consider the context of a society's lifestyle determined by these factors, and to review the interactions between these phenomena, before proceeding to postulate more specific hypotheses relevant to the two regions under investigation.

A number of empirical studies, for example of Scotland (Keating et al., 1991; Lynch, 1996; Stolz, 1997; Lange, 1998), Catalonia (Morata, 1996; Loughlin, Mathias et al., 1998), Baden-Württemberg (Cooke, 1992; Cooke and Morgan, 1998; Knodt, 1998) and other regions suggest that in terms of regional development, formerly less well-developed regions which over the last decade or so have managed to develop into quite strong regions appear to have followed a relatively similar path. In each case, combinations of regional actors have taken up the initiative and formed and implemented a regional development strategy comprising socio-economic, political and socio-cultural components. From that derives a model of regional development which takes these components into account and which can typically be characterised as a four-step process of problem recognition, quantitative infrastructure development, qualitative infrastructure development, and quality of life enhancement.

Problem recognition. In order to bring about a major regional transformation, it is essential that the socio-economic situation in a region is regarded as unsatisfactory by a sufficient number of public, semi-public and private actors in that region. Typical indicators of such a situation are: (i) a state of structural crises in the regional economy, whereby a number of, or all, traditional economic sectors becomes incapable of supporting the accustomed lifestyle of the regional society and its communities; (ii) a sharp increase in social problems, such as long-term mass unemployment, a much lower wage structure than in neighbouring regions, inadequate funding for health, education, cultural events and other public services in the community; and (iii) a lack of internal regional resources, physical and human, to act swiftly and decisively to overcome the problems, or to adapt to present and potential future challenges deriving from the outside, for example the need to compete successfully with other regions, on new terms and by new means. Such a crisis may be reinforced by a real or perceived lack of ability of the political system to provide appropriate legislative and executive leadership within the region, or to provide an effective representation of regional interests towards higher levels of government, other regions, and the private sector – attracting inward investment.

The initial step to trigger a sustained development effort, in the literature frequently referred to as 'regional mobilisation' (Négrier, 1998; Loughlin, Mathias et al., 1998) would be to recognise the need for action. This process has to start with a critical and honest problem assessment, and the subsequent realisation that a joint effort is required to secure economic, political and socio-cultural survival – the 'we are all in the same boat' syndrome. However, it is not always a straightforward exercise to identify exactly who those 'we' are. Even if external factors create similar problems for groups of actors – thus giving rise to a common interest – other considerations might prevent them from co-operating. Competitive rivalry among companies of the same sector may prevent them from joining forces even though they are all attempting to solve the same problem. Much the same goes for local economies such as the Welsh valleys and the Saxon *Regierungsbezirke* with their different socio-economic interest groups, as well as for public agencies and actors in political institutions.[13] In this scenario, it is essential to bring as many as possible interested actors to a regional 'round table', loosely starting to form what Keating (1997: 34–5) calls 'development coalitions', both sectoral and inter-sectoral. Here we also find a cultural dimension: the existence of an already mobilised interest group, such as a nationalist movement, or a very proactive socio-cultural or religious movement, may be a valuable asset as a rallying point for additional forces, and a generator of creative ideas to shape aims and specific regional means of development. By the same token, the absence of such a movement, or its lack of strength and popular support, causes a disadvantage which has to be overcome by additional political efforts.

Over the last few years, the EU has contributed significantly to the emergence of a homogeneous style of planning and decision-making on regional development throughout the Union. As national resources are no longer freely available, EU Structural Development Funds and other EU means of support are now regarded by most planners in less developed regions as absolutely essential for conducting any project of notable size. Therefore, a reasonable assumption is that once the preliminary planning decisions and organisational arrangements are made, the strategic development concept of a region is increasingly bound to follow the approach that is most likely to succeed, i.e. where at least start-up funding is likely to be available from the EU.

Quantitative infrastructure development. Often regarded as the first task to be tackled in regional development programmes, especially in areas that as yet have little or no physical infrastructure, or where the existing physical infrastructure is in need of urgent modernisation. The principle of quantitative infrastructure development is to design and implement large-scale projects to develop the physical infrastructure of the region, especially with regard to integrated transport networks and to utilities supply. The main aim of this is to generate a certain minimum level of development needed to start attracting inward investment.[14] Although it is true that some high-tech businesses can set up shop virtually wherever there is a place to house a computer and a telephone line, the manufacturing industry still needs a suitable site with enough space for future expansion, and both the manufacturing and the service industries look out for easy access to customers. Which industries to develop is also a most crucial decision with regard to employment. In the high-tech industries, the cost per job created is much higher than in manufacturing, while in the service industries the cost per job could be high (for example in banking), or low (for example in fast food retail). This in turn determines the sum of inward investment that needs to be attracted. No privately financed investment will come at all, though, if investors are not satisfied that to start an enterprise in that particular location will be worthwhile because of comparatively low costs and potentially high profits. The chance to develop businesses independently of the location of raw material, but near the location of prospective customers, favours regions that are already well developed, which do not necessarily coincide with the traditional industrial regions.

Qualitative infrastructure development. This is the key stage in a region's modernisation process. Here, the focus shifts to human resource development, to attracting inward investment on a more or less regular and steady basis, to developing a modern company base, and to active promotion of the region as a suitable partner for economic, political and cultural exchange. Again, the present EU Structural Development Funds provisions enable eligible regions to apply for support under the appropriate programmes. Occasionally, the EU provides further special incentives, such as the Regional Technology Plan (RTP). However, here – more than was the case with regard to quantitative infrastructure development – local and regional initiative, as well as reasonable and adequate planning according to real needs, and a sustained and honest effort to implement the measures fully are required. There would be no point in training or retraining people, giving them skills they are unlikely or unable to use, and investors are bound to find out sooner or later whether a location indeed offers all the advantages mentioned in the prospectus issued by the regional development agency. Moreover, despite the fact that evaluation and audit procedures by the EU still have room for improvement, it would be of advantage to a region if it were able to demonstrate that the funds received had been put to good use because initiatives had become, over time, self-sufficient, or because the problem at which the funds were directed had been successfully tackled.

To achieve these ends effectively, sufficient competence by regional actors is of the essence, and therefore the capabilities of the political system and the quality of public–private relationships are in demand. Learning from regions where policy implementation has been successful can play a major role here, in particular with regard to effective interest representation. After all, it can be argued that it is the problem of effective interest representation – i.e. a political function – that frequently causes demands for a change in the political rules.

However, once the basic economic requirements have been fulfilled, socio-cultural developments, including more elaborate manifestations of national or regional identity, can become a valuable asset. Not only will tourists appreciate the opportunity to explore the heritage and recreational facilities of the area, but also the local population is likely to realise its full creative potential more efficiently if the environment in which this has to be done is perceived as adequate.

Quality of life enhancement. This can be regarded as the final phase of making a region truly 'modern'. Having reached this stage, the region is endowed with an adequate physical infrastructure, a highly trained workforce, a reasonably well-established mixed company structure which is able to compete successfully in Europe and beyond, and a functioning political and administrative infrastructure. The latter is able not only to deliver and process creative ideas and exercise legislative and administrative leadership to steer and sustain the development process, but also to represent the region's interest to the outside world. Thus, the region is capable of generating sufficient output to direct surplus resources towards the provision of additional social security and services, the improvement of cultural and leisure facilities, and environmental protection beyond legal requirements. This also means that regions which regard themselves as nations are able to direct surplus into prestigious projects, political channels, and advertisements to enhance the nation's reputation, if it is perceived that these steps are worthwhile, as can be seen in the case of Catalonia. National and regional cultures blossom and smaller local initiatives can grow more freely as individual participants can afford to pay for more elaborate activities.[15] The influx of EU funds into the region declines sharply as the need for such funds – and thus eligibility – is no longer present. Only very few regions and cities have reached this stage, and it is reasonable to suspect that as yet Wales and Saxony are not among them.[16]

However, it has to be noted that in the practical process all four phases are to some extent intertwined. Measures attributed here to a certain phase may, if there is a specific reason or urgent need, in fact be carried out at any time. While, for instance, the physical infrastructure needs constant maintenance and improvements to remain up to current standards, measures designed to enhance the quality of life are always regarded as good vote-catchers at the next election.

This model of regional development comprises three constituent components of the development process. They are: (i) socio-economic issues, (ii) political structures and procedures, and (iii) socio-cultural components of the society's lifestyle in the region. Progress can be defined as an adequate development of all three components through means of regional mobilisation and the successful implementation of various practical projects deriving therefrom. The nature of mobilisation activities or the type and size of individual projects vary according to a region's needs. However, given the same target of developing into a region that conforms to the criteria of a 'new region' able to pursue quality of life enhancement more or less at will – i.e. as defined by the regional actors – while maintaining the ability to respond to outside pressures, it is reasonable to assume that the development process itself is governed by a number of generally applicable principles which can be observed in the regions concerned, including Wales and Saxony.

The desire for economic and social development can be regarded as the key driving force behind a region's development efforts. Political concepts such as 'freedom', 'independence' or 'self-determination' derive from the interest definition of regional actors, and may subsequently be employed in the process of regional interest representation. If endowed with sufficient popular support, these political demands may take on a life of their own independently of the realisation of those interests for the promotion of which they were originally designed. But because of being political in nature, these demands remain a means to an end and do not become an end in themselves, however hard their proponents try to convince us that they do. Political projects in regions are usually run by regional élites, often self-proclaimed, pushing their interests to the fore. It is essential, however, to analyse the motives for their demands. Whether at the beginning of the process these demands are considered justified by, or even comprehensible to, outside observers may be questionable. Political projects usually come with universal claims that may attract or repel other actors during the process. However, whether the original claims were justified – and thus the standing of the proponents – is judged by the result of the process. This puts proactive actors at risk.

Political cultures and administrative structures matter insofar as they must be able to deliver at least some of the necessary feasible creative ideas and initiatives, as well as a suitable framework for effective action to steer and sustain the development process. This is the logical consequence of the hypothesis that a change in the nature of the state only occurs if the political entities replacing the old structures are not only in place but also capable of taking over. Otherwise, present holders of the powers of authoritative decision-making see no need for a hand-over, and former holders may be more than willing and capable to take back formerly devolved powers.

Regional culture, heritage, etc., can be powerful aides to the generation of ideas, to decision-making, and to rally popular support for proposed measures. However, the absence or lack of influence of regional culture or distinctiveness can be overcome by increased political efforts. The preservation of a regional culture, or the traditional lifestyle of a region or 'stateless nation' may appear to the people concerned as an end in itself. In conflicts with an ethnic dimension this may appear to the people as a clash of ends which needs to be settled by political means, or if necessary, by resorting to the use of force. Such a definition of ends, however, assumes that there actually is a threat to the culture or lifestyle concerned. In democratic societies, where outright discrimination on ethnic or similar grounds is outlawed, and national and international mechanisms are in place[17] to combat that kind of discrimination, such a threat can only be socio-economic in nature. The other side of this coin is the artificial manufacturing of a heritage or distinctiveness in present-day economic, political and even administrative regions which do not have significant historical roots. In those cases, popular support may be harder to achieve and maintain, but the practical outcome in terms of creating ideas and developing efficient structures of decision-making may be the same as in historical or traditional regions.

To test these hypotheses, we now turn to the empirical investigation of two EU regions which have very different historical and political backgrounds but share more socio-economic common ground than one would reasonably expect: the Celtic nation of Wales, for the time being part of the UK, and the Free State of Saxony, having just a decade ago returned into the common German fold. First, Chapter 2 will look at the historical background of the two regions, leading to an overview of the present socio-economic situation, and the present actor structure in the two regions. Secondly, Chapter 3 looks at regional interest formation, and investigates the behaviour of public actors, with particular reference to their involvement in regional development management. Finally, Chapter 4 consists of an analysis of the practice of regional governance in the regions, with particular reference to new forms of public–private relationships which may constitute a new mode of regional governance, changing the political system.

NOTES

1. Of course there are the occasional pro-integration alterations, e.g. the SEA and the TEU, but none of the treaties carries a time limit, let alone a dissolving procedure. While an intergovernmental treaty dissolving the EU is in theory, and in law, not totally unimaginable, any political interest to even think about this is at the moment virtually absent from the European scene, and about as likely to surface as a serious political demand as any move to dissolve the United States of America. This is not to say, however, that particular further integration steps would not be subject to a fierce political debate.
2. The RTP initiatives of the mid-1990s spring to mind.
3. Translation by author from the German text: 'Ich bin davon überzeugt, daß in den demokratischen Jahrhunderten, die uns bevorstehen, die individuelle Unabhängigkeit und die lokalen Freiheiten immer das Ergebnis künstlicher Bestrebungen sein werden. Die natürliche Regierung wird die Zentralisation sein.' (Tocqueville, 1990: 316).
4. Although the idea of subsidiarity – if not the name – had been around for some time (e.g. in the work of Hugo de Grotius), Pope Leo XIII is widely regarded as the first author to apply the concept of subsidiarity to socio-economic matters, in his 1891 Encyclical *Rerum novarum*. In its wake, Pope Pius XI's 1931 Encyclical *Quadrogesimo anno*, and various works by Oswald von Nell-Breuning SJ and others have expanded and updated that approach into the realms of political economy, and of government (see KAB, 1975).
5. The neofunctionalists' apparent satisfaction with this situation can probably only be explained by the fact that they would regard these suggestions not as being made by 'factional' interests in the negative or pejorative sense, but as representations of legitimate interests.
6. Sub-national territorial arrangements differ widely among the member states, and even within member states – Keating (1997) calls the latter 'asymmetrical government'. Moreover, regional political demands often come alongside demands for democratisation of the EU system ('Europe of the Citizens') and for safeguarding existing constitutional rights (e.g. in some of the German *Länder*, including Bavaria and Saxony).
7. This is closely related to the designation of economic regions; however, a possible distinction between the two is that economic regions can be regarded as indigenously grown, and already in existence as distinguishable entities, while the planning regions are just drawn up for the purpose of planning, and often only exist as regions in the planning documents which created them.
8. The emphasis here has to be on 'major'. In the UK, for instance, there was the West Lothian question, and a recent reshuffle of UK seats in the CoR, increasing the English representation by two seats, but reducing the number of Scottish and Welsh representatives (Evans, 1998: 2).
9. Purely for linguistic convenience, in the empirical part of this study actors are nevertheless referred to by the name of their institution or organisation (e.g. 'Welsh Office', 'Saxon Government', 'CBI', etc., instead of the persons in charge there). If the institutions and organisations as such are referred to, this will be indicated separately throughout the text.
10. Including opposition members of legislative bodies.
11. Strong private companies (e.g. Siemens, Volkswagen) have started to show a perfect willingness to turn their backs on their home regions and go elsewhere if in their opinion those regions fail to do enough to keep them there.
12. In Marks's sense, meaning a transfer of powers of authoritative decision-making.
13. In Germany, the rivalry among political institutions is not only practical reality, but even a constitutional demand under the concepts of 'federal separation of powers' and '*konkurrierende Gesetzgebung*'; i.e. the application of a principle akin to subsidiarity to legislative powers and to the right to issue executive orders (*Verwaltungsakte*).
14. Net inward investment by private actors (excluding funds provided by the EU and national governments as well as regional/local incentives given to private actors for coming to the region) is most crucial to the success of regional development, and therefore an important indicator of progress in that direction.

15. This is very similar to the US 'Country Club' phenomenon, and West German examples show that cultural initiatives tend to become social gatherings or societies (*Vereine*) of local élites – but not exclusively so.
16. Some of the regions and cities that are among the 'chosen few' are Baden-Württemberg, Emilia-Romagna, Tuscany, Barcelona (but not all of Catalonia), Hamburg, Munich, Frankfurt/M., Luxembourg, and – to some extent – Paris, London and the English 'Home Counties'.
17. This is not to say that such legal protection mechanisms are always effective, or easy to use. However, they are there, and the established wisdom in international law is that in conflicts which have an ethnic dimension and concern the right to self-determination the status quo shall prevail until the conflict can be resolved by peaceful means.

2

Regional Socio-economic Conditions, Interests and Strategies: Wales and Saxony

This chapter outlines the criteria for comparing Wales and Saxony, and analyses the socio-economic environment in which regional actors must function. It also introduces the actor structure in the two regions, investigating how this structure is linked to, even dependent on, both historical roots and present-day features of the socio-economic lifestyles of their two societies.

THE REGIONAL HERITAGE

Wales: A 'Stateless Nation'?

Along with Ireland and Scotland, Wales is one of the traditional nations[1] on the north-western fringes of Europe. It possesses a rich heritage in terms of culture, language, and community lifestyle upon which to draw as a focus for building a common identity. The first documented roots of this heritage reach back into the time of the Roman occupation in Britain, although the Druid cult, practised in the north-western corner of Wales, is presumed to be of even older origin. Christianity made its inroads into Wales during the Roman occupation (approximately AD 60–400), reaching its peak in the early twelfth century, with the See of St David's in West Wales developing into one of the predominant seats of power in what is today regarded as Welsh territory. In addition to the Norman feudal church, there was an alternative, Celtic ecclesiastical system, which was mainly based on monasteries and gained significance in many rural parts of Wales. The main secular seat of power was Ludlow, the capital of the Kingdom of Powys.[2] Before the Acts of Union of 1536 and 1548, that kingdom was, in the eleventh and twelfth centuries, the closest thing to territorial unity as a political entity ever achieved in Wales. At its peak it comprised about 70 per cent of today's territory of Wales, plus parts of the English counties of Herefordshire, Worcestershire and Shropshire. Up to the sixteenth century, and occasionally thereafter, the Marches straddling the border between England and Wales in the south-west were the scene of more or less continuous feuding between local warlords of both English and Welsh origin.

However, starting with the English occupation around 1535–36, the local warlords and secular and ecclesiastical gentry ruling in Wales and the Marches were forced to assimilate politically and administratively into the system of the English monarchy, developing closer economic, political and legal links with England than any other part of the UK. This still has considerable implications for the present system of governance. Today, usually there are much fewer Westminster Acts for Wales than there are for Scotland and Northern Ireland. The structures of the legal system, and of semi-public and private organisations, etc., are also very similar to those found in England (Mathias, 2000).

Within the constitutional framework of the UK, Wales's status as a distinct national entity, in the modern sense derived from the early nineteenth century, has never been questioned (Loughlin and Mathias, 1996: 182). However, until very recently the main manifestations of Welsh national identity belonged almost exclusively to the sphere of culture: the use of the language, including promotion schemes by and for those who still spoke it; annual folk art festivals (Eisteddfods) with prizes for the best achievements in Welsh music, art and literature and promotion of the national culture; national teams in football and rugby;[3] and not least the use of the Welsh national flag and the Welsh national anthem, either alongside or even without their UK equivalents, whenever deemed appropriate. Among those who cherished this heritage, it was this mixture of non-conformist religion and radical politics which proved to be a source of popular support for enhanced Welsh self-determination in other fields.

On the other hand, according to advocates of Welsh identity (for example, Osmond, 1995) it lacked adequate reflection in political, administrative and economic terms. Indeed, the absence of an elected form of regional government seems to be a strong argument for this claim. However, there have been functional equivalents for regional government, and since 1995[4] a process has been under way to establish a regional government.

The structural crisis in the late 1980s and early 1990s, comprising virtually all sectors of the economy, undermined the economic basis of many Welsh communities. These local communities used to be rather close-knit and egalitarian, probably due to the similarity of living conditions shared by most of the members, and the egalitarian tradition in the nonconformist religious communities of various descriptions.[5] Their economic way of life was largely dependent on coal, steel, the textile industry or agriculture, supplemented by fishery, forestry and various crafts. Socially, the highlights of the week were attending church or chapel on Sunday, and occasional visits to union meetings, choirs, the cinema or the pub. Except in Cardiff, Swansea and Newport, anything more was neither available nor affordable. However, the economic threat to these communities, with rocketing unemployment, a failing support system of family, friends and neighbours – as those became needy at the same time – and the lack of immediately available alternatives brought a swift end to the traditional system in the late 1980s. The unions lost many paying members, the cinemas and the pubs were closed, and the chapels encountered increasing difficulties in sustaining the intellectual leadership and supplementary social services which had been their main contribution to the communities.

Prime Minister Margaret Thatcher's strong policy of non-interference in the economy was not well received in the Welsh 'ex-industrial valleys' (Lovering, 1996: 8). Her similarly outspoken anti-union policy, on the other hand, went straight at the heart of a major pillar of Welsh public life: hard-core, left-wing unionism, with its close political and financial links to the Labour Party, which had reigned supreme and virtually unchallenged in the Valleys and beyond ever since the end of the Second World War. So, quite unintentionally, Thatcherism also contributed significantly to an increasingly widespread political belief that the Welsh people would be considerably better off if they were allowed to develop and manage their own socio-economic and cultural – and to some extent also political – domestic affairs while relying, but being less dependent, on the goodwill of London to lend a helping hand if and when required.

Not surprisingly, these developments also coincided with renewed demands by Welsh nationalists, and members of a newly emerging Welsh-speaking intellectual élite – especially in education and in the media – for greater recognition of Wales's status as a nation. One key expression of this demand was an increase in the active promotion of the Welsh language as a means of public communication. Nevertheless, general public support for these demands was, is, and is likely to remain, much smaller than some campaigners, including the nationalist party Plaid Cymru, would like to see. The business community in particular remained fairly sceptical, as expressed for instance in the rejection of the idea of a Welsh Assembly by the Confederation of British Industry (CBI) Wales in 1979 (Jones and Wilford, 1983: 224), and time and again in more recent surveys by CBI Wales itself (e.g. CBI, 1994), and by independent researchers.[6] It also needs to be pointed out that in 1991 only 18.7 per cent of the Welsh population spoke Welsh (Williams, 1995: 50),[7] and that many people who live in Wales regard themselves not only as 'Welsh' but equally strong as 'British'.

However, the link between economic and political demands on the one hand, and national and cultural demands on the other, constituted a new departure in the formation of territorial interests. Previous economic and political demands which had surfaced in the 1960s were met by the then Labour government with measures of economic regionalisation. However, apart from the creation of the Welsh Office (WO) in 1964, political regionalisation never went far beyond some feasibility studies undertaken by a special parliamentary committee. Although a Welsh Assembly was envisaged even then, the idea was washed away in the wake of the 1968/69 Local Government Reform for the entire UK. According to Morgan (1982: 385), the main contribution of the Welsh-language movement was that, partly influenced by student revolts, and other instances of political unrest elsewhere during 1968, 'in so far as it inspired the young and seemed to appeal to a traditional folk culture in contrast to the shoddiness and false glamour of commercialised capitalism, it helped to speed on militancy' in expressing these demands. The apparent failure to establish a close link between the two kinds of demand was also a contributing factor to the overwhelming rejection of the devolution project by the Welsh population in a referendum in March 1979.

Sensing that London's influence might dwindle if some of the Welsh demands were to be met, Thatcherite conservatism, gaining office later in the same year, would, of course, have none of this.[8] The result of Thatcherite policies can be summarised as a ruined industrial base, an intact yet widely disliked political system, a weakened but still fairly proud working-class identity, and a national tradition determined to protect the values of the past while searching for an alternative future.

Wales is, when all is said and done, not a stateless nation; it does have a state, the UK. Sections of the Welsh population might not regard this as an ideal solution, especially after their experience of the Conservative governments of the 1980s and early 1990s. What Wales does not have is a state of its own, but, differing from the SNP's outspokenness concerning 'independence in Europe', even the Party of Wales[9] is reluctant to openly demand a separate Welsh state – mainly because of much uncertainty about this issue within the party itself (Lynch, 1996). For better or worse, therefore, Wales remains part of the UK system for the time being, and the interests of Welsh actors are bound to focus on changes to that system in order to promote their interests more fully and more efficiently.

Saxony: A 'Nationless State'?

The Saxon tribe is one of the oldest in continental Europe. From the second to the eighth centuries, parts of it left their original territory – present-day Lower Saxony – to occupy new territories to the north-west as far as Britain (along with the Angles) and the south-east, leaving traces in some parts of Germany (Saxony-Anhalt, present-day Saxony) and beyond as far as northern Romania. However, their advance to the south and south-west was stopped by the Franks in a series of wars lasting almost three hundred years before being settled in the early eighth century, in what today is the territory of the German *Land* Hesse.

Having emerged from the Middle Ages as one of the larger German kingdoms, the Saxon king was one of the seven monarchs – the so-called 'Electors' – who had a vote in the election of the German emperor. At one time, in the middle of the eighteenth century, forming a dynastic union with Poland, Saxony developed into one of the more important players in pre-Napoleonic central European politics. However, in 1871 it was incorporated into Bismarck's German empire without too many questions being asked.

As an administrative unit, Saxony remained in existence as part of the various German states until 1952 when the then German Democratic Republic (GDR) decided to break up the traditional territorial structure and create new administrative regions (Bezirke), three of which were former Saxon territory: Dresden, Leipzig and Chemnitz.[10] Saxony was re-created as a distinct political and territorial entity only in the process of German unification: with the signals already green towards German unification, the *Volkskammer* (GDR parliament) on 22 June 1990 passed the *Ländereinführungsgesetz* (*Länder* Re-establishment Act),[11] which became valid at the very moment of unification, on 3 October 1990 (Wollmann, 1998: 20).

Other than in the very early days, and then still in the sense of being a Germanic tribe, the Saxons have never really regarded themselves as a nation in an ethnic sense. Key cultural elements of Saxon identity, for example the heritage in architecture, literature and the arts, are mostly derived from the days of the Kingdom of Saxony, and in particular from the eighteenth century. These have, to a large extent, survived the absence of Saxony as a territorial entity, but the people's sense of belonging has, well beyond living memory, rather been one of regional affiliation, best described by the German term *Heimat*, within the German nation. Often understood as 'home', this concept goes far beyond a purely territorial dimension and comprises other elements such as 'family and friends', 'local culture and traditions', 'one of us', and similar expressions of affection. A closely related concept would be 'roots'.[12] There is no Saxon language, but many people speak a distinct and easily recognisable regional dialect of German.

However, there is a small national minority, the Sorbs, whose territory (Sorabia) comprises the north-eastern part of Saxony, and the south-eastern tip of the neighbouring *Land*, Brandenburg. They were the original inhabitants of present-day Saxony but were forced east by the advancing Saxon warriors and settlers as late as the eleventh and twelfth centuries. The Sorbs are a Slavic people who have a deep-rooted sense of Slavonic cultural identity. A considerable – though declining – number of them speak Sorb, a Slavonic language, though nearly all Sorb speakers are bilingual. Sorb language schools can be found throughout the area, but these now face severe difficulties in attracting pupils as more and more parents perceive that being taught solely in the Sorb language will leave children at a disadvantage in later life, impairing career prospects. Well founded or not – official discrimination is, of course, outlawed – this perception is growing stronger as more and more people face the new reality of living in a capitalist system.

The Sorbs have their own customs and traditions, notably quite elaborate Easter celebrations, dances and equestrian events. Under the GDR system, Sorb nationalism was encouraged and funded only in a way that was deemed non-threatening to the East German political system. The Sorb mass organisation-cum-cultural forum, the *Domowina*, amounted to little more than political showmanship, as did the *Domowina's* token representation in the *Volkskammer*.[13]

Since 1990, however, attempts to revive a true Sorb national lifestyle have been hindered considerably by harsh financial restraints – the area is one of the poorest in Germany. The second largest city, Hoyerswerda, also became a centre of neo-nazi activities in the early 1990s, a development that was more than likely caused through economic hardship, along with an apparent inability of the new political system to provide answers for pressing local problems – for example illegal immigration from Poland, and all sorts of black-marketeering. The Sorb case is fairly illustrative of the limitations of opportunities available to minority cultures in ostensibly liberal free-market economies: if the market pressures are strong enough, even the best intentions all around are bound to lead nowhere unless they are backed up by sufficient resources.

The changes of 1989–90 also brought about the collapse of almost the entire Saxon economy, which was forced to adapt to the new free-market system within a very short period. What started the ball rolling was a mass exodus from East to West Germany both before and after the opening of the Iron Curtain on 9 November 1989. The economic and monetary union between East and West Germany, effective from 1 July 1990, followed by the re-establishment of the East German *Länder*[14] and the political union on 3 October 1990, can indeed be described as 'West German federalism ... [being] exported lock stock and barrel to the former GDR' (Anderson, 1995: 31).

This, however, is not a sufficient reason to assume that pre-1989 conditions had no bearing on both the socio-economic and the political ends in the emerging fight for survival under the new system. The GDR's political culture can be described as a fairly straightforward affair: play by the rules, do not ask inconvenient questions, and relax in the secure knowledge that if you stay out of harm's way the state will, subject to availability, tend to your basic needs. Of course, it helped to speak the 'language of the revolution',[15] but proactive behaviour beyond the party line of the day was usually doomed to fail – so why bother?

Therefore, the vast majority of the population was rather ill-prepared for the new experience of lack of social security. The risks and hazards of everyday life in Western societies, ranging from unemployment to crime and pushy salesmen, together with the need to act individually and proactively on one's own behalf, was duly noted by most Saxons. But what was largely missing was the knowledge of how to deal effectively with this situation. While some people were only too eager to please their new political and economic masters,[16] as many had done previously under the old regime, a significant number of people did not – and still do not – regard the new freedoms of speech and travel as sufficient compensation for the loss of an easily manageable lifestyle. Moreover, many East Germans do not see why they should be grateful for rights that West Germans take for granted. This is in particular the case among the younger generation, as their counterparts in the west played no part in the postwar reconstruction of West Germany known as the *Wirtschaftswunder* (economic miracle).

However, by and large, Saxon lost the economic fight within 18 months. The situation immediately after unification can be summarised as a ruined industrial base, an entirely new and as yet unknown but (elsewhere) proven political system, a half-hearted working-class identity, and a *Heimat* tradition determined to claim the best of both worlds by whatever means available.

Saxony is not a 'nationless state' in the same sense that Wales is not a 'stateless nation': as Wales is part of the UK state, Saxony is part of the German nation, which is now reunited. This belonging to the German nation forms an integral part of the Saxon identity, and gained particular importance between December 1989 and October 1990 in the drive for German unification. Since then, its mainstream manifestations have moved out of the political and into the cultural sphere. A key reason for this is that German nationalism in the political sphere is still a double-edged sword, fuelling lingering suspicions abroad about possible German interests in dominating the socio-economic lifestyle of Europe, and on the domestic scene being abused by neo-Nazi groupings. 'Ich bin stolz, ein Deutscher zu sein',[17] shouted by a neo-Nazi, is a frightening experience for most Germans, and Saxony has had considerable problems in that respect in the early 1990s. In addition, there is a strong, but often ill-defined, sense of regional *Heimat* affiliation among the population. While the present government of Saxony tries hard to fill this conceptual weakness by promoting its post-1990 achievements, its cultural origins in the eighteenth century still seem to be the predominant reason for its present popularity. The third dimension of Saxon identity is the relationship between Saxons and Sorbs, currently in a state of peaceful co-existence. However, this is not a relationship of equals; it hardly could be with 4.5 million Saxons on the one hand, and approximately 30,000 Sorbs on the other. So, while most Saxons take hardly any interest in Sorb affairs, the Sorbs are much keener on taking an interest in the Saxon socio-cultural activities. The Saxon government, and the local governments concerned, however, are taking political steps to ensure that relations remain amicable – fortunately, not a particularly difficult task.

ECONOMIC AND SOCIAL FEATURES OF THE REGIONS

Wales: The 'Celtic Phoenix'?

In terms of economic patterns, Wales is not a homogeneous region.[18] The Welsh territory can be divided roughly into four areas, the first three of which share a common feature: coastline. With more than two-thirds of the Welsh border consisting of coastline, this is an important economic asset and a major attraction for tourism to the region. Also, a thriving fishing industry can be found almost everywhere along the coast. The four areas are:

1. The industrialised south. A heavily industrialised belt stretches along the southern coast and the M4 motorway from Chepstow, near the English border, to Swansea, including the area to the north of Cardiff known as 'the Valleys'. All sectors of Welsh industry are represented here. It is also heavily populated, comprising roughly two-thirds of the Welsh population, and the three largest Welsh cities, Cardiff, Swansea and Newport, can be found here. The best quality soil in Wales can also be found in this area (Carter and Griffiths, 1987: 1.5a), but only just over 50 per cent of the land is used for agricultural purposes – the average for Wales as a whole is 81 per cent (WO, 1994: 144).

2. The semi-industrialised north. A string of smaller industrialised areas and towns and the A55 from Flint near the English border to Holyhead, an important ferry port on the Isle of Anglesey, serving a number of Irish destinations, are located along the northern coast. However, in terms of infrastructure this area has closer links to Merseyside and the north-west of England than to the south of Wales. The area also has a large agricultural sector.

3. The rural centre and north-west. Covering almost 75 per cent of Wales, this large, predominantly rural area with only minor pockets of usually small industrial estates stretches from the far south-west (Pembrokeshire) across the whole of central Wales to the southern parts of the former counties of Gwynedd and Clwyd, just south of the A55. Land use for agricultural purposes exceeds the Welsh average over the whole of this area (WO, 1994: 144–50).

4. The National Parks in the north-west and the south of central Wales. Almost 10 per cent of rural Wales is 'out of bounds' for the purpose of economic development. There are two large National Parks: Snowdonia in the north-west, and the Brecon Beacons in south-central Wales. In both areas, any kind of business activity, except some forestry, with a strong emphasis on environmental protection, and tightly controlled tourism, is prohibited by law (WO, 1994: 144). However, parts of both Snowdonia and the Brecon Beacons are used as training grounds for the Royal Air Force and the Special Air Service, respectively.

We can see from the above that the Welsh economy is a mixture of agriculture and industry, spread unevenly throughout the region. In terms of the number of businesses, agriculture (including forestry and fishery) is the largest sector, comprising some 19,500 enterprises (Blackaby, 1994: 194; WO, 1994: 72–80).

Construction is one of the more advanced sectors of the Welsh economy. The vast majority of construction firms are small and medium-sized enterprises (SMEs); (Blackaby, 1994: 222), based mainly in the south-east, which has benefited most from outside investment, including EU funds. Major infrastructure developments were implemented there in the 1990s. With these projects for the most part completed now, some of the medium-sized companies, and a number of self-employed individuals, have moved on to projects elsewhere, not least in East Germany.

The energy sector has seen a number of dramatic changes in recent years. Privatised from 1985 onwards, the main changes can be described as a farewell to coal, and a diversification of energy sources. The traditional

Welsh mining industry has seen a rapid decline: coal production output in 1993 declined to 1.98 million tonnes, from 16.1 million tonnes in 1970 (WO, 1994: 85). Since then, a number of revival efforts, focusing on the production of high-quality coal in small-scale operations, have been attempted. However, it is unlikely that they are going to compensate significantly for the severe reductions in terms of both production quantity and employment. Unlike Scotland, Wales has no oil of its own. Nevertheless, from the 1970s, a significant capacity for refining crude oil had been developed in Pembroke, reaching a peak in the late 1980s. Since 1996, however, capacity has been reduced there, which is fully in line with the overall UK trend.

The production and manufacturing industries are quite diversified: metals and metal products dominate; chemicals, transport equipment and food production are also of importance. In addition, printing and publishing, textiles and leather, and wood processing play a minor yet significant role (WO, 1994: 78). Mainly concentrated in the south, the manufacturing industry has undergone some changes in recent years. The most important trends are the attraction of subsidiary or branch plants of larger international corporations, further diversification, including the establishment of some high-technology companies, and the introduction of part-time work on a broader scale.

TABLE 2.1
DISTRIBUTION OF EMPLOYMENT IN WALES, 1989–94

	1989 (000s)	1994 (000s)	Change (%)
Employees	1,198	1.162	−3
Full-time	952	875	−8
Part-time	246	289	+17
Self-employed	185	181	−2
Unemployed benefit claimants	93	117	+26
Employees by sector			
Agriculture, forestry, fishery	19	18	−5
Energy (including coal mining)	29	17	−41
Manufacturing	237	221	−6
Construction	46	40	−13
Service industries	651	669	+ 3

Source: Lovering, 1996, p. 9.

Among the service industries, banking and financial and insurance services have performed well. Wales has only ever had one regional bank, the Bank of Wales, until it was recently bought by the Bank of Scotland.[19] Most services are provided by local branches of institutions operating UK-wide. Except for local bank branches, virtually the entire financial services industry of Wales is located in Cardiff. Other service industries, especially the small retail enterprises and restaurants and pubs, have to fight as hard as ever for survival against increasing competition from larger suburban units and each other. Although the number of registered businesses has remained almost constant in that sector, the turnover rate is high. The same is true of employment figures – an almost constant number of people employed in the sector by no means indicates individual job security. Moreover, in the service industries there is a high level of low-wage jobs, and the employment of part-time workers, including juveniles over the legal age limit of 16 but still at school, is more and more widespread, especially at larger retail units (Lovering, 1996).

One Welsh response to the difficult situation consists of attempts to seek assistance from the outside, in particular from the EU. This concept was by no means a Welsh invention; other regions, both within Britain and beyond, had embarked on similar courses as early as 1985–86 – i.e. even before the 1988 EU Structural Funds reform – and in many cases even before the crisis had reached 'Welsh dimensions' in their region.[20] However, the Welsh turn towards Europe was strongly facilitated by the fact that the remedies offered by the Conservative government in London amounted to little more than continued Thatcherite prescriptions such as privatisation and compulsory competitive tendering (CCT) of public services, the shifting of traditionally public responsibilities to non-departmental public bodies (NDPBs), or quasi-non-governmental organisations (quangos), and the promotion of an entrepreneurial culture aimed at cutting costs at all costs. Central government funding allocated to Wales for regional assistance saw a gradual downward trend, from £101.3m in 1988–89 to £74.4m in 1993–94 (WO, 1994a).

Since the late 1980s, the EU has offered more than a helping hand. The new EU instruments deriving from the 1988 reform seemed to be tailor-made for places like Wales. While this meant swallowing national pride for a moment and accepting being regarded as a region in Europe, upon which economically rather than politically defined status a territory's eligibility depends,[21] Welsh regional actors soon found out that there was much to gain from the reformed Structural Funds and accompanying measures. Virtually the whole Welsh territory has been entitled to receive funds under either Objective 2 (Industrial Regions in Decline; south Wales) or Objective 5b (Development of Rural Areas; central and north Wales). Both sub-regions were covered by their own Single Planning Documents, and Wales has done fairly well with regard to receiving EU funds, securing on average 12.5 per cent of all the UK's ERDF funds and 8.6 per cent of all the

UK's funding from the European Social Fund (ESF) between 1988 and 1992 (Cooke et al., 1993). These percentages have remained fairly constant.

TABLE 2.2
REGIONAL DEVELOPMENT FUNDING AVAILABLE IN THE INDUSTRIAL
SOUTH WALES (OBJECTIVE 2) AREA, 1994–96 (m. ECU)

Priority	Structural Fund contribution	National public funding	Private funding	Total
Disadvantaged urban communities	61.34	116.17	5.08	182.59
Industry and business	70.97	114.60	22.80	208.37
Knowledge-based industries	31.73	37.73	8.20	77.30
Tourism	23.03	28.15	5.02	56.20
Technical assistance	0.93	0.98	–	1.91
Total	188.00	297.63	41.10	526.37

Source: European Commission, 1995.

However, from the mid-1990s on, emphasis in the use of funds started to shift from pure physical infrastructure development to the creation of community projects that provide a network of support for sustainable development and enhanced quality of life, including housing, education, access to information, and communications (STAR/Telematique).

Compared to other UK regions, in the past Wales has not been particularly successful at participating in nationally administered programmes co-financed by the EU, obtaining only between 1 per cent (ESPRIT, BRIDGE) and 4 per cent (BRITE/EURAM) of the overall UK share (Price et al., 1994: 40). This is mainly because, although companies have invested in small-scale and secondary manufacturing in Wales, their research and development facilities usually remained elsewhere. However, largely through aid given to SMEs to do their own research and to team up with other SMEs and local academic institutions in order to create local research and development (R&D) units, advanced technology centres, and similar establishments, this situation is slowly improving. Of significant importance in this context is STRIDE, the EU programme for improved regional R&D capabilities. Although the emphasis of this programme is on the regional dimension, it has also proved to be successfully applicable on the sub-regional level in north Wales.

These efforts are supplemented by a number of measures aimed at improving the innovative capacity of SMEs. The more important programmes are SMART (since 1988), LINK (since 1989), and SPUR (since 1991). These are managed by the Department of Trade and Industry, and implemented in Wales by the Welsh Development Agency (WDA), in close co-operation with initially the WO and now with the Welsh Civil Service operating under the auspices of the NAW. One key focus of these programmes was the development of an 'infrastructure' of SMEs which could act as suppliers for potentially larger – mainly overseas – investors, thus hoping to make Wales more attractive as a location for their UK base. This decision has played a crucial role in the restructuring processes of the Welsh economy in the late 1980s and early 1990s. Since then, attracting larger investors has come to be regarded by political decision-makers as less crucial – though always welcome, of course – while the creation of significant SME clusters, mainly in southern and western Wales, has become an end in itself.

There is, however, no doubt that high levels of EU funding will not be available in future years. The EU's current enlargement plans are contributing to a not particularly favourable re-evaluation of the needs of the existing recipients of Structural Funds. A number of internal Welsh factors also indicate that a continuation of existing levels of support may no longer be appropriate: large infrastructure development projects in the South, on which much of the incoming money was spent, are almost complete now. On the other hand, the apparent shift of focus towards human resource development, though well publicised, has not yet gathered full momentum. Moreover, the worst socio-economic results of the industrial decline appear to have been curbed. Therefore, it is likely that Welsh actors are about to encounter increasing difficulties in proving that a general need still exists. This is not to say that incoming funds could not be put to good use, so individual projects are still likely to stand a reasonable chance of receiving EU funding – in particular in the 2000–06 Objective 1 area in west Wales and the Valleys. But the sense of urgency which dominated the debate in the late 1980s and early 1990s has disappeared – even if it was to some extent just 'talked away' in order to allow private actors and development agencies to 'sell' Wales more easily as a modern, forward-looking region to potential providers of inward investment.

What is of lasting value, however, is the actors' experience gained in those early days with regard to effectively gathering forces and proceeding along EU-prescribed lines of infrastructure development, access to new and/or alternative technologies, and relation-building with new political and business partners throughout the EU. After all, as the example of new role models such as Baden-Württemberg and Catalonia suggest, progress in both socio-economic and socio-cultural directions are by no means mutually exclusive.

The present situation in Wales can be characterised as a craving for attention by the outside world. Faced with diminished domestically available resources, sub-regional and local actors (public and private) have engaged in a new kind of 'planning competition' on both the domestic and the European scene, and occasionally even beyond. This constitutes the continuation of the traditional domestic competition between some old rivals, now dressed in new clothes: urban versus rural areas, one group of valleys against another, north versus south, and more recently east versus west. It is inevitable that there are winners and losers in this competition. So far, the big winners have been two of the three large cities of south Wales, Cardiff and Newport,[22] along with Merthyr Tydfil, just to the north of Cardiff. These are the areas that profited most from a number of huge development projects aimed at enhancing the physical infrastructure in the early 1990s, and have subsequently attracted the lion's share of inward investment into Wales. Some of the neighbouring areas, for example Blaenau Gwent, Caerphilly and Rhondda-Cynon-Taff, have so far fared rather less well – despite considerable efforts in terms of manpower, establishing local development agencies, and advertisement. While some physical factors[23] militate against them, a large proportion of the disappointment, repeatedly expressed by regional actors, must be attributed to very ambitious planning and overestimation of available or realistically obtainable resources.

Some other parts of Wales have fared even worse. The south-western tip, Pembroke, now has to pay the price for the industrial 'monoculture' of oil, gas and petro-chemicals. The oil tanker accident near Milford Haven in the spring of 1996 cast a dark shadow over Pembroke's future as an industrial location: due to natural restrictions the port cannot cope with the latest generation of supertankers. At least two major oil companies have reduced their refinery capacities in the area since then. The north-western tip of Wales, the island of Anglesey, is probably about the only place in the industrialised Western world today where people demonstrate *for* new road development projects regardless of environmental costs. North Wales has also had to pay a part of the 'peace dividend' after the end of the Cold War, as the Ministry of Defence decided to close a number of bases and maintenance establishments in the area. Many central and western parts of Wales suffer from an obvious lack of infrastructure development, and no potential investor is much impressed by regular power cuts and blocked access roads during the winter months.

However, some progress has indeed been made, but a general restructuring of the entire economic base of a region takes time – and both national and economic freedom also require that one also meets one's responsibilities and obligations. To achieve this, the EU has granted about two-thirds of the Welsh territory, with about 2 million inhabitants,

Objective 1 status for a period of seven years starting January 2000, on the understanding that thereafter hardly any EU funds will be available to Wales. Utilising these funds appropriately for the management of significant regional development will be the one key task the newly established NAW will have to address.

Saxony: 'Blühende Landschaften'?[24]
With regard to the spatial distribution of the Saxon economy, there is, generally speaking, not much division. Saxony is more or less industrialised throughout, with only the hilly rural areas along the southern and eastern borders falling behind. However, with a population of just over 4.54 million and an area of 18,431 sq. km (SLA, 1997: 32) Saxony is one of the larger and, in terms of industrial output by far the strongest of the East German *Länder*.

TABLE 2.3
GROSS DOMESTIC PRODUCT IN SAXONY, 1991–99

Year	GDP (m. DM)	Change from previous year (%)	Share of German GDP (%)
1991	60.030	n/a	2.3
1992	87.620	+28.8	2.8
1993	104.981	+19.8	3.2
1994	121.463	+15.7	3.6
1995	132.072	+8.7	3.7
1996	136.476	+3.1	3.7
1997	136.476	+0.2	3.6
1998	137.751	+0.9	3.6
1999	141.273	+2.6	3.6

Source: Statisisches Jahrbuch Sachsen, 2000, p. 664.

A key feature of all three governmental districts is the location of a heavily industrialised zone in close proximity to Dresden, Leipzig and Chemnitz, the district capitals, while the further one gets from these the degree of industrialisation declines. Chemnitz in particular used to be an important centre of 'heavy' industries, metallurgy and machine manufacturing. To some extent this tradition has been maintained, albeit on a somewhat smaller scale. The governmental district of Chemnitz, however, probably has the largest internal divisions, and also features some of the most deprived rural areas in the south.[25] The decline of the *Erzgebirge* sub-region, however, was not a product of misguided GDR economic policy or of German unification. Its demise started early in the twentieth century when the natural resources of iron and silver ore – which gave the mountain range its name – ran out. Subsequent efforts by the GDR to revitalise the area by deliberately locating SMEs there may have seemed appropriate at the time, but resulted in the creation of a fairly well-skilled but not particularly mobile workforce now located in places which, due to infrastructural underdevelopment, appear to be singularly unattractive for inward investment. Indeed, despite the best efforts by the *Regierungspräsidium* Chemnitz and local councils, what remains is tourism, health and other service industries, hill-farming, and small enterprises operating predominantly in the local market – such as there is.[26] These problems were compounded by the Saxon government's decision not to engage in large-scale infrastructure development south of the A9 Dresden to Chemnitz motorway.

The Dresden governmental district features a well-developed 'light' industry sector, headed by the electronics industry. One of the largest inward investment schemes, the opening of a chip manufacturing plant by the American company AMD near Dresden is, however, the only proof so far that development of light industry in this area is ongoing. AMD is now the largest manufacturing employer in the area, and it is the only service industry which has seen significant growth. This goes for both the city of Dresden itself and the area along the Czech border that attracts many tourists. In the northeast of the governmental district, along the Polish border and in Sorabia, the situation is less comfortable. Plagued by black-marketeering and shopping trips by Saxons across the nearby border, local businesses find it difficult to survive. There has never been a large-scale manufacturing sector in this area, which is probably the most rural corner of Saxony. Support initiatives by the Saxon Ministry of Agriculture, however, have gone a long way to alleviate the most pressing problems, as have some infrastructure improvements.[27] The most important of these are probably the extension of the A9 motorway to the Polish border, the improvement of railway links with the Czech Republic, and the improved facilities at Dresden Airport.

For centuries, Leipzig has always been a city of commerce and services. Despite a lack of support by the Saxon government, local politicians and officials have managed to keep this tradition alive. The new fairground and its surrounding business park to the north of the city are the most impressive examples of this. In addition, the focus of development planners has been on improving the infrastructure for businesses in which Leipzig has a proven track record, for example publishing (LBN, 1998: 1–3). Leipzig is also a centre for commercial and legal services, and division of the Federal Supreme Court (*Bundesgerichtshof*) and the Federal Administration Court (*Bundesverwaltungsgericht*) have relocated there.[28]

The rest of the governmental district, however, is by no means free from problems: the energy and chemical manufacturing sectors, based on open-cast lignite mining in the southern part of the district, have seen severe cut-backs. While the overall impact on the environment is very noticeable and generally welcome, alternative means of employment have yet to be developed. In the eastern part of the district, large-scale agricultural production units and SMEs in the food industry have found it difficult to adapt to EU market regulations.

In all governmental districts, however, mass unemployment is a major problem. The positive development in the service industries – the only growth sector in terms of employment – alone is not enough to stem the tide. Surprisingly, the retail industry, in which the most visible changes have occurred with the opening of new outlets and out-of-town retail parks virtually everywhere, has not significantly contributed to job creation. In addition, various qualification and job experience schemes, welcome as they are by the participants, often just provide a stopgap measure and do not lead to an enhancement of long-term employment prospects. Therefore, unemployment is likely to remain in the vicinity of 15 to 17 per cent for the foreseeable future.

TABLE 2.4
EMPLOYMENT IN SAXONY, BY SECTOR, 1991–99

Sector	Employees 1991*	Employees 1995**	Employees 1999**
Agriculture, forestry, fishery	101,337	66,200	53,100
Manufacturing	1,008,706	709,100	626,500
Trade and transport	350,747	429,800	423,100
Service industries	281,142	205,100	229,200
Public and semi-public institutions	451,250	569,000	566,200
Total	2,193,182	1,979,200	1,898,100

Source: * SLA, 1997: 201; ** SLA, 2000: 223.

In general, however, Saxony was to some extent more fortunate insofar as the German central government, although being politically to the right, behaved more sensitively to the needs of its newly acquired region after 1990. Not only came 'freedom under the law' but, like the other new *Länder*, Saxony also experienced a huge influx of economic development aid under the terms of the *Gemeinschaftsaufgabe* [Verbesserung der Regionalen Wirtschaftsstruktur] (GA). Translated into English as the joint task of improving regional economic structures, this scheme, surprisingly, is not a child of unification; it is in fact the result of a 1960s initiative:

Bonn's decision in 1969 to reform the national regional policy framework sprang from its desire to curb competitive bidding for mobile investment among the Länder. The Federal government granted the states a hand in federal policy-making in return for a measure of restraint in their own regional initiatives. The Länder retained the right to fund their own regional programs provided they did not undercut national regional economic objectives. Thus, regional policy after 1969 became a 'joint task'. ... Complex, multilateral negotiations between state and federal representatives resulted in annual framework plans that established crucial policy parameters ... Decision-making was highly transparent, involving clearly defined procedural rules and multiple statistical indicators for the designation of assisted areas. Bargaining was strictly an intergovernmental affair – firms, local authorities, and producer groups were absent from the process. (Anderson, 1995: 29–30)

Subsequently, Anderson lists two major changes in the system of governance deriving from the introduction of this scheme: the change in emphasis from party-political channels of regional interest representation to intergovernmental state–federal linkages, and compensation for the federal states' loss of independent decision-making by way of allowing them to act as gatekeepers between the federal government and sub-state territorial authorities in the field of regional policy (Anderson, 1995: 30–1).

After unification, the East German *Länder* were integrated into the GA, albeit under somewhat different rules: the economic indicators in the east were simply off the scale used to measure eligibility in the West German *Länder*. The federal and state governments introduced a special development initiative called *Gemeinschaftswerk 'Aufschwung Ost'* (Joint Initiative 'Boom East') designed to bring east Germany up to west German standards in key respects. Deliberately deviating from the exclusively intergovernmental set-up of the GA, the *Gemeinschaftswerk* involved not only the federal and state governments, but also key industrial organisations representing various sectors of the economy. The *Kanzlerrunde*, a consultative body of the organisations involved, were invited by the Chancellor to meet regularly to act as a think-tank and negotiating body. Responsibility for the provision of funds and the implementation of agreed policies rested with its several participants, who in turn formed individual partnerships to carry this out. This is the theory, anyway, and is regarded as an example of 'good practice' or, in the spirit of the TEU, implementing the 'principle of partnership' within the German federal system of government.

So there was a much less straightforward exercise of executive power by the federal government in Saxony than there is in Wales by London. However, with the *Rechtsstaat*[29] came the lawyers, accountants, civil servants, technical advisers, and all categories of senior personnel – including the proud new owners of the freshly privatised industries – from the west in order to facilitate the necessary transformation processes.[30]

The Saxon government tried hard to make the most of the new opportunities provided by EU membership. Objective 1 status was granted to all East German *Länder* immediately in 1990. The first transitional ERDF-dominated Operational Programme (1991–93) provided Saxony with ECU 464m. (SMWA, 1994).

TABLE 2.5
USE OF ERDF FUNDS IN SAXONY, 1991–93

Priority	Number of projects	Funds allocated (m. DM)
Economy-related infrastructure	348	381.97
Investment in manufacturing industry	2,598*	399.78
Human resource development	50	67.71
Improvement of rural areas	84*	47.20
Technical assistance	n/a	23.40
Total	3,080**	920.06

*   Of the 2,659 projects which received funds under these two headings, only nine were not SMEs
** Excluding technical assistance

Source: SMWA, 1994: 22–5.

In addition, Saxony has received DM 395m in ESF funds over the same period, out of which 16,334 individual projects have received some support (SMWA, 1995). The main theme of the 1994–1999 concept of regional development was to emphasise an integrated approach to the distribution and use of the several sources of funding available, according to the ERDF-dominated Operational Programme for Saxony for that period.

At first glance, the figures in Table 2.6 seem impressive indeed, as one would expect in an Objective 1 region. The two key problems, however, were how to administer the distribution appropriately, and how to use the money efficiently with a view to long-term sustainability of the projects which receive funding. As required by the Operational Programme, and a number of supplementary programmes (ESF, LEADER, RECHAR), the organisational structure of fund management, consultation and processing applications has been set up. Among the public actors, the appropriate Saxon ministries (*Staatsministerien*) are, within their departmental brief, in charge of the strategic planning of the entire *Land*. The Cabinet Office (*Staatskanzlei*) exercises general supervision and budgetary co-ordination. Except for very large – or prestigious – projects, however, the real front-line work of planning, liaising with semi-public and private actors, processing of applications and supervision of development is done at the sub-regional level, by the Offices of Economic Development of the *Regierungsbezirke*. The concept of taking an integrated approach is to be understood basically as the opportunity of sub-regional and local actors, co-ordinated by the respective *Regierungspräsidien* in charge, to bid for projects which are entitled to apply for funding from different sources by submitting one proposal rather than several. However, the *Regierungspräsidien* have tried hard to make sure that mixed sourcing does not lead to use of funds outside the confines of the relevant programme. The work of the *Regierungspräsidien* is being supported by similar offices that have been set up by the larger cities. In some cases a limited number of semi-public and private development agencies has been established, but usually on a small scale.

TABLE 2.6
REGIONAL DEVELOPMENT FUNDING AVAILABLE IN SAXONY, 1994–99 (m. ECU)

Task	Total	ERDF	ESF	EAGGF	Federal govern-ment	Regional govern-ment	Local govern-ment	Private invest-ment
Manufacturing and infrastructure	4,059.1	600.7	43.1	–	226.8	250.0	147.1	2,792.2
SME and service industry	3,556.4	483.3	111.7	–	134.7	221.4	–	2,605.3
R&D and innovations	410.9	141.0	80.3	–	–	90.2	–	99.4
Environment	860.5	342.4	262.6	–	–	141.4	114.4	–
Human resource development	889.5	325.8	295.8	–	267.9	159.3	108.6	–
Agriculture and fishery	1,671.0	100.7	43.1	471.4	116.6	145.2	48.5	745.5
Technical assistance	91.1	20.1	38.2	6.2	–	24.6	2.0	–
Total	11,538.5	2,014.0	874.8	477.6	746.0	1,032.1	420.3	6,242.4

Source: SMWA, 1995: 34.

The most pressing problem, however, was how to use available funds strategically in a way that enables individual projects to become self-sufficient in the long term. Except for some large infrastructure-related projects, there is precious little evidence so far that Saxony has made any progress in this direction. Despite considerable myth-building efforts by regional politicians and the media, it is still the exception rather than the rule that modernisation has indeed led to increased productivity.[31] Semi-public and voluntary sector organisations and projects find it virtually impossible to shift from a grant-maintained to a self-sufficient operation, not least because there is no sufficient local or regional company base in place to provide significant sponsorship. It also has to be mentioned that nowadays private actors usually do not hesitate to threaten with relocation – for example just a few miles across the border into Poland or the Czech Republic – if there is no promise of continued support, or if the conditions are not perfect to ensure a quick profit. On the other hand, Saxony's co-operation with its eastern neighbours has so far, despite a significant effort by public actors, not amounted to much as there is no network of semi-public and private bodies capable of implementing the bold views of the politicians[32] on either side of the border. Indeed, some of the efforts, such as the sub-regional development initiative along the border, *Sonderstruktur-programm 'Perlenkette entlang der Neiße'*, are already viewed by some actors, the *Sächsischer Rechnungshof* (Saxon Audit Commission – see their Annual Report, 1996: 141–6) among them, as inefficient use of funds and open to abuse.

So – *'Blühende Landschaften'*? The CDU politician Günter Nooke has suggested that

> The German Unity is a success story. There they really are, the blossoming landscapes Chancellor Helmut Kohl was talking about. For instance ... in the land reclamation schemes to clean up the areas devastated by lignite mining in the Lausitz area and in central Germany. Each laying of a foundation stone of a new building, each opening of a reconstructed architectural monument, each repaired bridge, each reconstructed railway station and each kilometre of motorway drives home the point forcefully: without reunification all this would not have happened. (Nooke, 1998: 65)[33]

Many steps towards reconstructing the East German infrastructure have been undertaken, and indeed, many reconstruction jobs would not have been done had the GDR not ceased to exist. However, the 'success story' is mitigated by the fact that many rejuvenation efforts were conducted with little consideration for the social costs. As in Wales, the Saxon valleys now look much greener – as little industry remains to spoil the view. The railway station modernisation programme was paid for by much-increased ticket prices. The *Deutsche Bahn AG* has one of the most expensive price structures in Europe – especially for regional and local travel. Sweeping generalisations of success stories, such as Nooke's, are about as helpful as the eternal doom-and-gloom scenarios painted by the PDS in their Bundestag and Saxon *Landtag* election campaigns 1990 and 1994.[34] Basically, the same bottom line that applied to Wales applies to Saxony, too: yes, regional mobilisation can work, but it takes time, and not only national but also regional freedom of manoeuvre needs to be earned by meeting one's responsibilities and obligations.

THE ORGANISATIONAL STRUCTURE OF REGIONAL ACTORS

Wales: 'New Masters of Their Destiny'?

The UK has been described as a 'multi-national state' (for example Rose, 1982) with different constitutional arrangements for its constituent parts. Wales, however, has been locked into England more closely than Scotland and Northern Ireland. It has only gradually obtained administrative recognition of its position as a distinct political and cultural entity. Much to the disappointment of a number of places which thought they had a stronger historical claim, Cardiff was recognised as its capital city in 1955. The Welsh Office was created in 1964 – some 80 years after its Scottish counterpart. Wales as part of the UK is in turn a member-region of the EU, with all the implications concerning the validity of EU law within Wales, except in those policy areas in which the UK has exercised its opt-out choice. There are five Welsh Members of the European Parliament (MEPs), and two Welsh members plus two alternate members of the CoR. By chance rather than design, at the moment Wales also has its 'own' commissioner, Neil Kinnock.[35]

The supreme legislative power in Wales is vested in the UK Parliament at Westminster. Wales is represented by 40 Members of Parliament (MPs), chosen by majority vote in their constituencies. As the south of Wales is more densely populated than the north, 25 of the 40 constituencies are located in the area along the southern coast. In terms of law-making, England and Wales form a union. There is no specific law as there is in Scotland, but there are a number of Acts which deal with specific Welsh matters (for example Welsh Language in Education Act 1991; Welsh Language Act 1993; etc.). Of particular relevance for Wales is the House of Commons Select Committee on Welsh Affairs, because, in matters concerning Wales only, the House hardly ever decides against the recommendations of the Committee. However, the Committee roughly reflects the majority situation in the House, i.e. not all Welsh MPs are a member of the Committee, and some members of the Committee have no direct political links to Wales.[36]

The supreme executive power in Wales has, until 1999, been vested in the UK government. It exercised this power mainly through one of its departments, the WO. The head of this department, the Secretary of State for Wales, was a member of the UK Cabinet. The WO co-ordinated the activities of the other Whitehall departments within Wales, and conducted some of the functions of these departments. On the other hand, some departments, such as Trade and Industry, and Defence, more often than not prefer to deal with Welsh matters directly, at least in cases in which not only Wales but also other parts of the UK are concerned.

Formally, until 1999, there was no regional government in Wales. The original concept for the WO was to represent Wales more fully and more directly at the UK level. It was founded in 1964, when the newly elected Labour government fulfilled a campaign pledge within days of winning office. However, during the Conservative era 1979–97, the Secretary of State's role of representing Wales gave away more and more to the role of implementing government policy in Wales. Internally, the WO was organised along functional divisions of labour, roughly resembling a regional government structure. Restructuring measures took place quite frequently, usually with the appointment of a new Secretary of State – on average once or twice per legislative period. Under the leadership of the Secretary of State, the groups and departments of the WO enjoyed a certain amount of freedom running public policies in Wales according to their brief. However, they were bound by the provisions of applicable law, and major activities as well as budgetary decisions were subject to parliamentary scrutiny. In cases of infringement between the WO and other UK government departments, the view of the Cabinet prevailed, with the Prime Minister having the final say. Some policy areas, such as foreign policy and defence, had to be considered 'out of bounds' for the WO. It must also be taken into consideration that the WO's political freedom of manoeuvre in terms of 'independent' Welsh policy-making has always been quite limited by London, and subject to close scrutiny by the Cabinet, both Houses of Parliament, and the National Audit Office.

Some political steering, especially in the field of economic policy were, and still are, conducted by the WDA. However, the WO ran a number of business services of its own, and closely supervised the major WDA activities. This co-operation has in the past been used as an indicator that both organisations, WO and WDA, together with a number of other quangos, notably the Development Board for Rural Wales (DBRW) and the Land Authority, were functionally taking on the role of a regional government of Wales. The devolution debate has shed a new light on that assumption. One of the main motives for introducing a National Assembly for Wales from 1999 was to establish a democratic system of regional government that offers more than a surrogate system of functional equivalents mainly used for implementing decisions taken elsewhere. The Assembly comprises 60 members, of whom 40 were chosen by the traditional First-Past-The-Post system based on the 40 Welsh Westminster constituencies, and 20 were chosen proportionally from sub-regional lists based on the five old Welsh Euro-constituencies. However, another element of the recently introduced electoral reforms is that since the 1999 EP elections on Wales has been treated as a single Euro-constituency, and the five Welsh MEPs are chosen by pure proportional representation from all-Wales party lists.

According to the present legislation,[37] the NAW does not deal with issues that used to be outside the WO's brief. Within the policy areas previously dealt with by the WO, the NAW does not have the right to pass primary legislation. There are no tax-altering powers for the NAW.[38] Parliamentary scrutiny of Welsh affairs will remain firmly in place. In short, the NAW 'will have less powers than Bremen City Council' (Luyken, 1998: 55). This assessment is somewhat misleading insofar as Bremen is a *Land* in its own right, so Bremen's *Bürgerschaft* (city parliament) enjoys the full rights and powers of a German *Landtag*. Nevertheless, compared to the level of influence that the German *Länder* have, the NAW's powers do not seem to be particularly impressive. This is reason enough for the protagonists of devolution, both within Plaid Cymru and within some groupings associated with the Welsh Labour Party, for example Welsh Labour Action, not to be entirely satisfied.

Compared to the previous UK situation, however, the powers that were granted to the NAW are still formidable. Most notably among these is the right to develop and implement specific Welsh policies, possibly quite different from what is done in the rest of the UK, and with the opportunity to develop a distinct Welsh policy style. Along with this comes the right to enact secondary legislation,[39] in most spheres of Welsh 'domestic' affairs. So, while the WA does not have control over how much public money is going to be spent in Wales,[40] it has the final say as to the distribution of these funds. In fact, it has been given the right to shape socio-economic development policies according to its own principles and choices, provided that these policies do not break EU law or unduly interfere with policies run by the UK government for the entire country, or by other regional parliaments such as the Scottish Parliament (SP) or the Northern Ireland Assembly. In addition, the NAW gained a number of other rights, among them the power to set up, abolish or alter the structure and leadership composition of Welsh NDPBs, to oversee local government in a similar way to the one previously conducted by the WO, and to make appointments to the Welsh Civil Service. The WO as such has been dissolved, and both its functions and its personnel were transferred onto the staff of the NAW. The NAW also gained the right to represent Wales in negotiations with semi-public and private actors from outside Wales (HoC, 1997: 17–19).

Welsh representation within the governmental system of the UK, and towards the EU, however, remains largely unaltered. To appease Scottish and Welsh Unionists, Prime Minister Blair and other senior government representatives have repeatedly stressed that further steps to devolution beyond what has been introduced so far can only be considered as part of a general overhaul of the UK's constitutional system, to be addressed during a second or even third term of a Labour government. Therefore, for the time being, the NAW will only have minimal formal opportunities to deal with foreign and EU affairs, the government's foreign policy monopoly remaining firmly in place – notwithstanding enhanced informal means of Welsh interest representation already emerging, and the possibility of extending formal means through appropriate use of partnership agreements and concordats (Poirier, 2001). Some of the responsibilities the NAW has taken on are nominating the Welsh CoR members, and becoming directly involved in the running of the Wales European Centre (WEC), Wales's unofficial representation in Brussels – a task which the WO was not allowed to do.

The previous Conservative government had already promised to send the Secretary of State to represent the UK in sessions of the Council of Ministers more frequently (HoC, 1995a: 9–10). The present government has widened this promise to include ministers of the newly established regional parliaments as and when this seems appropriate (HoC, 1997: 21–23). However, the Secretary of State's role has diminished considerably. The Secretary is continuing to represent Wales in the UK Cabinet and, when appropriate, in Europe. However, he has lost the responsibility for what was the WO and has now become the Welsh Civil Service under the control of the Welsh Executive. The Secretary has retained a comparatively small personal staff needed to conduct his role as liaison officer between Wales, the UK government and Europe. The post of Secretary of State will still be filled by a Westminster MP, not a member of the NAW, and he or she will hence remain primarily responsible to Parliament.[41] In no circumstances, however, will the holder of this office be responsible for the actions of the NAW – this is the role of the newly established First Secretary, chosen by the NAW from the ranks of its 60 members. The First Secretary is the Leader of the NAW,[42] and chief of the Welsh Executive – a group of approximately ten NAW members[43] who are in charge of certain functions of the NAW, and chair its respective committees. The role of these committees includes supervision of their respective branches of the Welsh Civil Service.

A number of responsibilities which in other European countries rest traditionally with regional governments, for example education in Germany, had in Wales been given to local authorities, acting under close supervision by – and which were almost completely financially dependent on – the UK government. The 1999 reforms changed this situation insofar as the NAW, by means of secondary legislation, and not a Whitehall department, is now responsible for the distribution of the funds made available by the government.

TABLE 2.7
WELSH LOCAL GOVERNMENT REFORM: TERRITORIAL CHANGES, 1996

Old counties	Old cities and districts	New unitary authorities*
Gwent	Monmouth	Monmouthshire
	Torfaen	Torfaen
	Newport	Newport
	Blaenau-Gwent	Blaenau-Gwent
	Islwyn	
South Glamorgan	Cardiff	Cardiff
	Vale of Glamorgan	Vale of Glamorgan
Mid Glamorgan	Rhymney Valley	Caerphilly
	Merthyr Tydfil	Merthyr Tydfil
	Cynon Valley	Rhondda Cynon Taff
	Rhondda	Bridgend
	Taff-Ely	Neath and Port Talbot
	Ogwr	
West Glamorgan	Port Talbot	Swansea
	Neath	
	Lliw Valley	
	Swansea	
Dyfed	Llanelli	Carmarthenshire
	Carmarthen	Pembrokeshire
	Dinefwr	Cardiganshire
	South Pembrokeshire	
	Preseli Pembrokeshire	
	Ceredigion	
Powys	Brecknock	Powys
	Radnorshire	
	Montgomeryshire	
Gwynedd	Meirionnydd	Caernarfonshire and Merionethshire
	Dwyfor	Anglesey (Ynys Mon)
	Arfon	Aberconwy and Colwyn
	Ynys Mon	
	Aberconwy	
Clwyd	Colwyn	Denbighshire
	Glyndwr	Flintshire
	Rhuddlan	Wrexham
	Delyn	
	Alyn and Deeside	
	Wrexham Maelor	

* These new territories are either called 'Counties' or 'County Boroughs'. There is no distinction in powers, size or functions associated with the two titles.

Source: Author's own compilation using information provided in WO 1994: 159–160

The system of local government in Wales saw a period of transition, lasting from May 1995 until April 1996. This was due to the provisions of the Local Government (Wales) Act 1993, which was first proposed by the then Conservative government in March 1993 (WO, 1993), and eventually became law in November 1993. The main feature of the Act is that the old two-tier structure of local government was replaced by a new single-tier structure (see Table 2.7). One of the main aims of these reforms was to increase efficiency in local government, to reduce bureaucratic workload, and to simplify administrative and budgetary procedures. There have been suggestions that these reforms would result in 'hidden gerrymandering' by the government, claims that cannot be dismissed off-hand, although first tests – the local elections in 1995 and 1999 – indicate that there was little evidence of success: as in Scotland, none of these new authorities is currently controlled by a Conservative majority.

The old two-tier system consisted of a higher tier (counties) and a lower tier (cities and districts). The councils ran local administrative units to conduct the day-to-day business of local government, and to carry out administrative tasks as required by law. All county councils and most of the district or city councils ran administrative units dealing with matters of local development, attracting inward investment, and looking for copartners. The organisational framework of these units varied widely, as did the levels and ranges of activity, but the most common forms were department (for example Cardiff), and agency, in either its full (for example South Pembrokeshire), or limited variety (for example Rhondda). Departments are the 'classic' way of running local development programmes in Wales; civil servants plan the measures and either put their own personnel – council workers – into the job, or hire private contractors. With the introduction of the legal requirement to submit CCT in the late 1980s, some local authorities decided to privatise the planning element as well by inviting private companies to bid for the entire job (full agency model), or by establishing a publicly owned company which invites private investment into their programmes (limited agency model). Although preliminary indications suggest that there is no direct link between the organisational form and the level and range of activity, it seems to be the case that a majority of the more active areas have opted for an agency model. On the other hand, there is a clear division concerning the levels of activity between south Wales (higher) and north Wales (lower), roughly coinciding with the territorial distribution of funds provided by EU and national programmes. Only very recently has the north begun to participate in these processes more fully.

Although the idea of semi-public actors is nothing new to British politics, there has been a vast increase in both their numbers and their spending power in recent years. A new semi-public actor was created almost every month between 1994 and 1999. For the first time in 1994 and ever since, together they spent more money in Wales than the government – although part of it derived from government grants. Although organisations vary widely in form, there are three basic categories of semi-public actors operating in Wales: regulatory bodies, managing bodies, and institutes of higher and further education.[44]

Regulatory bodies. There are usually two kinds of regulatory bodies: authorities and regulators. Authorities are the traditional kind. Set up by Act of Parliament, they look after one specific problem, ensuring compliance with the applicable law thereto – thus fulfilling an investigating and quasi-judicial role. Staffed by civil servants, their decision-making bodies (boards, etc.) are made up of publicly appointed experts in the field whose backgrounds reflect a variety of institutions. Although appointees are expected to be politically neutral, the appointment process ensures that the government can easily prevent potential critics from being selected. As the activities of authorities are subject to scrutiny by parliamentary committees, public control is formally assured, but more often than not this means that the government with its parliamentary majority can exercise considerable influence over vital issues. Usually authorities have the power to veto economic decisions by private actors and to impose financial sanctions for non-compliance with their decisions, subject to judicial review. Authorities operate nationwide, but most of them have one or more offices in Wales. Examples include the Office of Fair Trading, the Monopolies and Mergers Commission and the regionally organised health and safety authorities. Under the Conservatives, some of these authorities were privatised and relaunched as commercial enterprises, for example the Forestry Commission, now known as Forest Enterprise.

A comparatively new form of regulatory body is the regulator. Operating with only a small staff of experts, but in close contact with the government and the industries concerned, regulators are publicly appointed individuals who are given the job of exercising at least some form of public control over previously state-owned industries which were privatised from the mid-1980s on. This was deemed necessary once the government had decided to give up its majority of shares, thus creating private monopolies. A particular case in point are the utilities suppliers. Again, the appointment procedure constitutes a tool for the government to exercise influence. However, once appointed, the regulator's activities are not normally subject to parliamentary scrutiny, since the government as shareholder must be deemed biased, except in cases of alleged malpractice, which are to be investigated by a Special Select Committee. In some cases the work of the regulator is supplemented by private organisations such as the consumers' organisations.

Managing bodies. These have become the most influential and therefore most important category of semi-public actors. The different types and the nature of their economic activities have earned them the name 'quasi-non-governmental organisations' (quangos), which is often used pejoratively. Again, the decision-making members of the organisations are publicly appointed, with all the political implications mentioned above. The budgets – and therefore more or less all activities – of these organisations are subject to parliamentary scrutiny, both by way of direct report to the Public Accounts Committee and by way of independent audit by the Comptroller and Auditor General of the National Audit Office (Morgan and Roberts, 1993).

Ostensibly created to ensure administrative efficiency and optimum utilisation of public funds, these organisations have – despite some undeniable success – been severely criticised. The criticisms are: (i) in the 1980s, in the name of efficiency managing bodies were used to implement Thatcherite economic policies bypassing established parliamentary procedures and local governments, thus also causing concern with regard to democratic control; (ii) in the event of things going wrong, it has become possible for the government to deny responsibility by shedding blame on the organisations, but still to claim success if things go well; and (iii) in a long-term perspective, by shifting responsibilities away from the government and also running a 'favourable' appointment policy, it has become possible for the government to limit the freedom of manoeuvre of future governments (see also Majone, 1996).

There are usually three main types of managing body: agencies, boards or companies. Agencies are multi-purpose organisations which are given the task of looking after a specified area: the most typical example in Wales is the WDA. Founded by Act of Parliament in 1975, its spatial perimeter is the whole of Wales. Its main tasks are to facilitate economic and infrastructure development, to attract inward investment, to help implement EU and national development programmes, to establish international contacts as deemed appropriate, and to liaise with virtually everyone who might be in a position to contribute to achieving these ends. In addition to its headquarters in Cardiff, the agency runs three sub-regional offices (south, west and north), and has a 'share' in the WEC in Brussels. The agency is also the second-largest freehold owner in Wales, second only to the Crown, but has recently embarked on a policy of selling off those grounds that have been developed to the tenants who did the actual development, or even third parties – thus breaking promises to some investors they had attracted by promising long-term, low-cost tenancies. On a smaller territorial scale, a number of Local Development Agencies are doing the same. These were set up by those local councils which have not opted for the 'department' solution. There are also a number of Regional Development Agencies dealing with areas that have encountered specific problems. By far the largest of these is the DBRW.[45] Although agriculture and environment issues are among its major concerns, the Board, by shifting some of its emphasis into attracting small businesses into rural Wales, certainly qualifies as a multi-purpose agency. Recognising that shift of emphasis, the government decided in 1999 to merge the WDA and the DBRW along with the Land Authority for Wales[46] into a revamped 'powerhouse' WDA as the new clearing house for all regional planning and development tasks. Other agency examples are the Cardiff Bay Development Corporation[47] and the agency running The Valleys Initiative.

Boards are single-purpose managing bodies dealing with the budgetary and general economic and administrative management of publicly owned non-administrative institutions, such as trusts, NHS institutions and schools. Administrative institutions have their own in-house managing bodies consisting entirely of civil servants and belonging to the public sphere but running market-oriented policies (for example the Welsh Office Establishments Group), but boards of non-administrative institutions consist only in part of civil servants. Other members comprise representatives of concerned groups (such as senior medical staff, teachers, parents, arts experts, etc.) and 'independent' advisors hired from private consulting companies. Although most of these boards are to a large extent dependent on government grants, their real power derives from their ability to hand out service contracts to private companies (Weir and Hall, 1995). In some cases they are legally required to submit to CCT, in particular for services run by local authorities instead of hiring their own service personnel. On the other hand, boards tend to use voluntary workers whenever possible, especially with regard to functions which overlap with the work of charities – thus saving considerable sums of money. However, while some of these boards enjoy freedom of manoeuvre and exercise it ruthlessly – such as implementing cost cuts in the NHS – others lack even the opportunity to exercise 'consumer choice' because of the lack of sufficient funding, for example most school boards.

Publicly owned companies are a comparatively old form of semi-public actor, but quite recently the term has acquired a new characteristic. The common feature of both old and new forms of public ownership of companies is that the government directly or indirectly holds the majority of shares. However, while the old large monopolies in public transport and utilities have been sold off as far as possible, the new trend is to establish small and medium-sized, and, above all, very profitable companies dealing with special issues of support for the local business community. A typical example are the previously local and later sub-regional Training and Education Councils (TECs) until their merger into the education quango ELWA in 2002. There are similar – usually small – companies specialising in technology transfer, business communication facilities, and consulting; often being run not only in close co-operation, but also in direct competition, with similar service providers run by private organisations, such as the CBI Wales.[48]

Two main types of private actor in Wales can be distinguished: Welsh branches of national organisations, and indigenous Welsh organisations with (or without UK-wide affiliations). However, although almost all actors regard Wales as a specific territorial unit for both organisational and economic purposes, the overall landscape of private actors in Wales is very similar to that prevailing in England. Six main categories of private actors are predominant: general business organisations; industrial organisations; trade unions and associations of professionals; private companies; political parties; and voluntary sector organisations and single-issue social interest groups.[49]

General business organisations comprise chambers of commerce, trade and industry, employers' associations, and export organisations. The Wales Chamber of Commerce and Industry provides a wide range of services for its members, including training courses, trade missions and general market advice – particularly with regard to Europe. Affiliated to the Association of British Chambers of Commerce, it also supports the five Welsh sub-regional chambers: Cardiff, Newport & Gwent, North Wales, West Wales, and Wrexham. Among the employers' associations, the CBI Wales and the Welsh section of the Federation of Small Businesses (FSB) are the most important. The CBI Wales offers a comprehensive business support service for its members, permanently updated according to findings in annual demand surveys. The FSB mainly focuses on the awareness of its members on both additional sources of funding and new developments in technology. Other important activities include lobbying for favourable legislation, and helping members to establish good relations with their respective local governments. Also operating in Wales are the Institute of Directors and the Institute of Management. The largest export organisation is the British Exporters Association. One of its largest regional branches is the South Wales Exporters Association. Not surprisingly, exchange of information and advice on administrative and fiscal matters are the main activities. Close links exist with the other main export organisations, the Institute of Export, and the DTI Export Organisation.

Industrial organisations play a major part in representing their members at the political level, in addition to creating a positive image for their industry among the general public. In 2000 there were 39 industrial organisations operating in Wales (Balsom, 2000: 602–11), one for almost every branch of the economy. Unlike the situation in Scotland, the Welsh organisations are usually Welsh branches of national organisations, with only one exception: The Farmers' Union of Wales (FUW). However, there is also a Welsh branch of the National Farmers' Union (NFU), so farming is the only sector of the economy where there are two industrial organisations for the same line of business. Both unions have members throughout Wales, but while the FUW is stronger in the north and the west, the NFU is stronger in the central and southern parts. In other sectors of the economy, although they come under various guises (alliances, associations, confederations, federations, societies, and even unions), the industrial organisations' field of activity is very much the same: to lobby for favourable legislation, to act as a 'watchdog' for professional standards, and even to facilitate technology transfer. However, co-operation is limited by the fact that the members are often direct competitors.

Trade unions and associations of professionals are the employees' counterpart to the employers' associations. In 2000, 32 trade unions and associations of professionals had a territorial representation in Wales (Balsom, 2000: 693–5), but about as many, 35, operated in Wales without having dedicated offices there. There is often no direct link between a line of business and union representation. While, for instance, the Transport and General Workers' Union, one of the most powerful unions in the UK, represents transport workers and unskilled workers in a variety of industries, there are no less than four unions for teachers – and even five for nurses. In general, public employees are organised in a wide variety of unions, although UNISON is by far the largest and covers all areas of public service from a NWA driver via local government clerk and primary school teacher to NHS nurse. Private sector employees tend to have no more than two unions covering their trade. However, overlapping is most common – and not always advantageous in pay negotiations. Fifty-five of these organisations are members of the Trades Union Congress (TUC) and/or its unions' organisation, the General Federation of Trade Unions. Traditionally, there is a strong link between the trade union movement and the Labour Party.

The strongest party in Wales, in terms of both membership and electoral support, is the Labour Party. This strength derives from three main sources: the high concentration of working-class areas in south Wales, the link to the unions, and the relative weakness – in some places the virtual absence – of a conservative political élite capable of rallying middle-class popular support. Union membership often implies collective membership in the Labour Party, which used to be a main source of party funding: members are charged a political levy as part of the union membership fee. As a result of this, for many years the unions were able to exercise a significant influence with regard to Labour policy-making, as unions by definition carried about two-thirds of the votes at Labour Party conferences. However, this situation has changed significantly since Tony Blair's Labour Party reform which started in 1995. As the key focus of these reforms is on strengthening the roles of the constituencies and the individual party members, the unions' share of the vote has now come down to around 50 per cent. It is likely that the influence of the unions on the Labour Party is going to decline further. In 1998, the Welsh Labour Party operated an electoral college system for choosing who would be its candidate to contest the election to become the first First Secretary of the NWA. Under this system three groups held an equal number of votes: the unions, the panel of Labour candidates for the NWA, and the constituency party organisations.[50] This model, giving equal influence to unions, office holders and individual members, is likely to become the dominant way of taking policy decisions within the Welsh Labour Party – not only as far as the selection of personnel is concerned, but also in regular party conferences when issues of policy and strategy are to be decided.

TABLE 2.8
DISTRIBUTION OF WELSH WESTMINSTER SEATS AMONG THE PARTIES
IN THE 1992, 1997 AND 2001 GENERAL ELECTIONS

Party	1992 (38 seats)	1997 (40 seats)	2001 (40 seats)
Labour	27	34	34
Conservatives	6	0	0
Plaid Cymru	4	4	4
Liberals	1	2	2

Source: www.news.bbc.co.uk/vote2001/

All other parties in Wales lack institutional links to other large private organisations. The three other parties of importance in Wales are the Liberal Democratic Party, the Conservative Party, and the nationalist party Plaid Cymru.

The Liberal Democratic Party regards itself as an up-and-coming force in Welsh politics. It draws support from middle-class and professional people. As these people live all over Wales rather than concentrated in specific areas, the potential support by an average of around 20 per cent of the voters, as expressed in the last five general elections, translates only occasionally into winning a Westminster seat under the present electoral system. The policies of the Welsh Liberal Democratic Party does not deviate significantly from the policies of the UK party insofar as the latter, too, is committed to both devolution and proportional representation.[51] Indeed, as the then UK party leader Paddy Ashdown claimed in the devolution debate, what is being done now is what Liberals have demanded for a full century. This goes in particular for the introduction of an element of proportional representation for the NWA, and full proportional representation for elections to the EP. However, the Labour Party and the Liberal Democratic Party have found much common ground on constitutional issues over the last five years or so, and co-operation between the parties in this area could not be closer. Indeed, Ashdown went as far as to accept Labour's invitation to sit on the UK Cabinet Committee on Constitutional Reform.

Another party committed to devolution is Plaid Cymru. In terms of parliamentary representation, it can now claim to be the second-strongest party in Wales. This, however, has as much to do with the collapse of the Conservatives as with an increase in Plaid Cymru's influence. Its territorial strongholds are in the north and north-west, where all four of the parliamentary constituencies it currently holds are located. There, the party can rely on an electoral support of around 15 per cent. However, there is an emerging Plaid Cymru intellectual élite in south Wales, composed mainly of professionals in education and the media. As they have the ability to act as multiplicators of political opinion, their views are omnipresent in most Welsh media, publication establishments, think-tanks, and similar bodies. Nevertheless, up to 1998, in south Wales and the Valleys Labour has never experienced any difficulties in out-voting Plaid Cymru by a ratio of at least ten to one.[52] In terms of policy, Plaid Cymru supports devolution as a step in the right direction towards the maximum possible self-government for Wales. This was expressed in its 'Powerhouse Parliament' campaign, designed to demand further extension of the powers of the NWA. However, contrary to the SNP's policy of using the SP as a tool to bring about independence from the UK, Plaid Cymru – for the time being – wants the NWA to work within the UK system. This constitutes a shift in policy from the position held by the party from the early 1970s to about 1995, when – as is still the case for the SNP – 'independence in Europe' was the expressed target. However, from the 1979 referendum on, Plaid Cymru has learned the hard way that in Wales radical separatism is indirectly proportional to electoral strength. Up to now, it has never been in a position to have to make good on political promises other than on some local councils in north Wales. Guaranteed to be out of power anywhere else, it was free to float nationalist ideas without really having to say how to put them into practice, hence practical feasibility was not first and foremost in the party's policy-formulating process. One example of this approach is Plaid Cymru's still current demand for a separate Welsh seat in the EU Council of Ministers, based on the fact that Wales is a *nation*. That such a seat depends on being a member *state* is conveniently omitted in all official party documents. However, with the advent of the NWA this situation had to change. All three parties in favour of devolution agreed during the joint referendum campaign in 1997 that at least during the start-up phase of the NWA an inclusive policy style should be developed. Therefore, initially Plaid Cymru politicians found themselves in key positions, in particular as committee chairs, within the NWA. This is another reason why the party has recently toned down its public rhetoric, although it is extremely difficult to assess to what extent private opinions of key party members have really undergone a significant change since 1997. The launch of a coalition government between Labour and the Liberals in October 2000 has effectively removed Plaid Cymru representatives from key positions within the NWA. Now to all intents and purposes back in opposition, it is again free to entertain a more radical approach to its definition of 'self-government in Europe'. So far, however, a coherent answer with regard to the details of such 'self-government' has yet to emerge within the party.

The Conservative Party was the only party in Wales to oppose devolution. This, however, can only be regarded as a secondary reason for its recent collapse in popular support: many – indeed most – opponents of devolution were not supporters of the Conservatives in the first place, and opposition to devolution in 1997 did not translate itself into popular support for the party. The more likely reason for the Conservatives' wipe-out in Wales in the 1997 and 2001 general elections was the UK-wide trend of dissatisfaction after 18 years of continuous Conservative governments in London. In Wales, this trend was augmented by the experience of successive Englishmen as Secretary of State for Wales, including John Redwood and William Hague. Under their stewardship the WO increasingly assumed the function of enforcing government policy in Wales, thus becoming regarded as insensitive to specific Welsh problems and aspirations that did not fit in with the views held by Downing Street.

However, political conservatism is by no means non-existent in Wales, and among the middle classes and the business community in south Wales, Pembrokeshire, and along the English border, the party can still muster up to 20 per cent of electoral support. Now suffering – like the Liberals – from the effects of the present electoral system, the party is nevertheless represented in the NWA. As in Scotland, the Welsh Conservative Party has now realised that it would be counter-productive to insist on swimming against the tide, hence the party's determination to mount a proper opposition within the NWA. In the first legislative periods, the 9 Conservative Members of the Welsh Assembly (AMs) along with the 17 from Plaid Cymru formed the opposition to a Labour/Liberal coalition government which held 28 seats and 6 seats, respectively.

Saxony: 'The Free State'?

In 1990, Saxony chose to follow tradition, derived from the days of the Weimar Republic (Schmeitzner, 1997), and call itself a *Freistaat* (Free State). The point of this exercise was for Saxony to emphasise the concept of statehood – free, no less – in its name; however, the only practical result of this decision is a linguistic quagmire. As far as constitutional arrangements, political powers, and influence in federal and European affairs are concerned, the 3 *Freistaaten* Bavaria, Thuringia and Saxony are in no way distinct from the other 13 *Länder* with whom together they form the Federal Republic of Germany (FRG). The concepts of statehood, partial sovereignty, and legal powers are regulated by Articles 30, 31, and 70–5 of the federal constitution, the *Grundgesetz* (GG). In a nutshell, Articles 70–5 indicate which powers either have to, or may, be exercised by the federation. In the latter case, a *Land* may legislate on its own if there is no federal law, or within the provisions of federal law. In those cases, however, federal law always supersedes *Land* law (Article 31). In all other areas the *Länder* may legislate as they see fit (Article 30). In addition, Articles 23 and 50–3 of the GG grant the *Länder* a number of rights to be exercised jointly in Europe and in the Bundesrat, which is the second chamber of the federal parliament, and is composed of representatives of the 16 *Land* governments. Saxony has four votes in the Bundesrat and is represented by 39 *Mitgliedern des Bundestags* (MdBs) in the first chamber of the federal parliament, the Bundestag (Sächs. Staatskanzlei, 1998: 17).

According to the Saxon Constitution,[53] the legislative powers constitutionally granted to the German *Länder* are in Saxony vested in the Saxon *Landtag* (Regional Parliament). The executive powers in Saxony are vested in the *Regierung des Freistaates Sachsen* (Government of the Free State of Saxony), composed of the *Ministerpräsident* (Prime Minister) and his Cabinet, elected by the *Landtag*. The ministers each head a *Staatsministerium* (State Ministry) which conducts the state civil service functions of their departmental brief.

In addition, the newly formed *Land* of Saxony decided in 1990 to stay divided into three territories. Under the FRG these were renamed

Regierungsbezirke (governmental districts), just as it had been under the GDR, but to retain them as purely administrative units, managed by the *Regierungspräsidien* (district government offices) in Dresden, Leipzig and Chemnitz. However, there is no legislative body for these territories. The heads of these administrative units, the *Regierungspräsidenten*, are appointed by the *Land* government, but once appointed they enjoy considerable freedom of manoeuvre in the running of administrative affairs in their territory. The internal structure of the *Regierungspräsidien* largely mirrors the ministerial bureaucracy, albeit on a much smaller scale.

Local government in Saxony consists of a two-tier system for rural areas, and a one-tier system for urban areas. The upper tier for rural areas consists of 23 *Landkreise* (local government districts). This number has been reduced from 48 (under the GDR) through a process of territorial reform in 1991–92 (Seibel, 1993a: 482–3). The main thrust of this reform was the creation of political units which comprise socio-economic entities of a feasible size.[54] One key step consisted of reuniting the local government of larger cities with the local government of the suburban and rural areas surrounding those cities. This policy was not implemented in the two largest cities, Dresden and Leipzig, as the resulting super-districts would have had up to three times the average size of the other districts in terms of population.

In the less densely populated areas of southern Saxony and along the Polish border, however, large territories have been brought under one administrative roof. These *Landkreise* are not only administrative units, but also feature *Kreistage* (district legislative assemblies). The executive branch in the newly formed *Landkreise* is headed by a *Landrat*, who is the only elected official in the *Landratsamt* (Local Government District Office). The powers and obligations of these offices are limited, and are mainly concerned with looking after the joint interests of the towns and villages in their area. In the economic sphere, their main function is detailed spatial and ground use planning, along with land ownership registry and transport. Some minor special functions, such as vehicle registration, are also run by the *Landratsämter*.

The lower tier of local government in the rural areas of Saxony are the *Gemeinden*, i.e. towns and villages.[55] Their role is set out in the *Sächsische Gemeindeordnung* (Saxon Local Government Charter). The *Gemeinden* have an elected *Gemeinderat* (Legislative Council), which in turn elects the Mayor. Seibel (1993a: 482) states that having this system meant 'following the example of a number of South German *Länder*', but it has to be noted that this system was already in place before and during the Nazi and GDR periods (Wollmann, 1998: 23). To continue with it meant no formal change, although now the Gemeinderat usually has a leading group and an opposition along party-political lines. The number of council members is usually relatively small – rarely exceeding 20 – but their administrative staff is usually quite large because one of the main functions of the *Gemeinde* bureaucracy is the administration of most elements of the social security benefit system, excluding unemployment benefit and pensions.

The six largest Saxon cities have a one-tier system of local government. It comprises elements of both the *Landkreis* and the *Gemeinde* system, and combines the powers and responsibilities of both. Since 1998, these cities each have a directly elected Mayor,[56] who also fulfils the role of a *Landrat*, and a *Stadtverordnetenversammlung* (City Council) operating along the lines of both a *Kreistag* and a *Gemeinderat*. Each City Council runs a vast local civil service, whose department heads are politically appointed by the council.

Compared to the Welsh case, the landscape with regard to semi-public actors in Saxony is extremely underdeveloped. The main reason for this is that Germany has not embarked on the widespread farming-out of governmental supervisory functions to NDPBs and similar organisations. The wave of privatisation in the transport and utilities industries consisted of a straightforward sale of shares through the stock exchange, on the federal level. During this process it was assumed that the public interest would be sufficiently safeguarded by means of a contract between the company to be privatised and the federal government, with disagreements to be settled, if necessary through the courts, under the usual provisions of the civil code, the *Bürgerliches Gesetzbuch* (BGB). During the start-up phase, a more effective lever held by the government ministries, however, was that agreed subsidies or tax relief would not be forthcoming if the companies failed to live up to their contractual obligations. Over time, however, it is envisaged that these contracts will be phased out, with no public supervision of the performance of the privatised companies in place.

The privatisation process in East Germany, however, posed a much more complex problem since the vast majority of the country's industrial and infrastructural assets were in public ownership on the day of unification. To facilitate the process of privatisation, a semi-public agency was established which at one time in late 1990 was the biggest owner of industrial assets in the entire EU: the *Treuhandanstalt* (THA). The THA itself was, strictly speaking, not a product of the unification of Germany, it was established by a special act passed by the GDR Parliament on 17 June 1990.[57] However, Article 25 of the Treaty on German Unification (*Einigungsvertrag*), dated 31 August 1990, provides that the THA was to continue, after unification, focusing on its two main briefs: to sell all industrial assets in its ownership for which a private buyer could be found; and to manage those assets for which no buyer could be found, reorganising them to make them more attractive to potential investors. To these ends, the THA was to co-operate with public institutions, which were entitled (but not legally required) to buy shares in the industrial assets in their territories, and with representatives of the business communities of Germany and from abroad. The THA was entitled to negotiate sales contracts, to impose conditions on sales, and to both require and give undertakings with regard to the management of assets as if the THA itself were a private company. General economic development strategies and the implementation thereof, however, remained outside the THA's brief: Article 28 of the *Einigungsvertrag* specifies this to be a job for the public institutions. Hence, a situation emerged where on the sales side the THA could act as it saw fit, irrespective of the wishes of the public actors of the territories concerned. On the asset management side, however, THA-run companies had to bid for European and national means of financial support in competition with already privatised companies.

Apart from private companies, virtually all Saxon or private interest organisations are the Saxon branches of national organisations. However, in keeping with the German concept of federalism, in most organisations the national establishments allow their regional offspring a significant degree of independence in representing their specific regional interests. To appreciate fully the speedy development of the landscape with regard to organisations in Saxony, it is essential to have a closer look at the process of German unification beyond the constitutional and legal dimension. In general, three key forms of developing the landscape in respect of organisations can be distinguished: unification, take-over and branching-out. Of these, unification was the most common, its application ranging from political parties via business interest organisations, trade unions and voluntary organisations, to churches. The basic idea here was to merge an East German institution, organisation, or association, with its West German counterpart. Given the large number and various types of organisations that existed in East Germany, in most cases West German organisations wishing to get a foothold in the East experienced no difficulties in finding a suitable equivalent there. In some cases, for example the Red Cross, many socio-cultural fields, and sports, very similar or virtually identical organisations existed in both parts of the country. The trade union system too, though highly centralised in the GDR, was fairly similar because the umbrella organisation *Freier Deutscher Gewerkschaftsbund* (FDGB), the key element of the system, had still retained its formal organisational division of separate *Gewerke* (trades). Even in such unlikely cases as employers' associations there was usually a GDR version, for example the *Handwerkskammern*. However, the key issue in these unification processes usually was to reform the internal structure and range or kind of activities of the East German organisation. This was addressed either before or after unification took place. In some cases, such as the churches, pressure to reform was brought not by a West German counterpart, but by outside events, financial pressures and legal requirements.[58] It goes without saying that in virtually all unification cases the West German organisation was the role -model for the new unified organisation. Allowances and alterations to the statutes were usually limited to a transitional period, or amounted to little more than tokenism. However, this is no real surprise as it only mirrored events in the wider society. Most mergers were conducted within the first 18 months after political unification.

A less straightforward way of expanding into Saxony was to conduct a take-over. This mostly concerned private companies that had resulted from the THA's sales policy already mentioned. While in the early phase east German companies were taken over by larger West German companies from the same branch of industry, later on the sectoral link ceased to be a significant criterion until finally the THA resorted to just selling freeholds, which basically then led to branching-out.

Branching-out was required for those companies wishing to expand into Saxony which could not find a suitable East German company to take over, and for those organisations for which there simply was no East German equivalent. Examples of the latter include a number of voluntary organisations, for example the St John Ambulance Association and the Knights of Malta Ambulance Service, and special interest organisations, for example the *Arbeitslosenverband*, the organisation representing the unemployed.

A special case is the reform of the party system, where the relics of the old GDR system are still prevalent at every turn despite the fact that whenever possible unifications with FRG parties have taken place.[59] A first glance at the personal and electoral strengths of the parties in Saxony indicates that both criteria are not directly linked.

The dominant role of the Christian Democrats (*Christlich-Demokratische Union* – CDU) in Saxony on the electoral side is impressive by any standard. However, this is mitigated by the fact that the party lost almost half its membership between 1990 and 1999 (SLA, 2000: 218). One reason for this phenomenon is that the present CDU structures in East Germany were created by a unification of the old CDU which existed in the GDR and the GDR's Democratic Farmers' Party (Demokratische Bauernpartei Deutschlands – DPD) in 1990, which in turn merged with the West German CDU at the federal level. So, while the Saxon voters preferred the most radical change of regime possible within the spectrum of democratic alternatives, members of the old GDR parties – by definition the more politically active part of the population – were less enchanted with that change of regime and either left politics altogether or found a new home with the parties placed politically to the left of the CDU. What remains in the CDU is the stock of members, including a significant number of new members and immigrant members from West Germany, who fully support the course of the party. The CDU's territorial strongholds in Saxony are in the city of Dresden and in the southern parts of the Chemnitz and Dresden governmental districts.

TABLE 2.9
MEMBERSHIP OF PARTIES IN SAXONY, 1990–99, AND DISTRIBUTION OF SAXON
LANDTAG AND BUNDESTAG SEATS IN THE 1990, 1994 AND 1998/99 ELECTIONS

Party	1990 Members	1990 Landtag (160 seats)	1990 Bundestag (40 seats)
CDU	37,200	92	21
SDP	4,451*	32	8
PDS	72,000	17	4
FDP	35,000	9	5
GRÜNE	820**	10	2
	1994 Members	*1994 Landtag 120 seats*	*1994 Bundestag 39 seats*
CDU	23,200	77	21
SDP	5,207	22	9
PDS	32,000	21	6
FDP	7,000	0	1
GRÜNE	1,056	0	2
	1999 Members	*1999 Landtag 120 seats*	*1999 Bundestag 37 seats*
CDU	17,767	76	13
SDP	5,304	14	12
PDS	22,281	30	8
FDP	3,260	0	2
GRÜNE	1,050	0	2

* 1991;   ** 1992

Source: SLA, 1997: 196–9 (for 1990 and 1994 figures); SLA, 2000: 211–18 (for 1998/99 figures).

A similar phenomenon in terms of membership can be observed with regard to the Liberals (*Freie Demokratische Partei*, FDP). Its present party structure derives from the 1990 merger between the East German Liberal Democrats (*Liberal-Demokratische Partei Deutschlands* – LDPD) and National Democrats (*National-Demokratische Partei Deutschlands* – NDPD), to form a conglomerate which in turn joined up with the West German FDP. Their significant drop in electoral support has two likely explanations. One is that this followed the general nationwide downward trend that the party experienced, at least on the *Länd* level, though less so in federal elections (see Leicht, 1995: 1). On the other hand it is reasonable to assume that in the 1990 elections the party managed successfully to emphasise its commitment to civic liberalism – as in 'politically free' – which was of course one of the key desires of the newly 'liberated' east German electorate. Since then, this image has suffered severe dents as it has become increasingly clear that the party is generally more concerned with economic liberalism. Persistent calls by leading representatives of the party for the prolonged existence of a 'low-wage-zone' in East Germany were not particularly well received. Apart from the Halle-Merseburg area in Saxony-Anhalt,[60] a few miles to the north of Leipzig, the FDP does not have territorial strongholds anywhere in East Germany.

The other large party in Germany, the Social Democrats (*Sozial-demokratische Partei Deutschlands* – SPD) had the disadvantage of not being able to merge with a properly developed East German counterpart. The SPD, having been the predominant party in Saxony in the Weimar Republic, suffered dismantlement right at the beginning of both subsequent regime changes. Outlawed and persecuted under the Nazi regime, the SPD was re-established in the Soviet Zone of Occupation in July 1945 only to be incorporated into the new *Sozialistische Einheitspartei Deutschlands* (SED) by way of forced merger with the *Kommunistische Partei Deutschland* (KPD) in February 1946. Many members left the party rather than go along with that merger, and of those, only a few were still politically active at the time of unification.

The drive for Stalinisation within the SED, the purges of 1952 culminated in the SPD to the post-unification opinion that no former SED members should be admitted to the SPD. It was argued that no real social-democratic thinking could have survived within the SED, in particular since the existence of factions or wings within the SED was ruled out by that party's statute. The SPD's policy of non-admittance was only changed in the run-up to the 1998 general elections. By then, however, some 160 former SED members had already found their way into the Saxon SPD anyway. Asked about this, its *Landtag* Chief Whip Knauer stated that 'for us that is neither a problem nor an issue' (Leipziger Volkszeitung, 14/10/98: 2). Nevertheless, apart from immigrants from the West, the new generation of Social Democrats in Saxony consists almost entirely of political newcomers. Founded in the frenzy of organisation-building after the fall of the SED regime in late 1989, the creation of the East German SPD[61] went almost unnoticed. There is only so much that can be achieved through the support from West German party organisations, hence the party as an organisation is still struggling in East Germany, despite much political success in Brandenburg, Mecklenburg-West

Pomerania and Saxony-Anhalt. In Saxony, given the lack of electoral support, potential new recruits are still afraid to back a loser, or see no clear conceptual distinction between the two big parties. It is only at the sub-regional and local level, in particular in its electoral stronghold, comprising the city and governmental district of Leipzig, that the Saxon SPD has shown its full potential so far. However, with an SPD-led government now in power at the federal level, it is reasonable to assume that better times may be ahead for the SPD in Saxony as well. However, this trend did not materialise in the 1999 *Landtag* elections, the SPD trailing the CDU by about 40 per cent.

The *Partei des Demokratischen Sozialismus* (PDS) regards itself as the political home of all forms of socialist thinking in Germany. Nowadays the party tries to distance itself from its organisational origin, the SED, which was the ruling party in the GDR.[62] However, the shift from ruling communists to open-minded socialists came about as a dual process of internal reform and external pressure. The loss of power brought it home to the remaining party members – i.e. to those 15 per cent who did not burn their membership documents – that the party had to change itself considerably if it was to remain a significant player in the politics of the 'new' Germany. A new generation of party leaders, having served in 'unexposed' positions in the old party hierarchy, or having not served at all, was elected, and the party name was changed to PDS – for a while it used the double acronym SED-PDS, but this was discarded in the run-up to the *Volkskammer* elections of 18 March 1990. In addition, the party is now open to various forms of left-wing thinking. The creation of factions and wings, prohibited by the old statute, is now a statutory demand. Therefore, the party consists of various 'platforms' – the communist platform being by far the largest – within a federal party structure. Although the PDS has no particular territorial stronghold, it usually does better in cities than in rural areas. However, throughout the region it has an extensive territorial presence of which the other parties can only dream. One result of this is that the PDS does very well at the local level, with a significant number of very proactive and capable city councillors.

The Greens (*Bündnis 90/Die Grünen*) are a somewhat special case. Their organisational origin lies in the various movements and activist groups which started to operate within the GDR during the 1980s. Usually they were more or less loosely associated with the churches, which provided an institutional umbrella and some degree of protection from persecution by the GDR state authorities. Some of the groupings were formed in late 1989 or early 1990, i.e. after the fall of the GDR regime. However, only in a minority of cases were there underlying ecological motives – and even then often only as an example for the failures and shortcomings of the SED's policies in general. The main points of interest for these organisations were personal and civil liberties, human rights, and associated issues, for example freedom of education, right of conscientious objection, etc. German unification, however, was usually rather low on their agenda. When finally unification became inevitable, their campaign demanded the use of the constitutional option allowed for underArticle 146 of the GG, i.e. the convening of a constitutional convention to discuss and ratify the replacing of the GG with a new constitution able to cope with the extra demands imposed by east German *Länder* joining the – qualitatively unaltered – system of the Federal Republic. In the long run, however, there was no way forward for these not-quite-parties but to unite (hence *Bündnis 90*, for the federal general elections in December 1990), and then to merge with the west German Greens, who at the time had image problems and had lost all their seats in the federal parliament. This amalgamation paid dividend for the Greens in the 1990 and subsequent federal elections – since 1998 they have even been a junior partner in the federal government. At the regional level throughout East Germany, however, the Greens fared less well: having played a significant role initially in the making of legislation, they are now regarded to an increasing extent as outdated. The transition period is now regarded by most members of the electorate as well and truly over, so much so that the voters decided not to return any Greens to four of the five East German *Landtage*. In Saxony, one of the larger GDR opposition groups, *Neues Forum* (NF), was particularly unwilling to join this trend of dismissing the Greens and still chooses to enter into an electoral partnership with them only if their potential platforms are the same or similar: usually, at the national level, they choose to campaign with either the Greens or the PDS, while at the local level, they choose to campaign alone. At the time of writing, the Greens have no particular territorial stronghold in Saxony, and even Leipzig, the epicentre of protest against the GDR regime, has turned away from it 1989 heroes.

SUMMARY

With regard to the landscape of public, semi-public and private actors in Saxony and Wales, it can be said that a sufficient number of organisations is present in both regions to make a quantitative analysis viable. The Saxon scene of public actors has been changed completely over the last decade, while in Wales significant changes – local government reform, followed by the much more significant process of devolution – are under way at the time of writing. With regard to semi-public actors, there are significant differences between the two regions. Wales possesses a well-developed and well-entrenched landscape of actors of this type, giving rise to the notion of 'Quangoland Wales' (Morgan and Roberts, 1993: 2). The present Labour government is currently trying to scale back this extensive use of semi-public actors, and has endowed the NAW with the right to sort out the details. In Saxony, however, the government is very much against the extensive use of such actors, hence the absence of powerful regional organisations. As stated above, in general there are not many semi-public actors in Saxony semi-public; the few that are there are mostly concerned with steering socio-economic development at the local level, or are local branches of federal organisations. Both regions are endowed with an array of private actors. These are mainly composed of companies, as both regions can be regarded as largely industrialised, and a number of economic and social interest organisations. With regard to the companies, both regions have seen a significant restructuring of their industrial base over the last decade or so, therefore the problem of actor inexperience arises in both regions – although the problem is more pronounced in Saxony as there not only the industrial base but also the entire economic system has changed.

This also has a bearing on the question of interest representation. In Wales some tried-and-tested methods of interest representation, for example lobbying the government, can still be employed in much the same way as, say, 20 years ago. However, most actors also had to adapt to new ways of representing their interests. In Saxony, the system of interest representation must still be regarded as emerging. As virtually all actors are new on the scene, the establishment of effective working relationships between them is still an ongoing concern. Experience from the West German *Länder* has been imported on a large scale, but the process of adapting this for the specific East German situation still takes time, effort, and a measure of goodwill that has not always been shown by all actors concerned. Nevertheless, the basic principles have been established since 1990, making a first assessment viable.

Much the same goes for the question of a regional system of governance. Here, the two regions differ considerably. With regard to Saxony, key rules of authoritative decision-making were established swiftly during 1990–91, drawing heavily on the west German example. But governance goes beyond government, and Saxony still has not fully come to terms with this. On the other hand, until a very few years ago, there was no such thing as a Welsh regional system of governance. The WO, in co-operation with local government and a number of NDPBs was deemed to provide a sufficient functional equivalent. However, from 1996 on, a system of governance started to emerge, with the NAW and a re-launched local government structure as its centre-pieces.

Furthermore, Wales and Saxony share a range of economic interests, not least the restructuring of large traditional industrial areas which have suffered a decline in the 1980s and the early 1990s, plus the interest in developing rural and hilly non-industrial parts of the region. Political, social and cultural interests, however, differ considerably. Saxony is a well-established political region with fixed rights and obligations under the German constitution. The UK system is at present less rigid, as devolution is essentially a process to establish the constituent parts of the UK as political regions. Political parties are campaigning for various degrees of self-government for the various regions; a system of asymmetric government is therefore the most likely outcome in the short to medium term.

On the social and cultural side, Saxony is currently busy to assert itself as a fully-fledged region within the German nation. Proud of its history and mindful of the existence of a small national minority within its borders, the Saxons are embarked on a course of developing a socio-cultural lifestyle based on the principle of voluntary participation and the availability of a multitude of opportunities. The principle of voluntary participation constitutes a radical departure from the situation in the GDR, and many Saxons now exercise their right not to participate in political and socio-cultural activities. It has to be noted however, that this abstinence often has a background of economic hardship and dissatisfaction with the quality of life currently available to them. A multitude of opportunities, nevertheless, has developed in most parts of Saxony, with the exception of the remote hilly areas along the southern border.

Wales, on the other hand, is currently trying to press forward its status as a nation within the multinational UK state. This has various implications for different actors, especially in the political field, with regard to the degree of self-government that would befit such nation status. Culturally, one can identify a number of splits among the Welsh population, for example between those who speak Welsh and those who do not speak it, and with special interest groups such as ex-miners, farmers, fishermen and others adding their own special set of cultural interests to the overall picture. The principle of voluntary participation is violated in several ways, in particular with regard to the Welsh language, while a meaningful multitude of opportunities is available only in the larger cities along the southern coast, and in the north-eastern corner, there provided by the nearby Manchester–Liverpool area. Altogether, therefore, the scene is set for a viable comparison between Wales and Saxony in the terms outlined above.

NOTES

1. Wales is, in fact, one of the Celtic nations that were established in the British Isles even before Roman times. To what extent one could, that early, already speak of 'nations' in the modern sense is debatable. What little we know of the lifestyle of these societies seems to indicate tribal communities.

2. The borders of Powys have been redrawn many times since; today Ludlow and its surrounding area is part of Shropshire, England.

3. This is important insofar as it implies recognition of Wales as a nation by international organisations, i.e. the governing bodies of these sports.

4. This was the year that saw the ascendancy, within the Labour Party, of the idea to embark on a course for devolution upon winning office in Westminster. Pro-devolutionists had campaigned for this for decades, but especially after the defeated Scottish and Welsh referenda of 1979 they were outnumbered within the party's rank and file. The main pressure for a pro-devolutionist policy in the 1990s, however, came from Scotland, not Wales, the rationale being to combat more stringent demands made by the Scottish National Party (SNP) during their 1994 party conference, on the theme of 'Independence in Europe' which was regarded by the new UK party leadership as a serious political threat to Labour, not only in Scotland.

5. The English and Welsh church systems are quite different. None of the Anglican Welsh churches accept the Archbishop of Canterbury as their leader. The Church of England, on the other hand, was the established church in Wales as well, until it was disestablished in 1920 after a campaign by Welsh people (nearly all Welsh-speakers) who regarded the Church of England as an alien church. Today, there are three main groups of churches: Nonconformists, Anglicans (both divided into Welsh-speaking and non-Welsh-speaking parishes) and Roman Catholics. Since the 1960s a number of non-Christian churches and religious communities have been established in southern Wales.

6. E.g. Loughlin, Mathias et al., 1998, 1998a.

7. This is not to say that the language would be unimportant. It is regarded even by some who do not speak it as a means of defining identity, and those people are rather proud of their distinct Welsh dialect of English known as 'Wenglish', as the next best thing to speaking Welsh. When hearing this dialect, most non-Welsh listeners assume that the speaker's mother tongue is Welsh, hence the 'accent'. On the other hand, the fact remains that about three in four people, especially in the south, do not speak Welsh. In the heavily populated south, the compulsory teaching of Welsh, introduced in 1991, has been implemented in most schools with rather less enthusiasm and corresponding results, and adult education schemes have so far only been successful among professional people, not the general population.

8. It was not until John Major's premiership that some key pieces of legislation, in particular the Welsh Language in Education Act 1991, and the Welsh Language Act 1993, were passed, which can be regarded as some recognition by London of Welsh demands.

9. Plaid Cymru means 'Party of Wales' in Welsh. In 1999 the party changed its official name to include both the Welsh and English versions: 'Plaid Cymru – The Party of Wales'.

10. Chemnitz was renamed in the course of these reforms Karl-Marx-Stadt. The old name was re-established in 1990.

11. GBl. I Nr. 51 S. 955.

12. Very similar terms in the Welsh language are *hiraeth* and *bro*.

13. By agreement with the *Nationale Front*, i.e. the ruling coalition that comprised all political parties and all mass organisations which had parliamentary representation, the Domowina was allowed to have two members of the *Volkskammer* as part of the parliamentary group of the *Kulturbund*, a mixed cultural organisation ranging from stamp collectors to allotment gardeners and amateur actors.

14. According to the old Article 23 of the FRG Constitution only German *Länder* were entitled to join the FRG; therefore their re-establishment in East Germany was a precondition for political union. However, the first elections to the parliaments of the new *Länder* took place after unification, on 14 October 1990.

15. George Orwell's 'Newspeak' from his novel *1984* springs to mind, but for most East

Germans there was no way of knowing this as *1984* was not available in the GDR – at least not officially.

16. This group of people became known as the *Wendehälse* (turncoats).
17. 'I am proud to be a German.'
18. These patterns have grown historically, and, in the south, were changed significantly in the early 1900s due to the discovery of large coalfields.
19. Nevertheless, even though the bank is now part of the Bank of Scotland it still trades under the name 'Bank of Wales'.
20. E.g. City of Birmingham, Strathclyde Regional Council, Baden-Württemberg and to some extent even Catalonia (Loughlin, Mathias et al., 1998).
21. Other EU regions which regard themselves as nations have experienced the same phenomenon with regard to their chances of interest representation at the EU level, e.g. Catalonia (Nagel, 1994).
22. But not the third one, Swansea.
23. One example is the narrowness of many of the valleys, flanked on both sides by steep hills, which makes it virtually impossible to set aside large sites for commercial development. During the era of deep mining the shape of the surface was not a significant factor in location-finding, hence many former miners' villages are tightly packed into places that simply have no room for large industrial estates.
24. Meaning 'blossoming landscapes' – a phrase coined by the then German Chancellor Helmut Kohl during the 1990 general elections campaign to describe what the future would have in store for East Germany under a CDU government.
25. Interview, Regierungspräsidium Chemnitz, 1997.
26. Ibid.
27. Interview, Saxon Ministry of Agriculture, 1997.
28. Until 1945, the German Supreme Court (*Reichsgericht*) was based in Leipzig.
29. This is a rather complex German concept which goes beyond the simple 'rule of law'. In a nutshell, it can be described as state-organised rule of law which in turn organises both state and society.
30. This is not the place to discuss their personal motivations for 'going East'. Suffice to say that pure altruism must be regarded as the exception rather than the rule.
31. This is an indicator frequently used by business interest organisations and West German liberals alike to demand that East Germany should remain a low-wage zone for much longer than initially intended by the Christian Democrats (see also Kurth, 1997).
32. For these visions see Piehl, 1995, *passim*.
33. Translation by author from the German original.
34. Their 1998 Bundestag and 1999 *Landtag* campaigns put much less emphasis on alleged general system failures, focusing instead on manifest individual social needs.
35. At the moment, the Kinnock family is well represented in Brussels: his wife and daughter-in-law are MEPs and his son works as a middle-rank bureaucrat for the Commission.
36. This situation became most dramatic when the Conservatives failed to win a single seat in Wales in both the 1997 and the 2001 general elections – hence none of the Conservative MPs currently serving on the Committee have constituency links to Wales.
37. Government of Wales Act 1998.
38. The Scottish Parliament has the power to alter Scottish tax levels (Scottish Office, 1997: 21).
39. This goes way beyond the right to enact 'bylaws', which had already been enjoyed by local councils. Councils retain their power to enact local bylaws in the usual way.
40. That decision is to be made in Westminster and Whitehall. There will be an allocation, the so-called Block Grant, in the annual UK budget.
41. Nevertheless, the Secretary of State has the right to attend and speak at NAW sessions. To facilitate this, a special chair (not seat, coloured red instead of charcoal) is reserved for him in the WA's meeting chamber.
42. Not to be mixed up with the post of Presiding Officer (Speaker).
43. There is no legal requirement that at member of the Welsh Executive must hold an NAW mandate – in theory the NAW could elect virtually anyone. However, it is very unlikely that the WA makes use of this opportunity.

44.   As the latter are not part of the system of governance as such, they will not be discussed at length here; however, they play a major part in running R&D policies.
45.   There are some inconsistencies in the use of the terms 'agency' and 'board'. Functionally, the Development Board for Rural Wales is an agency.
46.   Yet another agency, in charge of registering land ownership and general spatial planning.
47.   This corporation was dissolved in March 2000 and its assets and liabilities transferred to Cardiff County Council.
48.   Interview, South Glamorgan TEC, 1996.
49.   Private companies have been dealt with under the heading of socio-economic features above. Voluntary organisations and single-issue social interest groups (e.g. Greenpeace) have only a minimal bearing – if any – on the theme of this book and therefore need not be considered in detail here.
50.   Within the latter, each individual party member had one vote. The candidate with the most votes in a constituency then obtained both votes of that constituency in the electoral college.
51.   Interview, Liberal Democrats Wales, 1995.
52.   This changed considerably in the 1999 series of elections: the NAW and the Local Government elections of 6 May, and the EP elections of 10 June all showed a substantial increase in Plaid Cymru's vote in south Wales. Here, the party unexpectedly gained two NAW seats, and took control of two local councils. In the EP elections, it even achieved parity with Labour in Wales in terms of MEPs elected (two each).
53.   *Verfassung des Freistaates Sachsen vom 27. Mai 1992* (Sächsische Landeszentrale für Politische Bildung, 1999).
54.   On average 125,000 citizens (Seibel, 1993a: 482).
55.   In the case of very small villages located next to each other, they may form *Verwaltungsgemeinschaften* (Joint Administrations) on the executive side.
56.   Until 1998, the Mayor was elected by the City Council.
57.   *Gesetz zur Privatisierung und Reorganisation des volkseigenen Vermögens* (*Treuhandgesetz*), GBl. I Nr. 33 S. 300.
58.   Now, for instance, Saxon priests can be drafted in by school authorities to teach religious studies in schools – a common practice in the FRG.
59.   The developments in the party system described here are not specific to Saxony, but apply in more or less similar ways to the entire former GDR territory, except Berlin, where there have been unifications with existing west Berlin party structures on the *Land* level. In particular, the SPD has profited from this.
60.   The birthplace of the immensely popular former party leader Hans-Dietrich Genscher, who as Federal Minister for Foreign Affairs played a key part in the 1989–90 events leading up to unification.
61.   Initially founded as the Social-Democratic Party (SDP), the name was only changed into SPD in the run-up to the 1990 *Volkskammer* elections.
62.   It needs to be pointed out that the SED ruled in coalition with *all* the other GDR parties.

3

Public Actors in Regional Development

Public actors have been defined as groups of people running state institutions during a particular period in time. This chapter focuses on the roles, the perceptions and self-perceptions, and the key management activities of these public actors when taking on their supposed responsibility for a broad cluster of policy areas affecting large parts of the lifestyle in their societies. The key point here is that whereas private interest organisations, including political parties, are free to express and pursue their particular – factional – interests, public office comes with responsibilities for a wider range of policies and functions that the public actors have to take on *ex officio*, whether they wish to or not. Before proceeding to this analysis, however, we have to discuss whether the presumption that state institutions do not hold political interests *per se*, as outlined by Marks (1996: 22), holds true in the two cases under investigation here, Wales and Saxony.

REGIONAL INTERESTS: '*CONTRAT D'ETAT*' OR FACTIONAL 'SHOPPING LISTS'?

The question whether state institutions are free of inherent political interests gains particular salience under the specific conditions shaped by the Germanic tradition of legalising and institutionalising, or even constitutionalising the accommodation of – possibly contradictory – political interests. This entails the creation of detailed constitutional and legal prescriptions for these functions and responsibilities.

One case in point is Saxony. In addition to the functions regulated by federal constitutional law (in particular, Articles 30–1 and 70–5 GG), Saxony has given itself a *Land* constitution, which came into force on 6 June 1992. Articles 7–12 of this constitution contain a series of *Staatsziele* (aims of the state). Ostensibly, therefore, the Free State of Saxony, as an institution, ceased to be politically neutral or inert. A *Staatsziel* is a legal construct whose status differs from both basic rights and state functions. *Staatsziele* cannot be enforced by individuals through the court system – basic rights can, by the individuals concerned. So can state functions, on application by federal or state organs, or other members of the federation.

In the Saxon constitution,[1] the basic rights (Articles 14–38) simply restate a series of provisions laid down in federal constitutional and criminal justice law, that would be binding in Saxony anyway, just as they would be in the rest of the German federation (federal law supersedes *Land* law; Article 31 GG). The state functions mentioned in the Saxon constitution (Articles 70–108), i.e. the production of state legislation, administration of justice, general public administration, administration of the state finances, and provision of public education, contain no surprises either. Their main contents, and the limits of creative freedom of manoeuvre, are clearly defined by superseding federal legislation. Fulfilment of these federal norms is, so to speak, a condition of a *Land's* membership in the Federal Republic; the federation would be entitled to force a *Land* to comply (*Bundeszwang*; Article 37 GG). So, from the outset, there were severe checks imposed upon the framers of the Saxon constitution in these fields – and the outcome of their deliberations is correspondingly uninspiring.

Staatsziele, on the other hand, may be regarded as mere pick-and-choose shopping lists of political aims which ought to be pursued by whatever party or administration is in power. One way to make sure that this is done consistently over a long period, regardless of the possibly varying political circumstances of the day, is to endow the *Staatsziele* with the status of constitutional demands. The decision on whether a government of the day has done a proper job in that respect, however, is made by political debate, and ultimately in the ballot box.

Saxony's list of aims is, compared to those of the other east German *Länder*, comparatively short (Kilian, 1997: 20–1). The Saxon aims include the provision of some basic social needs (jobs, adequate accommodation, and education; Article 7); gender equality (Article 8); the protection of minors (Article 9); protection of the environment (Article 10); the promotion of arts, culture, science and sports (Article 11); and, uniquely among the *Staatsziele* of the German *Länder*, cross-border regional co-operation (Article 12). Article 13 states that the *Land* has the duty to do the best it can to implement the above aims, and to shape its state actions accordingly.

This tendency to regulate political ambitions has been criticised by a number of interest groups. According to Kilian (1997: 24–5), the left complains that the social aims are not bold enough, while the right thinks that they are too bold, and not amenable to meaningful implementation.[2]

One key criticism is that interest groups not mentioned in the text justifiably feel neglected: the inclusion of some and the exclusion of others would constitute a breach of Article 18 which proclaims the equality of all people before the law. The omission of some interest groups as such, however, must be regarded as a political balancing act. On the one hand, the framers of the constitution did not wish to overburden the state with responsibilities which are either best left to be dealt with by the free play of vested interests in the political debate, or belong to the purely private sphere of individuals. On the other hand, not to mention social interest groups at all, or to leave the provisions for some of them deliberately vague, served the interest of the government to retain full control over access to decision-making procedures and public funds. The idea here, apparently, was not to deny such access altogether, but not to make it a constitutional right either – thus allowing the government to steer this process as it sees fit.

A possible justification for the establishment and constitutional proclamation of state aims would be that there is a broad consensus in the society as to which features of the daily life of this society ought to be promoted. Indeed, who would be prepared to state publicly that he or she is against jobs for all? Or, for that matter, against cross-border regional co-operation? Appropriate or not, to the extent that political ambitions and wishes are promoted to constitutional status it is justified to claim that vested state interests have been established. This is mitigated, however, by the lack of meaningful legal means to enforce these aims against a government, in cases where it is regarded as failing to do its best to serve these interests. Hence the implementation of the *Contrat d'Etat*, or general consensus plan, is brought back firmly into the realm of political debate, along with any other interests and individual policy proposals.

Wales, on the other hand, seems to follow the traditional Anglo-Saxon model of identifying and pursuing state interests. Constitutional provisions, such as there are, generally remain free of proclamations of state interests. Instead, private actors, in particular political parties, present their own programmatic agendas – or shopping lists of interests – to the public, hoping to be supported and/or elected on these indications of intent. If successful, these actors proceed to implement their agenda, not necessarily identical with the previously published one, again hoping to convince enough citizens that their policies are better for them than the opposition's alternative suggestions. A year or so before the end of the legislative period the actors, having come full circle, start again. This procedure is even employed for constitutional changes such as those that have been brought about by the current devolution process. The basic point here is the supposed 'absolute' sovereignty of the Westminster

Parliament, which is deemed to be in a position to do anything it sees fit; including altering constitutional arrangements. If not even matters relating to the structure of government are legally protected by constitutional means, the much weaker legal concept of state aims would be of very limited utility in the context of the UK constitutional framework.

A new policy style, propagated in particular by pro-devolution campaigners in Scotland and Wales, emphasises the principle of inclusiveness in decision-making and implementation of development programmes. This should, in their opinion, prevent any negative consequences of the new principle of taking decisions which are to be binding beyond the current legislative period. However, both in long-term strategic planning[3] and day-to-day policy-making the principle of a straightforward political battle between concepts, ideas and factional interests remains firmly in place. What is new are new rights, and new forms, of actor participation in decision-making processes. Examples of these are the introduction of elements of proportional representation for regional elections in Scotland and Wales, almost inevitably leading to situations of no overall control over the SP or the NAW by a single political party, and enhanced consultation procedures to be conducted by the SP and NAW with private actors in Scotland and Wales. The state and its institutions, however, are still supposedly neutral in terms of interest holding. Just as in Saxony, in the end it is the current constellation of actors, and in particular public actors, at a given point in time, who identify and shape regional interests, and take the key decisions concerning the pursuit of these interests.

In the devolved UK system, the ultimate success is measured by the ballot box; however, there is a general constitutional understanding – though not a written law – that no parliament or legislative assembly must through its acts of legislation bind its successor. This rule, in theory, prevents the constitutionalisation of vested state interests, and indeed this has so far never been attempted in the UK. Nevertheless, the concept of the unacceptability of decisions by legislatures which would bind their successors has taken on an increasingly fictional character. Key decisions taken by the Conservatives, such as the decision to join the EC, in 1973, and the large-scale privatisation and deregulation of national industrial assets, decided and implemented between the mid-1980s and the mid-1990s, have set the pattern in that direction. Under Labour, a continued privatisation programme, the devolution agenda, and, not least, reform of the House of Lords are but a few examples of how Westminster has now taken upon itself to make decisions designed to last well into the new millennium. Both the SP and the NAW are likely to follow that trend, given the fact that the very nature of doing business in a first ever legislative period inevitably involves setting precedents for further action by successors.

PUBLIC ACTORS AND REGIONAL DEVELOPMENT POLICY MANAGEMENT

As outlined above, regional mobilisation can be described as a complex set of measures employed by regional and sub-regional actors in order to facilitate challenges and changes in their respective fields of activity, and in order to make the most of the opportunities provided by EU regional policy-making. This set of measures comprises three analytically distinct but practically intertwined steps of increasing intensity of involvement: (i) problem recognition and manpower commitment, (ii) search for suitable partners and contacts, i.e. networking, and (iii) long-term substantial co-operation (Loughlin, Mathias et al., 1998: 194). The remainder of this chapter deals with structural and organisational measures taken by public actors to make themselves fit for their steering role in the development process. Chapter 4 then investigates the role of private actors, including new forms of public–private interaction, networking and long-term co-operation.

Public Actors managing Welsh Regional Development Policy[4]

Given the absence of a legally fixed system of public interests in Wales, public actors are, in principle, free to set their own agendas and pronounce them to be Wales's regional or national interests. However, in this process these actors are nevertheless faced with external factors limiting the scope of their choice in shaping the regional agenda. Politics and policy in Europe are today conducted increasingly as a system of multi-level governance: the local, the regional, the state, and the European levels are all involved in regional policy-making (Loughlin, 1997: 10).

The REGE Wales respondents were asked to evaluate the relative importance of these different levels. The findings, dating from 1996, indicated that an overwhelming 92.4 per cent of respondents perceived the national level to be most important, but significant majorities also acknowledged the importance of the regional (80.1 per cent) and the European (71.8 per cent) levels. Almost half (48.2 per cent) thought the local level was important. This may be regarded as an indicator that indeed most regional actors have experienced the complexity of MLG-style structures in practice. Apparently, however, the local level seems to be somewhat under-represented within these structures.

The REGE panellists were also asked about the nature of politics in

Wales. Interestingly, more than three-quarters of the respondents (76.4 per cent) thought that the political character of Wales is more traditional than innovative. Smaller majorities (62.7 and 52.8 per cent, respectively) thought it to be more oriented towards consensus than controversy and to be more state interventionist in the conduct of socio-economic affairs, rather than inclined to foster an unchecked play of market forces. With regard to the question as to whether political actors in Wales are more inclined to pursue a more 'interventionist' course of action, a majority of public actors think that this is the case (60.7 per cent), as do a majority of semi-public actors (56 per cent), while only a minority of private actors (31 per cent) shares this opinion. So public actors perceive themselves to be more interventionist than they are perceived by private actors. Among public actors, interventionist behaviour was strictly discouraged by the Thatcher government – and by 1996 some public administrators still seemed to be exercising a certain self-control in that respect. This result can also be regarded as an indication of a situation where what goes as public interest is determined by specific interest groups clustered around political parties. After all, 85.7 per cent of the business interest organisations thought Welsh politics to be more lined up along party-political divisions than focusing on interpersonal relations between individuals, a view in which, not surprisingly, 66.7 per cent of the legislative bodies concur. On the other hand, the Thatcherite agenda of creating a Britain based on neo-liberal principles and based on 'market' approaches seems to have made a less strong impact in Wales than generally assumed. It remains to be investigated to what extent these views have seen significant change since 1996. Clearly, here lies an enormous challenge for the newly created Welsh actors, not least the NAW.

Another series of REGE questions investigated the panellists' perceptions of key public sector institutions, in particular the WO and the WDA. Did these two bodies usually set the right priorities for economic development in Wales? Overall, only 43.7 per cent of respondents agreed that the WO was setting the right priorities. The agreement rate for the WDA was significantly higher: 62.7 per cent. The business community displayed a remarkable split between its organisations (CBI, chambers of commerce, and others) on the one hand, and its individual members (managers of companies) on the other. While the business officialdom gave an overwhelmingly positive verdict on the WO's leadership role, almost 53 per cent of the managers joined significant majorities of both semi-public and local public actors in giving a generally negative opinion. Two possible reasons for this split emerged from the REGE study.[5] First, there is a positive correlation between those managers who held a rather negative view on the WO and those who indicated that they found it difficult or not worthwhile participating in specific development projects. Secondly, a similar – though weaker – correlation exists between a negative verdict on the WO and the lack of direct contact with it.[6] The positive opinion about the WDA is shared by all actor categories, except members of legislative bodies and public administrations, whose opinions were evenly split (50–50).

With regard to the general relationship between the public and private sectors, a rather negative opinion of the WO emerged: 64.1 per cent of REGE respondents thought that this body never, almost never, or rarely acts as the primary organisation which develops economic initiatives. Furthermore, 50.8 per cent of respondents thought that politicians and civil servants are not open to suggestions from the business community and the wider community. Finally, 54.8 per cent of respondents felt that, in public policy-making, the interests of important economic and social groups were more or less routinely disregarded. This appears to be a fairly clear indication of some considerable dissatisfaction with regard to public–private relationships in Wales, and a feeling that key groups are excluded from the decision-making process. This is confirmed by a breakdown of the replies by actor category: all three of the chambers of commerce; 60 per cent of trade unions; and 59.1 per cent of semi-public organisations felt excluded.

The picture of Welsh politics and policy-making that emerges is of a society and economic system that, in 1996, was still quite conservative rather than innovative, with a partisan interest promotion. This is probably a consequence of the dominant role of the Labour Party in Wales at the time, although overall, at Westminster it was still in opposition. Since then, the desirability of a 'market-based' approach to economic development has become a hotly contested issue within the Welsh Labour Party – probably a contributory factor to Labour's difficulties in the 1999 elections (Evans and George, 1999: 16–17).[7]

Steps to analyse not only the problems, but also the opportunities arising from socio-economic development issues, and in particular their European dimension, have been taken by virtually all public actors in Wales, albeit to varying degrees of scope and intensity. In the 1990s, the foremost document produced in this respect was the House of Commons Welsh Affairs Committee's Report *Wales in Europe* (HoC, 1995a). This report was the outcome of an enquiry conducted by the Committee between February and October 1995. The main themes of the investigation were 'to examine the relations between Wales and the central institutions of the EU' (para. 1) and to assess 'the links which the WO has established with regions within Europe' (para. 2). Evidence was taken from a number of public, semi-public and private organisations, including the WO, the WDA, the WEC, Welsh members of EU institutions (for example MEPs), local development corporations, and several private businesses (Mathias, 1996).

The report gave the overall impression that while basic needs of establishing Wales as a region in Europe had been served, there was considerable room for improvement concerning decision-making, and with regard to administration and implementation of European policies. The problems which, in the opinion of the Committee, had prevented better progress were identified as consisting of a mixture of both home-made rules, for example the prevalent dominance of Whitehall (HoC, 1995a: para. 6), and external circumstances, among them the reluctance of non-UK partners to commit themselves to more formalised co-operation (for example Rhône-Alpes in the 'Four Motors' group; para. 57). One can only conclude from this, therefore, that the Committee felt that, up until 1995, Wales had been unable to make the most of given or potential opportunities.

The structure of the report follows the dual strategy set out in the Committee's terms of reference. However, going through the text it becomes increasingly clear that relations with the central EU institutions and with the other regions can only be developed as two elements of a comprehensive European strategy. But this would have meant asking for active policy-making by the WO in this field – a suggestion strictly rejected by the report (para. 7). Only policy-monitoring and the development of reactive strategies should be allowed (para. 25), with the UK government remaining the actor responsible for strategic decision-making with regard to Wales's socio-economic development and interest representation in Europe.

What remained, then, were administrative and organisational measures to ensure optimum utilisation of opportunities within the scope of the externally determined political freedom of manoeuvre. The report provided a thorough quantitative analysis and qualitative assessment of recent and ongoing activities in this field. Particular emphasis was given to the development of Wales's relations with the 'Four Motors' initiative. The report shows that the political links established between the WO and the regional governments of these regions, though not always formalised, had been useful for promoting Welsh interests directly in Europe. But while those partnerships, exchanges and other co-operation measures had only started to reap at least some of the intended benefits, the key impression remained that Wales was still very much the junior partner, gradually learning by doing how to play successfully in this 'upper league'. On some occasions the report went beyond analytical features. Key recommendations included the demand for WO representation in the Council of Ministers as and when appropriate, more WO support for NDPBs involved in co-operation projects with other regions, especially the 'Four Motors', and a transfer of the responsibility for running the ESF in Wales to the WO.

However, in general, the recommendations, although quite specific and detailed, resembled a patchwork of possibly useful ideas rather than a comprehensive approach to reform – and perhaps inevitably so: one must not forget that this is a House of Commons Committee Report and not a Government White Paper. Although the Conservative government started to implement some of the report's recommendations, such as the increased frequency of appearances of the Secretary of State for Wales in the EU Council of Ministers, it did not lead to a significant change in the government's policy on Wales.[8] Yet by virtue of reviewing key elements of Wales's ongoing attempt to develop itself into a truly European region, the report contributed significantly to a better understanding of these processes, among both public and private actors. Throughout 1995–97, policy documents produced by local councils, development agencies, and even business interest organisations frequently referred to the report. Therefore, it has had a considerable influence on the strategic thinking and planning of Welsh actors.

All of the 56 public actors on the REGE panel saw, between 1990 and 1996, the need for some kind of internal reorganisation due to changes and opportunities facilitated by Wales's involvement in the process of European integration. Such reorganisation has taken various forms, from just asking someone to gather some information, to the creation of a fully fledged new department or desk.

With the interest of public actors in European issues clearly in evidence, the most important limiting factor of their internal reorganisation efforts was the availability of financial resources. For those who could afford it, the creation of new departments and desks was very popular with public and semi-public bodies. The WO was not really hampered by financial constraints in this respect, as the UK government at the time saw a potential benefit in terms of attracting both inward investment and ERDF/ESF funds. Therefore, it was decided to create a new department, the European Division, to deal with the political interest representation, and with legal issues, i.e. the distribution of information, and monitoring the implementation of EU regulation in Wales. It was further decided to broaden the scope of activities of an existing department, the Business Services Division; its promotional activities taking on a new, distinctly European dimension.[9] The WDA had already created an International Division, with two main functions: co-ordination of all international activities of the Agency, and the provision of business services. In the early 1990s, the main territorial focus of the division shifted considerably from operations in Southeast Asia to continental Europe.[10]

On a smaller scale, local authorities tried to follow suit, although in general financial constraints were much more in evidence. In particular, local authorities outside the area of Objective 2 eligibility concluded after preliminary enquiries and interest representation experiments[11] that a significant individual effort to establish a presence in Europe would not be worthwhile. Although in most cases a desk or a small, often part-time, working group was established within existing economic development departments or public works departments, the councils concerned usually decided to go for some form of joint or indirect representation of their particular interests, via the Association of Welsh Counties (AWC), and after the local government reform of 1996 even more so via the Welsh Local Government Association (WLGA), and/or via the WO, the WDA and the DBRW.

However, inside the area of Objective 2 eligibility a slightly different picture emerges. The councils of the three Glamorgans, and of Gwent, had most to gain from marketing their territories internationally. Frequently encouraged by the then MEP for South Wales Central, Wayne David (Labour),[12] all four councils formed new departments in their local administration, and later went on to set up their own local development agencies, which were controlled, but not wholly owned by the council in question. This tradition has largely survived the local government reform of 1996, although control and ownership of some of the agencies did change, for example in the case of the Cardiff Bay Development Corporation. The new Newport County Borough Council, on the other hand, restructured the existing agency. The Newport Development Board, which has played a major role in the large-scale infrastructure developments in South Wales, remains under predominantly public control, a partnership with the council, the WDA and the private sector.[13] However, in former Mid Glamorgan, where mostly the old districts became the new territorial basis for the unitary local authorities, the district (now county borough) councils split up existing manpower and organisational resources to form smaller units, either wholly or partly in public ownership. In the process their drive for independent, individual interest representation has been lost. Current efforts tend to follow the joint representation approach, mostly via the WLGA.

This is not to say, however, that this transition went entirely without difficulties. One possible reason for this is that the new WLGA not only comprises former AWC representatives, used to acting at the (pro-European) county level, but also representatives of the former lower tier, the districts, which mostly did not really think it worth their while to establish an elaborate European policy. A number of interviews with representatives of the new local authorities in the Valleys[14] in 1996 and 1997 also revealed that a certain degree of planning competition between the new unitary local authorities had broken out, and that neither the WO nor the WDA succeeded fully in their efforts to prevent this. Whether the

NAW, now in charge of economic development in Wales, will be able to do a better job in that direction remains to be seen.

In general, it has to be noted that not so well-endowed smaller organisations usually had to make do with some alterations in procedural arrangements in order to take into account the European dimension. In some cases, the organisations concerned decided to hire outside expertise for specific purposes and for a limited amount of time – the latter with some mixed success. What is significant, however, is that, in approximately three quarters of the REGE Wales public actor respondents, the changes introduced have resulted in a quantifiable increase in the manpower committed to dealing with EU matters.

With regard to how to pursue interest representation in Europe, the decisions on how to proceed mainly depended on the legal status of the organisation concerned, the target of interest representation, i.e. whether the measure was, in the Hrbek and Weyand terminology, 'horizontal' or 'vertical' integration, and, inevitably, on the available resources.

In the case of the WO, the key elements of the legal framework were (i) its status as a UK government department, (ii) its function of secondary decision-making on development policy and implementation, and (iii) its role as a vetting agency for EU funding applications by Welsh private actors. The status as a UK government department can be considered as somewhat of a mixed blessing with regard to vertical interest representation. A clearly limiting factor in this respect was the UK government's prerogative, spearheaded by the Foreign Office, in terms of foreign policy. In addition, the Department of Trade and Industry also had an important say in conducting investment policies in the various parts of the UK. The WO's direct and formal access to organs of the EU was thus limited to instances in which it was acting with the agreement, or on behalf, of the government. A typical example would be the – infrequent – appearance of the Secretary of State for Wales in the EU Council of Ministers. Furthermore, the WO was unable to become a full partner in the WEC partnership, although informal practical relations were established. Indirect representation, on the other hand, was legally safeguarded via the Secretary of State's presence in the UK Cabinet. This was a two-edged sword: it can be argued that the two last Conservative secretaries of state, John Redwood and William Hague, were the representatives of the UK government in Wales, rather than vice versa. Their Labour successor, Ron Davies, who took office in May 1997, was an outspoken devolutionist and had little difficulty in projecting himself as the representative of Wales both toward the UK government of which he was a member, and toward the EU. Formally, his role was restrained by the same legal arrangements, but the Blair government was regarded as giving him a much longer political leash than Thatcher and Major gave Redwood and Hague. During his 18 months in office, Davies took the lead in shaping Labour's devolution plans for Wales, but was forced to resign for personal reasons before these plans came to fruition. In 1999 he was nevertheless elected to the NAW. However, Davies' successor Alun Michael, who in 1999 also became First Secretary of the NAW, was a Blairite by choice and therefore did not need a leash. This form of Welsh interest representation in pre-devolution days must be regarded as a somewhat imperfect tool.

The WO's functions as information provider, application vetting agency, and guardian of the implementation of both EU law and EU-funded projects were mostly responsible for securing it a strong influence in all aspects of regional development in Wales. The key feature here was that it was the only public actor which possessed the right to manage Wales's EU funds, including the right to withhold payment – albeit on behalf of the government. Project participants had to deal with the WO at both the application stage[15] and the implementation stage. On the other hand, it was chiefly the responsibility of the WO to identify and obtain sources of matching funds under the Objective 2 co-financing regulations. This is not to say that the matching funds had to come out of the WO's own budget. Frequently used solutions were representations to the UK government to provide the money, helping local government to use their own resources to greater effect, negotiating with private businesses for participation in projects, and low-interest loans.

Organisationally, the WO's main steps to develop the political steerage capability of the development process were internal co-operation and the utilisation of semi-public actors. Internally, it had to ensure that the Trade and Industry, European, Agriculture, and Business Services divisions were all working towards the same ends. This was done through a working party chaired by one of the under-secretaries of state; from 1997, under Labour, Peter Hain, a junior minister of state. By that time, however, most of the economic management functions with regard to state-owned assets had already been handed over to the WDA, which was thus entrusted with what, prior to 1975, used to be state functions (see Morgan and Roberts, 1993; WDA, 1994; Weir and Hall, 1995). From the late 1980s, the financial management of EU funds was franchised out to a firm of chartered accountants in Bristol – much to the disappointment of both project participants and Labour activists who thought that this contract, if franchised out at all, should be given to a Welsh firm[16] rather than be handled by people outside Wales, who allegedly had no direct interest in the progress of projects, as they were not personally affected by the decisions taken.[17] The REGE Wales survey detected no such dissatisfaction. However, a total of 12 public actors blamed the WO directly for what they experienced as slow and sometimes inefficient handling of funds approved by the EU.

The WO was also involved in measures of 'horizontal' interest representation; after all, there is no doubt that even the former Conservative government saw some advantages of establishing Wales as a modern region in Europe. The most notable example, much hailed by the above-mentioned House of Commons report (HoC, 1995a), was the WO's involvement in negotiating and managing the association agreement with the 'Four Motors Consortium'. However, this was no breach of the established policy as stated in the report, that the WO should only be allowed to conduct policy-monitoring, and to develop reactive strategies in the field of economic development policy. Politically, this was designed as an exercise in policy learning from the best; and certainly there is nothing wrong with the inner logic of wanting to learn from the best (Morgan, 1995; Cooke and Morgan, 1998). After all, the 'Four Motors' initiative was originally formed by Baden-Württemberg, Catalonia, Lombardy and Rhône-Alpes as an interregional organisation of some of the strongest regions in the EU (Cooke et al., 1993; Knodt, 1998, Fischer and Frech, 2001).

The House of Commons report claimed that between 1990 and 1995 a regular exchange of information, and some business agreements had been the fruits of these arrangements. In the case of Catalonia, the main emphasis of co-operation had been on cultural exchange, but in terms of economic co-operation only the Baden-Württemberg partners had shown any serious interest, backed by some financial commitment in the form of investment in Welsh industry. This co-operation was managed to a large extent by a joint working group of officials from the WO, the Baden-Württemberg *Land* government, and a number of interested industrial and cultural organisations. The WDA had established a permanent representation in Lombardy (Milan), which runs a joint 'introduction service' for businesses with the Milan Chamber of Commerce, established within the framework of the EU's EUROLINK programme. As of October 1995, the WDA claimed that this programme led to 'some 20 to 25 substantiated links', without giving further specifications (HoC, 1995b: para. 35–64). Even less information is available on details of co-operation with Rhône-Alpes.

The information in the report was well publicised at the time, and used both for arguments claiming success, and for arguments alleging failure of the WO's involvement with the 'Four Motors'. The reality, however, is somewhere in between. The WO's short-term gain in political prestige did not turn into quantifiable long-term economic gain, while on the practical side, it was the WDA rather than the WO that took on the task of fulfilling the political ambitions by instigating economic co-operation among private actors from the regions concerned.

Among the local public actors in Wales, both 'vertical' and 'horizontal' means of interest representation were established or altered to accommodate a growing interest in Europe. Characteristically, such interest representation took the form of joint rather than individual activities by the local authorities concerned. After all, the same restrictions concerning financial and manpower resources that were in evidence with regard to internal management reform also applied to external interest representation. On the 'vertical' side, the two local government associations, the AWC (for old-style county councils) and, to a lesser extent, also the Association of District Councils (ADC) (for old-style district councils) acted as forums for debate, and attempted to fulfil the role of a clearing house for joint interests, to be forwarded to the WO and the WDA.

The local government reform of 1996 has had an important effect on European consciousness in Wales. The AWC was strongly pro-European, individual councils and the ADC less so. By abolishing the counties – and with them the AWC – the Conservative government delivered a devastating blow against this European consciousness. The WLGA, on the other hand, has had a bad start due to internal rows over membership contributions.[18] This also diminished the effectiveness of their interest representation efforts towards the WO, and towards European partners. It remains to be seen, however, to what extent an appropriate working relationship between the WLGA and the economic development officers of the NAW can be established in the newly created forum for this task, the Partnership Council, with a view to both the effective management of projects in the different parts of Wales, and an effective approach to joint regional and local interest representation towards Europe.

The picture that emerges from the REGE Wales responses and additional interviews is that, normally, local authorities have not been in direct contact with EU officials, apart from being called to give evidence to the Objective 2 Monitoring Committee, and some limited involvement in informal discussions on the implementation of projects. However, it was repeatedly indicated that the WO was seen as a surrogate agency, channelling requests up and money down. A similar role, though less formal and not involving the handling of funds, was fulfilled by Welsh MEPs, who were reasonably accessible to their constituents and provided a useful link to normally somewhat remote echelons of EU officialdom.[19] A number of REGE respondents and interviewees from south Wales praised the MEPs Wayne David[20] and Glennys Kinnock, the wife of Commissioner Neil Kinnock. There was a distinct party-political dimension to this, as all the councils concerned were controlled by Labour, dealing with Labour

MEPs and a commissioner who used to be leader of the Labour Party, thus gaining a vehicle to bypass the WO, which was controlled by the Conservatives. There were, however, political and legal limits to what could be achieved in this way. It is therefore extremely difficult to quantify any success or failure of this approach, apart from the moral boost of confidence gained from being seen, by both voters and private actors, in the vicinity of key decision-makers.

The AWC was also instrumental in the establishment and running of the WEC in Brussels. This followed a UK-wide trend in the late 1980s and early 1990s, of establishing a presence in Brussels in order to gain access to EU decision-makers, develop favourable contacts, and generally fly the flag for one's region there.[21] Originally developed as a channel of vertical interest representation, it soon became obvious that the WEC's role in this respect was even more limited than that of Welsh MEPs. By 1996, it had no legal status whatever in the system of EU governance, but this is not to say that it was not useful to Welsh actors. Its main functions were information-gathering for public and private actors in Wales except the WO, developing contacts with other regional representations – i.e. 'horizontal' networking – and providing a venue for hosting Welsh promotion activities and other events.[22] Although informal, all three were at some point or other useful to Welsh public actors. In 1997, even the WO started to co-operate with the WEC, and the NAW has started to enhance the role of the WEC, using it as an unofficial 'Welsh embassy' in Brussels.

With the exception of Wales's affiliation to the 'Four Motors Consortium', the membership of Wales in interregional associations was also mainly organised jointly via the AWC and later the WLGA. Usually referred to as the 'Welsh member', they were formally represented by the AWC's and later the WLGA's secretary-general in associations such as the Assembly of European Regions (AER), the Conference of Peripheral Maritime Regions (CPMR), and the European Centre for Regional Development (CEDRE). The county councils in the South Wales Objective 2 area were joint members of the Association of European Regions of Industrial Technology (RETI; often referred to as the association for industrial regions in decline – see McAleavey, 1994). The only instance of individual membership of a single Welsh council in an interregional association was Dyfed's membership in the Association of European Border Regions (AEBR). This is remarkable insofar as among English and Scottish councils who embarked on a similar approach individual membership in these associations was – and still is – the rule rather than the exception (Loughlin and Mathias, 1996: 179). However, when asked about this both in the REGE survey and in subsequent interviews, only

Mid Glamorgan Council placed a high value on these activities.[23] Probably this is not surprising, as their territory comprised a number of Valleys which were the main beneficiaries of Objective 2 projects in the early 1990s. Any sort of involvement in the European scene was therefore given a high priority.[24] After the local government reform of 1996, the Merthyr Tydfil and Rhondda-Cynon-Taff CBCs, whose territories comprise most of the old Mid Glamorgan area, decided to continue with this policy of maximum involvement.[25] In general, though, according to the REGE responses, involvement in interregional associations was not ranked highly among Welsh local public actors, only 26 per cent agreeing that it was important to them; good relations with the WO (60 per cent), the WDA (57 per cent), the Welsh MPs (57 per cent) and MEPs (54 per cent), and the DBRW (27 per cent) were seen as being more important.

With the foundation of the CoR in 1994, Welsh public actors gained a new vehicle for both external interest representation at the EU level, and 'horizontal' networking with peers from all EU member states. During the CoR's first mandate period, Wales's allocation of seats consisted of three members and three alternates. From the second mandate period on, this dropped to two members and two alternates. Both Scotland and Wales had to hand one seat and one alternate seat to England in order to redress an imbalance in terms of the population size represented by each CoR member (Evans, 1998: 1). The members and alternates were appointed by the Secretary of State for Wales upon nomination by the AWC. In Scotland, these arrangements were the same, but in England local government associations were free to name their representatives without interference from the government.

During the first mandate period, the party-political affiliation of the Welsh CoR members neither reflected the electoral strength of the Welsh parties, nor the party-political control of councils in the AWC: Labour, the Conservatives and Plaid Cymru each obtained one member and one alternate seat. As requested by the Secretary of State, these appointments usually follow the British tradition of nominating an equal number of Labour and Conservative representatives to EU positions, as, for instance, is the case with British EU Commissioners. So, how did Plaid Cymru manage to get in on the act? According to Labour allegegations made at the time, it was as a result of Plaid Cymru's 'yes' vote on the TEU in the House of Commons; however, both Plaid and the Conservatives have always denied that this was the case. The Welsh Liberals lost out altogether concerning CoR involvement. Following its sweeping success in the 1997 General Election, Labour, by now in control of the WO, but acting in full agreement with the likewise Labour-controlled WLGA, used the 1998 round of appointments to redress the balance heavily in their favour: from 1998 on both Welsh members and one of the alternates were members of the Labour Party, while the second alternate position went to a Plaid member. This reflected the 1997 position of the parties in terms of electoral strength in Wales, with Plaid as the second-strongest party. From 2002 on, the NAW took on the responsibility for selecting and appointing the Welsh CoR members and alternates. It is likely that the party-political make-up of this group will roughly reflect the relative strength of parties in the Assembly at any given time. In 1998 John Evans, then a Welsh CoR member, stated that during the first mandate period the Welsh members had failed to develop a significant role in the CoR, the main reasons for this being the somewhat disorganised working conditions in the CoR itself (see also Christiansen, 1995, 1997), and the absence of any significant support by the Conservative government (Evans, 1998: 1–3).

It is likewise difficult to assess the Welsh CoR members' success in terms of horizontal networking (Farrows and McCarthy, 1997; Schwaiger, 1997). Initially, the potential beneficiaries at home were apparently unimpressed. During the first mandate period, the REGE survey revealed that among those surveyed only 37 per cent of the members' legislative bodies and 48 per cent of the public administrations regarded the CoR as important. Even fewer, 17 and 24 per cent, respectively, had made the effort to get in contact with the Welsh CoR representatives. With a more settled working procedure in the CoR now established, a more interested government in charge in the UK, and devolved regional actors such as the NAW influencing the selection of personnel, it is reasonable to speculate that this channel of interest representation is likely to improve. However, so far, it is too early to attempt to come to firm conclusions about this.

Overall, Welsh public actors have tried quite hard to come to terms with the changing environment of regional policy-making, in particular with regard to economic and social development. Structural and organisational changes introduced since 1990 have shaken up the established public actor culture of Labour-dominated local actor 'heavy-handedness' on the one hand, and Conservative-dominated WO 'colonial administration' on the other. The local government reform and the devolution measures introduced have provided a new organisational framework for public interest formation and public interest representation. One feature of this framework appears to be a greater role for non-traditional bodies, of both the public and the semi-public variety. However, whether this framework will be able to keep its potential promise of greater Welsh self-determination and efficiency in interest representation remains to be seen.

Public Actors Managing Saxon Regional Development Policy[26]

To speak of the changes to the landscape of public actors in Saxony that have occurred since 1990 merely in terms of 'reform' would be an understatement. At the beginning of 1990, the 'Saxon policy environment', let alone the public actors themselves, did not even exist. Only through German unification did Saxony develop its political system, its institutions, and its organisational procedures of governance.

In general, the Saxon government seemed determined to proceed faster and more ruthlessly – and initially indeed more successfully – than their counterparts in the other new *Länder* when it came to developing and implementing strategies for restructuring the whole society. However, to get a grip on the pressing needs for public action in a number of policy areas, a first important step was the restructuring of the civil service system inherited from the GDR. This process had begun prior to unification. It was the *Volkskammer* which, through the *Ländereinführungsgesetz*, the ratification of the Treaty on German Unification, and the GDR Local Government Self-Administration Act, 1990,[27] formalised a three-way split in the allocation of functions and civil service personnel.[28]

According to the Treaty on German Unification, Articles 13–15, GDR institutions whose functions were equivalent to federal functions in the FRG were to be made part of the federal administration. The Local Government Self-Administration Act left local and sub-regional administrations free to make their own arrangements within the limits prescribed by the Act, until such time as the new *Länder* produced subsequent legislation on the matter.[29] For the new *Länder*, the starting date for the reform was 14 October 1990, when the first *Land* elections were held. Article 15 of the Treaty handed over the administration of the GDR *Bezirke* to the *Länder* from the moment a *Land* prime minister was elected. Institutions not fitting any of these categories were to be disbanded with effect from 3 October 1990, and their personnel suspended for a period of six months during which time they would be trained, and, then, either reassigned to new institutions, or made redundant by default (*abgewickelt*).

Benz (1993: 471–2) characterises the 'strategy of institution-building' that followed the unification as consisting of four closely intertwined key elements: (i) time-limited administrative support, (ii) decentralisation 'from below', (iii) need-based financial support, and (iv) co-operation between the *Länder*.

The first of these, the provision of administrative aid, is also outlined in Article 15 of the Treaty on German Unification. Giving a time limit of 30 June 1991, it provided that upon request by a prime minister of a new *Land* both the west German *Länder* and the federal government were to send experienced personnel to help with the establishment of the *Land* government. The costs for this were to be borne by the federal government, or the sending, not the receiving *Land*, for the first six months. If a post-holder was to be retained thereafter, the financial responsibility for this would shift to the new *Land*.

In Saxony, the newly elected CDU government, headed by the experienced former secretary-general of the CDU, Kurt Biedenkopf,[30] decided to do most of the recruiting of its senior and medium-level administrative personnel for the *Staatskanzlei* (Cabinet Office) and the state ministries in Baden-Württemberg and Bavaria. It is therefore no surprise that the internal organisational structures and procedures originally set up in Saxony reflected to a large extent the established practice in those two West German *Länder*. Both Baden-Württemberg and Bavaria with their long tradition of government by right-of-centre parties, the CDU and the CSU, respectively, were generally perceived as somewhat conservative in the political environment of Germany. However, quite apart from party-political affiliations, the rationale for choosing this model was that both *Länder* had established a track record of above-average performance in economic and social development in the recent past. Baden-Württemberg, the German '*Musterländle*'(role-model *Land*) – and the work ethics to go with it – was top of most socio-economic performance indicators, including GDP per head and unemployment rate, usually around half the west German average. Since the late 1970s, Bavaria had seen a development drive unparalleled in West Germany since the days of the *Wirtschaftswunder* in the 1950s, resulting in the *Freistaat* becoming a net contributor to the *Länderfinanzausgleich*. A former professor of economics, Biedenkopf,[31] therefore, could hardly resist this opportunity to learn about policy from the best. On the other hand, having become accustomed to the rather favourable conditions in their home regions, the senior personnel thus recruited were faced with a set of economic and administrative problems which they had never encountered before. Some of the structures and functional divisions of labour within the Saxon ministerial bureaucracy had therefore to be reviewed to accommodate specific tasks, not least the handling of ERDF and ESF funds.

The double task of building both the administrative and the socio-economic structures more or less from scratch forced the political and the administrative leadership onto a course of learning by doing, with mixed success. It must be regarded as a significant success that the Saxon ministerial bureaucracy was established somewhat faster than elsewhere in East Germany;[32] however, this could not have been done without the administrative help of experienced West German personnel. Saxony suffered less than the other east German *Länder* from the phenomenon of recruiting junior west German personnel into senior positions, as was the case for instance in Saxony-Anhalt and Mecklenburg-West Pomerania, where there was a quick turnover of post-holders and little progress before satisfactory appointments could be made.

The difficulty of getting the new state institutions up and running – and the need for west German personnel – was further increased at the *Land* level by the loss of experienced East German personnel who had served in higher and medium-level positions in the East German regional administration. This was caused by the Saxon government's decision to embark on a course of action whereby it sacrificed the experience and knowledge of the region of that generation of civil servants for the safety and well-being of the new administration: in effect, it did not want to appoint people who might be unwilling to implement the new policies to the best of their ability. Also, Saxon state laws prohibiting the employment of people who served in 'exposed' public positions under the old regime are tougher than elsewhere. Thus, while it was common throughout the East German public sector not to employ agents and informers of the *Ministerium für Staatssicherheit*, the GDR Secret Service, Saxon law also excluded former members of the GDR armed services (other than national servicemen and junior policemen), and people who held managerial positions in regional administration, education and higher-education establishments, and even the public health service, regardless of their professional and academic qualifications. For non-managerial positions, including teachers, lecturers, medical personnel and secretarial staff, the usual policy was to terminate existing contracts, and to offer re-employment subject to satisfactory checks of qualifications and loyalty, known as *Evaluierung* (evaluation).[33]

Speedy decision-making, not only in the field of institution-building but in virtually all other fields of state activities as well, was helped considerably by the fact that the CDU enjoyed an absolute majority in the Saxon *Landtag*, with the parliamentary opposition politically split and apparently unable to develop constructive suggestions for alternative courses of action. While the SPD was – not very reluctantly – ready to agree to most actions taken by the government, the PDS was at the time still digesting the total change in the political system, and thus not in a position to come forward with viable ideas consistent with the new policy environment.

This situation provided the government with two major advantages: proven electoral support, and the absence of political competition with regard to ways and means to reconstruct various aspects of Saxon society. The government was therefore both tempted and empowered to push through its agenda in a speedy and more or less ruthless fashion, with political and social exclusion at the core. This was a luxury not enjoyed by the governments of the other east German *Länder*, and enabled the Saxon government swiftly to acquire a reputation of proactive behaviour and decisiveness.

This is not to say, however, that everyone was completely satisfied with the government's activities, in particular with regard to its economic and social policies. During 1990–91, a winter full of social unrest and almost daily demonstrations outside government buildings by one or another pressure group – except employers' associations (those were let inside to make their representations) – convinced the government of two things: that it was on the right course – the more radical the changes, the sooner the envisaged 'blossoming landscapes' would develop – and that law and order had to rank high on its list of priorities. This drive for law and order was spearheaded by one of the five East Germans in the first Biedenkopf Cabinet, the Minister of the Interior, Heinz Eggert.[34] As a result, the Saxon Police Act is the toughest in Germany – to the extent that certain provisions have been declared unconstitutional by the *Sächsischer Verfassungs- gerichtshof* (Saxon Constitutional Court), as being incompatible with the basic rights guaranteed in the Saxon constitution, and/or violating superseding federal legislation.[35]

The principle of 'decentralisation from below' as outlined by Benz (1993: 471) was therefore adhered to by the Saxon government at the *Land* level with enthusiasm and decisiveness, using all available legal and political resources at its disposal when it came to dismantle the old GDR administrative structures, and in the take-over of functions formerly conducted by GDR national administrations (for example police, education, higher education). This contributed not only to Saxony's speedy integration into the federal system of the FRG, but also to the strengthening of the government's own position as the key regional actor. However, the Saxon government proved to be much less enthusiastic about decentrali- sation 'from below' with regard to the reorganisation of sub-regional administrations. The *Regierungspräsidien* in the three administrative districts of Dresden, Leipzig and Chemnitz were clearly designed as secondary administrative units. While formally this is in line with established practice in the larger German *Länder*, the amount of day-to-day control exercised by the *Staatskanzlei*, and to a lesser extent the ministries, initially exceeded what can be regarded as standard practice in the west German *Länder*.[36] While a certain amount of anxiety by the government was understandable in the start-up phase, it also fuelled suspicions that the government was engaged in undemocratic practices to politicise the civil service. These suspicions were particularly strong among those opposition groups, in particular *Neues Forum*, whose members had been in opposition to the GDR regime, campaigning not least for open, transparent and impartial government and administration.[37] One factor which contributed to alleviating these fears was the policy of filling most (including senior) positions with East German personnel, usually experts in their particular field who had not served in managerial positions in the GDR administration. In cases where West German expertise was indispensable, in particular concerning economic policy, private consultants or external agencies were used extensively – a not always very cost-efficient solution, but appropriate as this was designed to be a short-term measure until suitably qualified civil servants became available.

Today, the main thrust of the activities of the *Regierungspräsidien* still consists of policy implementation and secondary decision-making according to directives issued by the *Land* government. However, in terms of practical policy, the *Regierungspräsidien* have been able to establish a larger influence. This goes both for decision-making, by suggesting practical solutions to the *Land* government, and for the ways and means of policy implementation. In addition, they are frequently called upon to act as mediators in conflicts of interest between the *Land* and local government, and, in the case of economic development policy, between the various levels of government within the state, and private actors.[38] To facilitate the latter, the *Regierungspräsidien* were the first units of public administration to recognise the potential value of semi-public actors – sub-regional and local development agencies – and public–private partnerships.

Up to 1996, most of the representatives of organisations and institutions interviewed in Saxony indicated that it may still be too early to pass judgement on the success of the government's efforts to develop a viable and efficient administrative structure. Most public actors at the *Land* level pointed out the progress and achievements made in their area of responsibility, implying that more could hardly have been done in the time available. In addition, some interviewees – in particular administrative personnel from the Germany – mentioned that due to the all-encompassing state of economic crisis, combined with the institutional inexperience of the newly created actors, networks of co-operation and support systems usually available to West German *Land* governments and administrations were not available yet in Saxony. Among the public actors, the *Staatskanzlei* in particular was generally regarded as doing a good job at crisis management, trying to co-ordinate and facilitate the manifold reconstruction jobs. However, a considerable minority of private actors did not even consider the *Staatskanzlei* an important actor, since their dealings with the Saxon government were normally with the State Ministry of their particular sector, and/or the *Regierungspräsidium* responsible for their territory.

In the administration of ERDF and ESF funds, this view is under-standable, as the *Regierungspräsidien* and the ministries took the lead in applying and monitoring procedures. Among the private actors, and in particular the business community, opinions on whether the Saxon administration was doing a good job, setting the right priorities, mostly depended on whether or not they had received financial support from a public or EU source. In a cash-short economy such as Saxony's, this narrow view does not come as a surprise, but on the other hand can be regarded as institutional inexperience on the part of the private actors concerned. It is also an indicator for the still widespread belief that the state was duty-bound to act to solve problems in virtually all spheres of the society's socio-economic life – again a 'culture of dependency', as the Thatcherites had accused Wales of having. However, the motives behind this appear to be varied, ranging from a lack of experience concerning the political and economic decision-making processes in free-market systems to the straightforward – though usually not openly admitted – desire to make a quick profit. Strangely, the *Staatsziele* definitions were usually only used by public actors to justify their decisions. Private actors, even those who were active among the *Staatsziele*, did not explicitly refer to them. When prompted, the responses ranged from an admission of not knowing to complaints about the virtual impossibility of enforcing them.

Saxony must be regarded as a very pro-European society. Not a single actor, public or private, failed to acknowledge that the EU (and its institutions) was an extremely important decision-maker when it came to their activities. This assessment was not linked to whether ERDF, ESF or EAGGF (European Agricultural Guidance and Guarantee Fund) funds had been received. Criticism, regarding delays in obtaining necessary informa-tion, failure to secure funding, or inadequacies in the administration and implementation of projects was mostly levied at the Saxon government and its ministries, in particular the State Ministry for Economics and Employment (SMWA). However, the State Ministry for Agriculture, Food and Forestry largely escaped such blame,[39] and was widely perceived as having done a very good job in extremely difficult circumstances. In general though, the Saxon government, faced with the need to comply with the complex EU rule-making and administrative process on the one hand, and a set of pro-European private actors in the region on the other, found it increasingly difficult to maintain its own pro-European stance – at least at the political level, much less so within the administration.

Initially, one of the most difficult tasks for the Saxon government and the ministerial bureaucracy was to overcome hesitant approaches to decision-making on economic and social development matters. Such hesitation was in evidence from both public and private actors at the sub-regional and local levels, especially in rural and less developed areas.[40] Under the GDR, these actors were accustomed to 'higher authorities' telling them what their planning targets had to be, and, as far as possible, providing them with the means to achieve these targets. So the same 'why bother' culture that prevailed at the individual level could be observed on the institutional level as well. Needless to say this attitude had to change dramatically if adverse effects for the area were to be avoided. Indeed, many, but by no means all, local actors proved to be fast learners as soon as it became apparent – around late 1992, when the funds initially granted under the terms of the *Gemeinschaftsaufgabe* ran out – that they would lose out considerably if they did not shift their work to a more proactive mode. In particular, the city of Leipzig became the forerunner of developing local renewal strategies independently of Saxon government activities.

Still, the Saxon government remains adamant that it knows best how to develop Saxony; and advice, whether from Bonn or from Brussels, is usually welcome only if accompanied by funding, an attitude that was fostered when the system of EU funding for east Germany was changed. Between 1991 and 1993, a joint programme (*Gemeinschaftliches Förderkonzept*) was in operation for all east German *Länder* and east Berlin. Saxony, with the largest population, received the largest share of available funding (except from the EAGGF), but, under the co-financing rules, had to come up with the largest joint federal and *Land* contributions, as well as having to attract the most private investments (see Table 3.1).

TABLE 3.1
REGIONAL DEVELOPMENT FUNDING FOR
THE NEW *LÄNDER*, 1991–93 (m. ECU)

Land	Total	ERDF	ESF	EAGGF	Joint federal and Land	Local govern-ment	Private funds
Brandenberg	2,231.1	239.9	103.7	132.2	625.8	116.3	1,103.2
East Berlin	819.1	116.2	46.2	1.8	163.5	50.6	440.8
Mecklenburg-West Pomerania	2,015.2	177.3	80.1	151.8	586.5	89.5	930.0
Saxony	3,618.0	444.0	182.2	105.9	848.8	202.5	1,834.0
Saxony-Anhalt	2,473.7	268.2	114.9	122.3	644.8	127.5	1,196.0
Thuringia	2,127.9	244.4	102.3	86.0	529.6	114.6	1,501.0
Total*	13,285.0	1,490.0	629.4	600.0	3,399.0	701.0	7005.0

* In addition, 450m ecu not regionally earmarked ESF funds and 110m ecu technical assistance were available.

Source: Kommision der Europäischen Gemeinschaften (eds), 1991.

The principle of treating east German *Länder* jointly and similarly under the special rules outlined in the *Gemeinschaftliches Förderkonzept*, rather than under standard Objective 1 rules, was abandoned on 1 January 1994. From that date on, each *Land* ran individual operational programmes, which followed standard Objective 1 rules – whose eligibility criteria were met by all east German *Länder*. However, politically, each *Länder* now became responsible for running their own regional economic development affairs. This also included an increased responsibility for negotiating their affairs with the EU institutions, something that Saxony was able to do rather well, measured by securing their continued significant support.[41]

However, the political consequences of these changes in external rules were significant. The government noted that enhanced means of representation of Saxon interests were required in the long term. By 1994 it was still proactive in decision-making, having gained increased confidence by winning the second *Landtag* elections, again securing an absolute majority. It marked the occasion by giving up its position as a joint representative of all east German *Länder*, preferring instead to represent only Saxony's interests in Brussels. While that did not go down well with the other east German *Land* governments, it set the tone for a series of steps to disassociate Saxony from the rest of the new *Länder*, culminating in Biedenkopf's claim that 'we are not the East, we are Saxony' (Biedenkopf, 1998a: 1).[42]

From the summer of 1996, Biedenkopf repeatedly elaborated on the theme of strengthening the role of regions within the EU. In the *Landtag* debate on Saxony's position on the 1996 IGC (Sächsischer Landtag, 1995), CDU parliamentarians demanded that the principle of subsidiarity be applied to all levels of government within the EU, and in particular to the running of regional development policies. The vision outlined in the policy statement issued by the CDU in the *Landtag* included better individual[43] direct access to EU institutions by German *Land* representatives, and the demand that the regions be given a greater say in the use of funds, which were to be less rigidly earmarked – all in the name of close ties with the people and enhanced democracy in decision-making.

One cannot fail to notice that these demands were the exact equivalent of those which were of significance to Welsh devolutionists both in the referendum campaign and in the 1999 NAW elections campaign. In the circumstances of the Welsh political scene, they seemed to make sense, given the weak status of indigenous Welsh actors prior to devolution. However, within the German constitutional and political context, the appropriateness of these demands must be questioned. Voicing them implied that the majority group in the Saxon *Landtag* was not satisfied with the provisions at the time – a view echoed only by the Bavarian CSU, and not in the other *Länder*. The *Bundesrat* had adopted a less rigid stance in 1995 (*Bundesrat*, 1995).

However, the CDU group in the *Landtag* even went as far as demanding that the EU become a 'league of states' rather than a 'centralised state', integrated, yet safeguarding existing distinctions (*Sächsischer Landtag*, 1995). This vision of a 'league of states' demanded more or less equal status for territorial entities which regard themselves as states, whether or not they are members of the EU in their own right or only as part of a federation. Following the rationale that the constituent elements of such a league would be states, and that Saxony is a state, the argument culminated in the demand that Saxony was to become a signatory state of international treaties and a member of international organisations – implicitly demanding individual EU membership (ibid: 6). With the opposition rightly ridiculing this stance in the debate, exposing the motion's deliberately confusing – and even unconstitutional – use of the term 'state', the then Saxon Secretary of State for Federal and European Affairs, Ermisch (CDU), had to retract this idea in his statement on behalf of the government,[44] pointing out that this would infringe the distribution of competencies as outlined in Article 23 GG.

The withdrawal of these demands, however, did not mark the end of this line of thinking in the Saxon government or the Saxon CDU. In an interview with *Der Spiegel* at the time, Biedenkopf stated bluntly that for him it would be 'completely unthinkable' for Brussels to decide how East Germany is to be reconstructed.[45] Such statements have clearly attracted significant popular support – and the government does its utmost to maintain this. One course on which the *Staatskanzlei* has recently embarked is to cash in on the *Heimat* tradition.[46] The aim of this policy is twofold. First, making people feel proud and valued as Saxons – or Sorbs, if preferred – might help to overcome a certain general perception among the population of being treated as east (i.e. second-class) Germans. However, while this will give them a more positive view of themselves, it will be more difficult to explain away the disadvantages of being an east German living in a west German economy. Secondly, a region able to show a flourishing community life might present itself more favourably to potential investors.

One reason why the Saxon government is still able to get away with such rhetoric can be seen in the apparent inability of the other main party, the SPD, to mount an opposition worthy of the name. Apart from the debate on general European affairs mentioned above, prior to the SPD's change of stance in early 1997, the only instance in which it took issue with the government over a practical measure of regional development policy was when it sided with the European Commission in a row between the Commission and the Saxon government over the application of Article 92(2)c EEC Treaty with regard to subsidies for the Volkswagen AG plant at

Mosel near Zwickau (Krehl, 1996: 1). In general, however, at the regional level the SPD has yet to come up with a coherent policy of regional development in Saxony within the EU. At the local level, the SPD clearly has fared better, not least in the only large Saxon city in which it had control of the council: Leipzig.[47] However, local actors think – understandably – predominantly locally, so for the people of Leipzig 'inter-regional co-operation' usually does not go too far beyond developing an uneasy relationship with their neighbours in the Halle-Merseburg area (Saxony-Anhalt), running a joint RTP region across the *Land* border. It was not until late 1996 that the regional party leadership became aware of the SPD's lack of ideas concerning a feasible alternative strategy to government policy. A number of fact-finding studies was commissioned by the party's *Arbeitsgruppe Europa* in late 1996 and early 1997. In addition, the Leipzig MEP Konstanze Krehl (SPD), who has since become leader of the regional party, has been able to start flying the European flag for the Saxon SPD, offering information and independent advice for individuals and Saxon private actors. However, lacking the political power to implement one's ideas has had a demotivating influence on SPD activists in Saxony.[48] The 1999 *Landtag* election result was correspondingly catastrophic for the SPD: having won just 10.7 per cent of the popular vote, the SPD is now only the third-strongest party in Saxony, 11.5 per cent behind the PDS and an astonishing 46.2 per cent behind the CDU (SLA, 2000: 210).

Facing both a hostile regional government and – until September 1998 – a hostile federal government, has so far made it extremely difficult for all parties, except the CDU, to see their ideas put into practice. A similar problem surfaced with regard to arguments from interest groups which during the first few post-unification years were, in the opinion of the Saxon government, not in a position to contribute meaningfully to the creation of a new Saxony, among them trade unions, voluntary organisations, and most of the academic community. Whether such a policy of arbitrary social and political exclusion was appropriate even at an early stage of the reform process must be open to doubt. In the opinion of the government, the short-term economic advantages over the other new *Länder* have outweighed the disadvantages encountered through the failure to establish a sustainable political culture of open debate and inclusive, transparent decision-making. When asked about this,[49] the CDU just tend to refer to their absolute majority in the *Landtag*, and suggest that they – and they alone – have a popular mandate to decide and implement policies.

However, having successfully kept potential critics, including the political opposition, as well as potential allies, at arm's length means – of necessity – that one is out there on one's own. Ten years on, the other east German *Länder* have caught up with Saxony in terms of regional development, and the Saxon government's political *élan*, so vigorously displayed in the first legislative period, seems to have run dry around late 1998, changing its policy-making style to a more reactive mode. The Saxon electorate, however, still expressed its satisfaction in the 1999 *Landtag* elections by giving the CDU an absolute majority for the third consecutive legislative period.

In 1998, a SPD-led government was returned at the federal elections. The first *Regierungserklärung*[50] of the new Chancellor, Schröder, was outlined on 10 November 1998 and was an exercise in fairly simplistic and practical can-do central steering. The entire governmental programme was geared towards a new work ethic, involving virtually all sectors and groups in German society. 'Off benefit and into work' was a concept taken straight out of Blair's 'New Britain' copybook. Federal funds were to be directed at job creation schemes (an extended and enhanced version of Kohl's stopgap measures introduced shortly before the election), at jobs for women, at various means of adult education and qualification – traditionally the *Länder's* responsibility – and at combating youth unemployment. However, in each of these cases federal funds would only be forthcoming if the appropriate interest organisations and private sector partners joined in these initiatives – the well-publicised '*Bündnis für Arbeit*', designed to go beyond Kohl's *Kanzlerrunde*, and to be at the heart of the government's activities. Accompanying measures such as the (ill-fated) tax reform, and a continued strong engagement in the EU, too, were to be part of this drive – exercising the government's traditional role of promoting favourable external conditions for the domestic agenda.

As far as regional development is concerned, neither the term nor the west German *Länder* were even mentioned in the *Regierungserklärung*. The new government seemed to be content to let the Western *Länder* get on with their own agendas, by the traditional means of self-reliance, *Länderfinanzausgleich* and *Gemeinschaftsaufgabe*.

The new government's policy towards the east German *Länder*, however, was to be completely different from this. Judging the previous government's efforts to have failed, Schröder's remedy seemed to be centralisation:

> As Chancellor, I have declared the development of East Germany to be a personal priority of mine. The appropriate competencies for this task will be combined. I will be aided in this task by a Minister of State in the Chancellery, who will be responsible for a very close liaison with the Land governments of the East German Länder. The Federal Cabinet will meet every two months in one of the new Länder, to discuss the situation with the Land governments concerned, and to initiate specific projects in accordance with the situation there. (Schröder, 1998).[51]

Personal scrutiny by the Chancellor, an 'east German supremo' with the rank of junior minister in the Chancellery, the federal Cabinet descending on each of the five east German *Länder* and their governments at least once a year not only to discuss the situation but even to become directly involved in individual projects – those who still believe that Germany is a truly federal republic must have been shocked by that prospect. The intention, though, seemed benign enough, showing serious commitment where the previous government had limited itself to grand gestures and short-term, knee-jerk reactions to problems as and when discontent in the regions had reached unacceptable levels.

However, the announced shift in federal policy style has not materialised. Contacts between the Federal Cabinet and the eastern *Land* governments have tended to be low-key and informal. Hardly anybody in the eastern *Länder* is quite sure what exactly the 'East German Supremo', Chancellery Minister Rolf Schwanitz, is doing. The federal government has managed to become quite unpopular in a very short time, as indicated by the 1999 election results in many of the *Länder*, including all the ones in the east. For Biedenkopf and his government in Saxony, the situation could therefore not be better, although they are hardly in a position to claim this as their success. Nevertheless, the Saxon government has so far not seen fit to implement any adaptations of policy style to accommodate the changed external circumstances. Given the lack of effectiveness of the federal action plan so far, the Saxon policy of disassociation from the rest of the eastern *Länder*, and the determination to pursue a policy style more in line with the usual approach taken by most west German *Länder*, i.e. to take what advantages are available from the outside world but otherwise just to get on with things, may still prove to be a winner.

As we have seen, both Wales and Saxony were by 2000 endowed with a structure of public actors which is legally endowed with the right to engage in managing regional development management, and politically most willing to take on that role. A further common feature is a significant dependence on outside (mostly EU) funding for certain development tasks. The policy styles observable in the two regions, however, vary. While in Saxony a remarkably self-confident government has managed to establish itself as master of proceedings, the new Welsh public actors are still in a process of finding their way beyond the trodden paths previously marked out by Westminster and the WO. Nevertheless, due to the diversity, complexity and costliness of a truly comprehensive regional development effort, both the Welsh and the Saxon public actors have realised that it is essential to co-operate to a large extent with private actors within the region.

NOTES

1. Information taken from the text published by the *Sächsische Landeszentrale für Politische Bildung*, 1999.
2. For instance, a *Land* employee who is made redundant cannot sue the *Land* government for having violated Article 7 by taking state action to put him out of his job.
3. The term preferred by devolutionists for this process is 'vision', despite its mystical connotations.
4. This section is based mainly on REGE Wales data, as described in Appendix A, where a copy of the full REGE Wales questionnaire is also provided.
5. To some extent – but not 'beyond reasonable doubt' confirmed by subsequent interviews (see Appendix A).
6. As measured by REGE question 23; see Appendix A3.
7. While it is difficult to establish tangible evidence for a split between rather 'old Labour' grassroots in Wales and a more 'New Labour' party leadership in Westminster, both party activists and the electorate seem to believe in the existence of a split. To some extent this was indicated by the election results of May 1999, where Plaid Cymru did particularly well in areas, such as the traditional south Wales coalfield communities, where they managed to portray themselves as a political force standing for socialist values which 'official' Labour seemed to have abandoned (Evans and George, 1999: 8–10).
8. As it turned out, Secretaries of State Redwood and Hague, widely regarded as being quite biased in an anti-European way, have not been particularly powerful advocates for such change anyway.
9. Interview, WO, Business Services Division, 1997.
10. Interview, WDA, International Division, 1997.
11. In the early 1990s, the annual Welsh European Business Fair was used by most local authorities as a testing ground.
12. At the time leader of the UK Labour MEPs, and deputy leader of the Socialist group in the EP.
13. Interview, Newport Development Board, 1997.
14. Representatives of the following councils were interviewed: Rhondda-Cynnon-Taff, Blaenau-Gwent, Neath and Port Talbot, and Merthyr Tydfil.
15. The term 'vetting' was not used officially, but compulsory consultation procedures and the requirement of private actors and local government to submit applications via the WO effectively guaranteed the WO's influence at this stage.
16. Interview, Wales Labour Party domestic politics expert, 1999.
17. Interview, Merthyr Tydfil County Borough Council, 1997.
18. In the case of Cardiff, the disagreements were so severe that the Cardiff representatives stopped participating in WLGA activities for some months in 1999/2000.
19. The constituency link was broken in the 1999 EP elections when Wales became a single constituency; the five Welsh seats being allocated by proportional representation (Home Office, 1999: 2–4).
20. In 1999 he did not stand again in the EP elections, instead staging an unsuccessful attempt to win a seat in the NAW.
21. For a detailed account of this trend, see Jeffery, 1996b: 183–203.
22. Notable among these are quite elaborate St David's Day (1 March) celebrations.
23. Interview, Mid Glamorgan County Council, 1996.
24. Interview, Wales Labour Party, EU expert, 1995.
25. Interviews, Merthyr Tydfil and Rhondda-Cynon-Taff CBCs, 1996–97.
26. This section is based mainly on interviews with public actors in Saxony, held between July 1995 and May 2000 (see listing in Appendix A).
27. *Gesetz über die Selbstverwaltung der Gemeinden und Landkreise in der DDR.*
28. In practice, this three-way split was already established in the GDR but fluctuations of not politically appointed personnel among the three administrative levels of central government, administrative districts (Bezirke), and local/sub-regional government were rather uncommon.
29. Saxony did so in 1992, passing a legally binding Local Government Charter (*Sächsische Gemeindeordnung*).

30. Having been a key figure in the West German CDU in the 1970s and early 1980s, Biedenkopf – like many others – fell victim to Helmut Kohl's drive to secure his place at the helm of the party in the mid-1980s, and was removed from his office as secretary-general. The post-unification need for political experience, however, provided him with a new lease of life in the top echelon of German politicians.

31. Prior to his political career, Biedenkopf had held professorial positions in West German universities in the late 1960s. During the 1990 election campaign, he took up a guest professorship in economics at the University of Leipzig.

32. Except Berlin, where somewhat different rules for the merger of West and East Berlin institutions applied.

33. The latter usually consists of an enquiry with the Gauck Agency, which took over the files of the *Ministerium für Staatssicherheit*, a check with the police for criminal convictions (convictions for political misbehaviour in the GDR usually were an asset rather than a problem, though), and the request to sign a declaration to the effect that one would not engage in practices designed to undermine the *freiheitlich-demokratische Grundordnung*, i.e. the constitutional and political system of the FRG.

34. A former Lutheran clergyman and victim of political repression under the GDR system (he claims to have been forced into inpatient psychiatric treatment), he was later dismissed from the government amidst allegations – not proved – of sexual misconduct.

35. In particular para. 22(7) SächsPolG (Police Arrest), and paras 39 and 40 SächsPolG (Data Protection during undercover investigations). See *Polizeigesetz des Freistaates Sachsen*, of 30 July 1991 (*Sächs. Gesetz- und Verordnungsblatt*, No. 20/91) as altered by the *Gesetz zur Änderung des Polizeigesetzes*, of 24 May 1994 (*Sächs. Gesetz- und Verordnungsblatt*, No. 30/94) and the Constitutional Court's judgement Vf 44-II–94, of 14 May 1996 (*Sächs. Verwaltungsblätter*, No. 7/8, 1996).

36. Interview, *Regierungspräsidium* Leipzig, 1997.

37. Interview, NF, 1996. It was pointed out that a totally politicised public administration was the main means by which the GDR regime exercised political power.

38. Interview, *Regierungspräsidium* Chemnitz, 1996.

39. Apart from the *Südmilch* affair, 1995–97.

40. Interview, *Sächsische Staatskanzlei*, 1996.

41. For financial details see Table 2.6.

42. Original text: 'Wir sind nicht der Osten, wir sind Sachsen'. The claim was repeated, ibid: 16.

43. Rather than jointly via the *Bundesrat* or other federal means of interest representation, as outlined in Article 23 GG.

44. Unpublished letter to the President of the *Landtag*, of 24 October 1996.

45. Original text: 'Für mich ist völlig undenkbar, daß in Brüssel darüber entschieden wird, wie Ostdeutschland aufgebaut wird.' (Ihlau and Pieper, 1996)

46. One case in point is the publication of a song book (see Sagurna and Müller, 1996) by the *Staatskanzlei*, the contents of which stirs up quite uncomfortable memories of similar efforts by the GDR to mobilise some *Heimat* feelings among the citizens. The book was distributed free of charge to all Saxon households.

47. The SPD lost this control in the 1999 local elections. However, it retained the office of Mayor, who was directly elected in 1998.

48. Interview, SPD *Landesvorstand*, 1996.

49. Interviews, CDU Group in the Saxon Landtag, 1997, and CDU Leipzig, 1998.

50. Germany's equivalent to the UK's Queen's Speech or the US President's State of the Union Address.

51. Translation by the author. Original text: 'Ich habe als Bundeskanzler erklärt, den Aufbau Ost zur Chefsache zu machen. Die Kompetenzen dafür werden gebündelt. Mir wird ein Staatsminister im Bundeskanzleramt zur Seite stehen, der vor allem für eine sehr enge Koordination mit den Landesregierungen in den ostdeutschen Ländern sorgen wird. Das Bundeskabinett wird alle zwei Monate in einem der neuen Länder tagen, um mit den dortigen Landesregierungen die Lage zu erörtern und konkrete Projekte auf den Weg zu bringen, die der Situation dort gerechtwerden.'

4

New Forms of Public–Private Interaction in Wales and Saxony

Numerous empirical studies (for example Cooke et al., 1993; Nagel, 1994; Kohler-Koch, 1996, 1998; Loughlin, 1996a; Knodt, 1998; Lange, 1998) have emphasised that regional development efforts are usually heavily dependent on functioning public–private relationships, within a wider framework of co-operation between various types of actors within the region. Regional mobilisation and political exchange are seen as facilitators of success. The basic idea here is that the pooling of regional resources and a joint approach to regional interest representation helps to establish a region in both economic and political terms, as a worthwhile place to live and invest in, and as a serious partner to do business with. However, this also raises the question to what extent this process may lead to a significant – and possibly unduly large – influence by specific private interests in the process of regional interest formation and public policy-making, thus altering the nature of regional governance. This chapter addresses the question: what are chances for and the constraints on public–private co-operation in the specific environments of the Welsh and Saxon polities, and what will be the influence of these interactions on the practical conduct of regional governance?

Despite the constraints on modern governments to deal effectively with private or factional interests, the right to run state institutions still remains in the hands of public actors. These actors therefore retain the means – political power – to act in pursuit of what they perceive as the public interest. This goes a long way in understanding why these actors perceive it as their responsibility to use this power to promote public interests when interacting with representatives of private interests. Depending on the degree of convergence between public and private interests in a given situation, the nature of such interaction may be either predominantly confrontational or predominantly co-operative; both to a lesser or stronger degree.

If governments, including regional governments and local authorities, perceive a certain private interest as not sufficiently in line with the public interest, the public actors will seek to exercise control over the issue, producing regulative or fiscal legislation, or taking administrative rules and similarly restrictive decisions, collectively – and pejoratively – known as 'red tape', in order to curb the private interest in question. On the other hand, if those governments perceive that there is a sufficient degree of convergence between public and private interests in a given field of policy-making, they are likely to co-operate with the representatives of these private interests, even though the motivation for doing so may differ considerably between the public and the private partners. Similarly different are the resources these partners usually put at each others' disposal: influence on authoritative decision-making on the one hand, cash and expertise on the other. Négrier (1997, 1998) has analysed this phenomenon in terms of 'political exchange' among various public, semi-public and private partners within a given territory. The concept of regional mobilisation goes beyond that insofar as it argues that synergetic effects of sustained co-operation among various public, semi-public and private partners within a territory (for example a region) are likely to enhance the state of socio-economic development in that region beyond what could be reasonably expected if co-operation procedures were limited to straightforward exchange operations. The concept of regional mobilisation is based on the view that such development is indeed in the interest of both the general public and the individual private groupings within that region.[1] Control, in this scenario, is usually exercised by public actors outside the region concerned, such as central governments or EU institutions. These external actors are motivated by their own set of interests and targets. Standardisation features large among these, as witnessed for instance by the German government's task of equalising living conditions across Germany, and the EU's twin aims of 'ever closer union' and 'cohesion'. In the practical political process, however, control and co-operation are often alternated, or used complementarily to each other: 'carrot and stick'.

CONTROL

Wales: 'Less State'?

The effects of Thatcherite monetarism on the discharge of what used to be regarded as governmental functions have already been well documented elsewhere (Jessop et al., 1988; Young, 1989; Richardson, 1994; and others). Much the same goes for shifts in regional policy from the mid-1980s to date (see Rhodes, 1993 (UK); Elcock, 1997 (England); Keating, Midwinter and Mitchell, 1991 (Scotland); and Cooke et al., 1993 (Wales), among others).

The tension between the political drive for 'less state' and the need for political steering – or governance, if one prefers – is a EU-wide problem, and nowhere more so than in Britain. As Majone (1996: 10–11) pointed out, 'In Britain dissatisfaction with the performance of nationalised industries led to repeated attempts by government to prescribe more specific objectives.' However, Thatcherite activism went far beyond traditional prescription methods – subsequently mentioned by Majone – employed by pre-1979 British governments. To undergo financial, administrative and regulatory reforms, along with large-scale privatisation, all more or less at once, created a new qualitative dimension of public governance in Britain.

The core contents of these reforms was an enormous reshuffle in the landscape of socio-economic and political institutions, creating a network of old and new actors – both public and private, but particular creativity was shown by the Thatcher government in creating a whole host of semi-public actors in various organisational forms. This to some extent blurred the lines between these actor categories. The new actors tried to go about their various tasks by co-operating where sensible, but basically became competitors for ever more scarce resources in terms of funds, influence in decision-making processes, and status in society. To create this new network and put it in charge of vital socio-economic processes in British society can be regarded as an enormous experiment in social engineering by Thatcher and her entourage. In effect, it can be seen as an attempt to rebuild the state and society on a completely new basis, very different from previous systems – and thus changing, or at least challenging, the very nature of the state itself. The key principles of this would be to reduce the scope of state activities, to commercialise as far as possible the remaining core activities, and to use the 'surplus energy' thus gained to tighten governmental control and oversight over not only the state itself, but also the entire socio-economic lifestyle of society (see also Jessop et al., 1988).

The Thatcherite demand for 'value for money' was only too often interpreted as 'cheapest is best' by newly promoted senior Whitehall civil servants and also a number of local and regional administrative establishments; and Downing Street, under both Thatcher and Major, apparently did little to change this view – even though that meant that in many cases the 'value' received declined sharply. Let us first have a brief look at the underlying concepts that seemed to lend support to the notion that indeed 'less state' was forthcoming. The foremost idea, repeatedly expressed by leading Tory politicians at the time, was a strict curbing of direct public expenditure – i.e. money spent directly by Whitehall departments. Having heavily opposed the 'tax and spend' mentality of successive Labour governments from the postwar period to the mid-1970s, the old arguments of wasting public resources through bureaucratic inefficiency and not keeping a tight check on implementation and running costs for new and ongoing projects[2] were repeated over and over again.

The Thatcherite agenda, based on neo-liberal theories of policy, wished to reduce government intervention at all levels, and particularly with regard to any policies that smacked of what they defined as the 'dependency culture' (Loughlin and Mathias, 1996). The first solution to reduce direct public spending was simply to stop doing it. The 1980 and 1981 budgets saw severe cuts in most departments' allocations. However, without clear indications as to precisely in which areas of activity the cuts were to be made, most departments had to decide on an across-the-board reduction in expenditure. While this can be seen as easing the burden for individual sectors by distributing it among many different shoulders, this also meant that virtually none had enough to get on with their tasks as previously. Later on, this practice led to the argument, repeatedly stated by representatives of various interest groups, that the now chronic cash crisis in important sectors dates back to this period. This applies not only to welfare, health and education, etc., but also to other, perhaps less obvious areas of state activity, for example support for ailing regions (Thomas, 1987).

As early as the mid-1980s, however, the first doubts were raised whether this approach was working. Nevertheless, successive Tory governments under both Thatcher and Major went on with direct expenditure cuts whenever they thought they could get away with it. One case in point was the money available for local government. Grant cuts were imposed summarily, leaving it to the individual councils – who presumably then would be held responsible by the voters – how to find the extra money or where to make the service cuts.[3]

But does 'less cash' really equal 'less state'? In a first instance, a tight-fisted Treasury necessarily implies less state interference in the running of the economy, as a self-imposed reduction in purchasing power results in less ability to act in the market place. All those audits, along with numerous reshuffles among the rank and file of civil servants, bear witness to Mrs Thatcher's determination to keep a tight check on the activities of each department; and cutting the public payroll was perceived as a nice – if secondary – little earner, too. However, the question here is not whether under Thatcher the pendulum might have swung too far in the other direction, creating 'less state' by stopping to carry out necessary or at least highly desirable functions. The more interesting phenomenon is that one might well argue that 'more state' has actually been forthcoming, in the sense of increased centralised checks and audits, with the necessary bureaucracy to go with it, and by means of producing new 'red tape' through re-regulation rather than deregulation.

Jessop et al. (1988) identify four components of what they describe as Thatcherite economic 'Neo-Liberal Accumulation strategy': (i) a commitment to privatisation, deregulation and the application of commercial criteria to the remaining state activities; (ii) deregulation in the financial sector, in particular the City; (iii) some sponsoring of inward investment, SME development and technology transfer; and (iv) a long-term approach to promote Britain internationally by establishing a 'tricontinental multinational presence' in the UK economy. These measures were implemented more or less simultaneously, in the hope of creating some symbiotic effect among them. However, in Wales the Thatcher government found an ideal field for testing various reform ideas in terms of privatising or franchising out not only public works services but also public administration functions. The result of these efforts has become commonly known as 'Quangoland Wales' (Morgan and Roberts, 1993).

In the processes of privatisation, Britain has indeed achieved more market and 'less state'. It is debatable whether it was worthwhile to do away with many of the old ways of governmental interference, but one thing that can be said about the changes is that most of the conflicts of interest are now out in the open and much more closely watched and publicly debated by those on the receiving end, the consumers and their associations. This in itself constitutes some progress.

However, beyond nationalised industries, for which privatisation was the Tory answer, there were many more areas of state activity in which for one reason or another privatisation was deemed either impractical or inappropriate, in particular because it was felt that the government should not give up its direct control. However, from a strictly monetarist perspective there was no reason why in these areas commercial viability criteria should not be introduced. The answer lay in the creation of agencies known as Executive Quangos or Management Bodies, run like private companies, in which the state holds enough 'shares' to exercise sufficient influence in the boardroom. The role of the regulator here was vested not in a single body but by establishing dual control through direct parliamentary scrutiny via the Public Accounts Committee, and through independent audit by the National Audit Commission, in turn reporting to the Treasury, the Cabinet, and finally Parliament. Agencies have become the most influential and therefore most important category of semi-public actors.

The example was already there, as it was a Labour government which in 1975 created the first of these agencies: the Scottish Development Agency (SDA) and the Welsh Development Agency (WDA). In Scotland, the Conservative government went one step further between 1988 and 1990, by commercialising the SDA. Now called Scottish Enterprise, it offers business services on a commercial basis and bids for EU funds

(ERDF/ESF) in direct competition with other providers such as the CBI and local development agencies. In 1991, 13 local development agencies were launched as subsidiaries of Scottish Enterprise. International representation of Scottish business interests became the task of yet another new agency, Scottish Trade International, jointly run by the Scottish Office (SO) and Scottish Enterprise. The initiative for this reform came mainly from Bill Hughes,[4] one of Thatcher's favourite Scottish businessmen (Mitchell, 1997: 400), while the then Secretary of State for Scotland, Malcom Rifkind – appointed in 1986 but still mindful of a Cabinet career that had just begun[5] – apparently was only too eager to agree with whatever Thatcher wanted.

In Wales, however, a different strategy was adopted – not least because the Secretary of State for Wales at the time, Peter Walker, was opposed to a commercialising of the WDA and threatened to resign over the issue.[6] So the solution was to let the WDA stick to creating development plans and some representation abroad, while the business services were kept within the WO. Numerous studies of their record can be found elsewhere (for example Morgan and Roberts, 1993; Loughlin, 1997). The latest development in the Welsh case was the merger – finally implemented by Labour in September 1999 – of the three largest Executive Quangos there, the WDA, the DBRW and the Land Authority for Wales. The rationale behind this decision was to prevent a further development of the already emerging planning competition between these agencies due to overlapping briefs and an apparent lack of adequate co-operation procedures. Whether this 'powerhouse agency' will also be able to deliver the openness and democratic accountability that is found wanting under the pre-1999 arrangements (see Morgan and Roberts, 1993), and that was repeatedly promised by Labour during both 1997 campaigns,[7] remains to be seen.

At the UK level, the agency model was extended into a number of fields, creating a host of new agencies: National Health Service Trusts for health-care, the Benefits Agency for the administration of all social security payments,[8] and the Child Support Agency for child welfare, were but a few examples. The key idea with regard to social security provisions was not only to save on staff, but also to combat fraud by running claimants through a cross-checking procedure. This is not the place to discuss the actual political decisions to cut down on benefits, for example the introduction of Jobseekers' Allowance to replace the old Unemployment Benefit.[9] However, from the point of view of the people on the receiving end all that this system achieved was to add another layer of bureaucracy, the Benefits Agency. The need to administer the sharpened procedures, such as fortnightly checks whether claimants do indeed seek work, and the need to establish adequate co-operation procedures between the various outlets of the two departments and the Benefits Agency, in the end itself created a large administrative bill. The fight against fraud, on the other hand, seems to have produced far smaller results than anticipated. How else is it understandable that in the last days of the Major government the Benefits Agency felt the need to open a 'Hotline' which people were encouraged to call – free of charge and confidentially – to report on suspected culprits?

Stuart Weir's investigation into quangos (Weir and Hall, 1995) emphasises that in particular the spending power of Executive Quangos – £15.08 bn in 1994, of which 92.2 per cent was spent by the largest 40 Executive Quangos – hardly receives the public scrutiny it deserves. A number of his other findings focus on the question of general public accountability of these establishments (see Table 4.1).

TABLE 4.1
PUBLIC ACCOUNTABILITY OF QUANGOS IN THE UK, 1995

	Executive quangos	Advisory quangos	NHS bodies	[Others]	Total
Number of quangos	358	807	629	4,534	6,328
Subject to code of open government	124	0	0	0	124
Public right to:					
• inspect register of members' interests	6	0	0	2,668	2,674
• attend board or committee meetings	6	0	298	0	304
• see policy papers and documents	0	0	0	0	0
Quangos required by law to:					
• publish annual accounts	191	n/a	248	4,534	4,973
• publish annual reports	201	163	248	1,596	2,178
• hold public meetings	2	12	314	105	433

Source: Weir and Hall, 1995.

Just a brief glance at the sheer quantity of quangos that seem to be outside close public scrutiny gives an impression of the accountability problem – let alone individual planning, policy or appointment decisions. Therefore, the Conservatives were probably right at least to ask the question whether government and its administrative branches really need to bother either to shoulder the workload directly, or to double it all up by exercising permanent scrutiny. However, while the answer to the first option is probably no, the second part – scrutiny – ought to be regarded as essential to safeguarding the public interest in a democratic society, even if that means a little less 'efficiency savings'.

However, there seems to be little public alarm over the apparent lack of democratic control, both among the organisations involved in co-operating with quangos, and among the consumers of services provided by them. The key to understanding the widespread complacency towards quangos probably is the perception among those concerned that this system works reasonably well. Most of the well-publicised benefits of the quango system can certainly be safely discarded as hype, or at least embellishment of facts. Nevertheless, despite criticism levied at individual projects and personalities, the Executive Quangos have done a reasonably good job. Apparently the public is prepared to accept this practical outcome as the only criterion for granting a large leeway in terms of accountability and control.

Within the context of this study, though, it is most noteworthy that virtually all the key decisions in this field were taken by state- (i.e. UK-) level actors. Here, the absence of a regional government was felt most clearly in Wales, as the WO, finally, had no alternative but to defer to whatever Westminster and Whitehall demanded – thus earning a reputation as 'colonial government' among the more dissatisfied public and private actors in Wales. In general, the activities of the quangos, less accountable and approachable than the government itself, did very little indeed to alleviate this situation.

Saxony: 'Vater Staat'?

Given the forceful and self-confident policy style displayed by the Saxon government with regard to most aspects of life in Saxon society, one would reasonably expect the same phenomenon to occur with regard to the development of public–private relationships in Saxony. In most public affairs, control was the one aspect of governance the Saxon government was least reluctant to deploy. However, public–private relations are a clear exception to that rule. One can from the outset observe two reasons for this. First, the key element in developing new public-private relationships was the privatisation of state-owned East German companies, but that was a federal task, conducted by the THA. Beyond this task, the Saxon scene was virtually deprived of any meaningful private actors, with new indigenous businesses and private interest organisations emerging only very slowly. So, secondly, the government had to be grateful for any activities at all by the private and voluntary sectors developing in Saxony. After all, a vibrant economy with high levels of employment was among the *Staatsziele*. Therefore, the exercise of too much control was seen as counterproductive at the time – hence the reverse policy of not only giving private economic interests a free reign, but actively suppressing those private interests judged to be not in a position to contribute meaningfully to Saxon economic and social progress.

A suitable political selling point for this approach – and used argumentatively with a vengeance – was found in the state interference that was predominant in the old GDR system. There, control was the main – indeed, virtually the only – means of running economic affairs: to the extent of negating the very existence of private interests beyond the supposed unity of interests between the state and the entire population.

In the early post-unification days, though, all east German *Land* governments were busy sorting out their own legal and administrative system, while public–private relations were dealt with at the federal level by the THA and, to a much lesser extent, on the local level. During late 1990 and early 1991, the THA's reigned supreme in this field, and *Land* governments basically did what the THA wanted, period. However, over time this shifted considerably as the THA's work neared completion.

The work of the THA encompasses three distinct periods. The first, lasting from the THA's formation until early 1992, can be characterised as a straightforward fulfilment of its double brief of selling and restructuring. Industrial assets were sold to the highest bidder. THA managers tried also to conduct a reform of those companies that could not be sold straight-away, although due to lack of own personnel the THA often was left with little choice but to leave the old management in place, and to limit its own role to one of audit and more or less stringent supervision. Nevertheless, as it turned out, these were the golden days of progress, with investors queuing in THA offices, the German Chancellor, Kohl, daydreaming of 'blossoming landscapes' in the east, and a west German business community only too happy to be offered the opportunity to buy up its potential East German competitors at very favourable prices. This was also the only time in which there was significant interest from foreign private investors in East Germany, mainly from France, Italy, Belgium, the USA, and Russia. The French and American interests were not sector-specific. The Italian interest focused on metallurgy and the chemical industry, while Belgian companies bought up significant parts of the construction industry. The Russian interest was due to their attempt to safeguard existing trade links established under the COMECON, mainly in the oil, gas and chemical industries. However, far from establishing a 'tricontinental multinational presence' – as Jessop et al. (1987) had diagnosed for Britain – in the east German economy, the interest of foreign investors was limited to a few bids to the THA for larger east German assets which had previously established an international reputation. There were also some cases of establishing new greenfield developments by foreign investors; the best-known example in that category being the American high-tech components factory AMD on the outskirts of Dresden – Saxony's answer to Silicon Valley – a project originally planned under the old GDR regime (*Halbleiterwerk Dresden*). But from spring 1993 on, fresh initiatives of non-German investment into east Germany has virtually come to a halt, some smaller individual co-operation and participation by East German companies – mostly now part of larger German conglomerates – in multinational deals notwithstanding.

All this, however, was largely over the heads of the *Land* governments. The key economic development decisions remained a federal matter. The Saxon government, in the early days, was keen to secure influence over the economic redevelopment process of their *Land* by buying shares in some larger companies, in particular transport and infrastructure-related assets, and the utilities. The manufacturing industry's pleas for *Land* government involvement, however, were turned down flatly: for the government to buy assets in the manufacturing industry would be contradictory to the main aim of privatisation. So the government, in particular the Ministry of Economic Affairs and Employment, confined itself to helping with the promotion of Saxony as a place with a future,[10] providing contacts, negotiating deals, and in general creating a political atmosphere of optimism and progress, however artificial.

The second phase of the THA's work, lasting from early 1992 to the summer of 1994, can be described as enforced consolidation, culminating in a *Torschlußpanik* (deadline frenzy) that saw mind-blowing deals combined with disregard for social consequences. On the sales side, the THA was left with those assets that needed significant investment after the purchase – hence a number of considerable assets were sold at rock-bottom prices, often as little as 1 DM, on condition that a specific sum of investment into the asset had to be made by the purchaser after the acquisition, and that a specific number of jobs had to be safeguarded. It did not take the business community too long, however, to find out that there was no effective policy in operation to enforce the conditions imposed in the sales contract. Claiming adverse market conditions, which to some extent really did exist, the new owners found it easy to avoid sanctions.

On the reform side, the impact of this policy was obvious: the THA's diminishing profits from sales meant little spare cash to spend on renewal efforts, and although the THA was by law entitled to take out loans, private lenders were reluctant to extend credit to projects that might collapse and be sold for scrap in the near future anyway. Unable to modernise, the value of those assets declined further, with interested parties sitting tight until they could snap up the asset virtually for free and without restrictions regarding the future use of the site. This was the third phase, best described as 'offloading', ending in the winding-up of the THA itself by late 1996. Regional offices in each of the *Länder* are now in charge of sorting out loose ends, but no new business is conducted there any more. Most interesting in this context is that the THA usually opposed buyouts by the management or employees' consortia during the first and second phases. This has to be regarded as a political rather than an economic decision, apparently designed to prevent any form of *Volkseigentum* from re-establishing itself.

Faced with this situation, it appeared that the Saxon government was not particularly gravely concerned. However, this is misleading insofar as it was rather a very careful policy of non-interference that was being pursued. This seems to be a logical and rational policy approach if a free-market economy is to be created, and one has to acknowledge the Saxon government's persistence in trying to achieve this end. This, most of all, is the main result of Saxony's quest for new public–private relationships: neo-liberalism had a field day. To this extent, Prime Minister Biedenkopf's economic development policy became Saxony's answer to Thatcherism. The key elements, as defined by Jessop et al. (1988) were all there: a commitment to deregulation and to applying commercial criteria to state activities; some sponsoring of inward investment, i.e. mostly coming up with matched funding for the EU's ERDF and ESF grants; and conducting a long-term promotion strategy for the region. Matters relating to financial deregulation were outside the remit of a *Land* government, but this is not to say that it could not make a useful contribution to promoting the Euro. However, the government curbed its efforts in the latter direction once it realised what joining the Euro would mean for most Saxons (who were apparently so glad to finally have the Deutschmark): that the absolute figures in their savings accounts would be halved again so soon after the creation of German economic and monetary union in July 1990.[11]

However, the business community was less grateful than could have been expected because, having participated in West German corporatism for decades, it was accustomed to being able to turn to the government for help – usually tax breaks or even straightforward subsidies – in time of need. Biedenkopf's government, on the other hand, was helping businesses in other ways, for example by keeping critics and social interest groups at bay, but in general was leaving them to their own devices, which was to a large extent a new experience for them. The one time the Saxon government did open its coffers – in the ill-fated Volkswagen deal – it got it horribly wrong. However, in general the Saxon government stuck to its policy of non-interference and 'socio-economic climate management', with significant consequences for a regional mobilisation project, or rather the absence thereof.

CO-OPERATION AND MOBILISATION

Wales: Regional Mobilisation 'from below'?

It is quite indicative for public–private relations in Wales since the late 1980s that the first, and probably most obvious, of the new relations is clearly not a product of regional mobilisation, but a spin-off of control. The idea of 'cutting costs at all costs' was quite forcefully driven home to the local administrations by the Thatcher and Major governments. Here, the version of 'less state' was CCT. This principle was nothing new to British politics, and had already been the rule rather than the exception for Whitehall departments wishing to purchase goods and services. Typical examples include the widespread use of civil contractors for the production of military equipment, and the use of private construction contractors for roads, motorways, public buildings and similar establishments. The full implementation of this principle in the UK itself had only marginal effects despite producing some strange oddities. The contracting-out of cleaning and canteen services within the Whitehall buildings probably makes perfect sense. The legal requirement for the military to privatise their food and provisions procurement – and let their mess hall compete with the concert hall or nightclub next door – does not.

On the other hand, CCT virtually revolutionised the way of doing business by the local authorities. Some of the traditional services run by local councils had already been in some form of 'competition' – or rather coexistence – with providers from the private or voluntary sectors, for example in housing, child care and facilities for the elderly. However, the mandatory legal requirement either to hire an outside contractor, or to give the contract or franchise to the council's own services – where retained – only if they were the cheapest bidder, led to a virtual collapse of public services in the original meaning of the term. This applied to most services, including what little companies a city or county might have owned.[12] With regard to housing, Welsh Labour-controlled councils usually put up a fierce resistance, but even there the traditional council worker[13] was a rapidly disappearing breed. In practice, 'value for money' had to be translated into 'minimum standards at the cheapest price'.

This immediately led to two closely related problems. Private tenders, contrary to councils, had to make a profit from their operations. The councils, being told by the government that this scheme was designed to save them money, were not prepared to pay more for the hire of these tenders than they had spent previously on their own services. Hence the profit margin had to come from 'efficiency savings' or rationalisation, which usually amounted to little more than cutting corners on service provision. With councils finding it difficult to attract bidders prepared to meet the full specifications set out in the advertisement, the corner-cutting usually started right at the beginning: in the negotiations between councils and potential contractors. Moreover, afraid of breaking the law by not choosing the cheapest bidder, councils were often prepared to make more concessions than would have been necessary according to the letter of the law. By and large, ill-informed (and often ill-advised) part-time councillors usually proved to be no match for hard-nosed negotiators from the business community.

Welsh Labour councils in particular found it difficult to behave like proper businessmen, and became easy prey for private contractors. The easy way out for these councils was to bite the bullet and stick to less-than-favourable contracts, recouping the money by increasing Council Tax bills much more sharply than Conservative councils in other parts of the UK dared. The reason why they got away with this is fairly simple: Labour supporters, usually more inclined to distrust anything labelled 'private', were – and mostly still are – happy to pay more than they needed to in order to protect the provision of public services. Needless to say that Labour councillors and directors of financial services did their utmost to place the blame on the Conservative government in London rather than their own lack of ability to deal with these matters (for example Bettinson, 1996). Under the new slogan 'Best Value', the Blair government has launched a new initiative in this field. The main change here is that a private sector provider is not automatically chosen over a public provider prepared to match the quality standards. The government is now urging local governments to mind the quality of goods and services even if that means spending a little more, adding a warning that councils failing to do so might get some decision-making powers taken away from them.

Beyond the day-to-day politics, there is a question mark against just how much democratic scrutiny there is at the local level because no independent means of supervision were introduced along with this drive for privatisation. While the government executed its offloading operation, there were no UK or even regional regulators. Therefore by default the responsibility for imposing proper checks on the activities of private contract-holders remains with the local councils. Being parties to the contracts rather than independent adjudicators, they find it extremely difficult to exercise this scrutiny in a meaningful way. If a contractor is seen to be stepping out of line, the only straightforward remedy for councils is the through the courts, with the burden of proof firmly on the council, and accompanied by incurring mounting legal bills. To cancel a contract or withdraw a franchise prematurely without being able legally to prove a breach of contract usually incurs even larger financial losses.

In pre-CCT days, when councils still had the power to make their own political decisions on the levels of service to be provided and the funding to put into these services, and the public was able to judge these decisions politically at the next elections, the public interest was protected – perhaps imperfectly, but still fairly adequately. Now, with the councils having to slip into the role of economic decision-makers, and no way of voting contractors out of office at the next elections, there is no system worthy of the name in place to protect the public interest.

As mentioned above, there is no functional equivalent to regulators at the regional or local level in the UK. While some UK regulators, such as the Health and Safety Executive, have established outposts in the regions, they remain firmly within the central structure. Problems that by law have to be regulated locally – for example a number of environmental and trading standards problems – are still being dealt with by council departments and have not been branched out. However, outside expertise, such as laboratory services, are bought in rather than run directly, as required by CCT.

One area where there has been a huge restructuring in local authorities' activities is economic development. This term must be interpreted in a broad sense, including also social and cultural issues and, where applicable, the protection of traditional community lifestyles. Therefore, the term 'community development' has been used more frequently in the recent past by both practitioners and academics. Virtually all local government bodies have set up administrative units dealing with matters of local development, attracting inward investment, looking for partners, and so on. Here we approach the sphere where regional mobilisation usually finds its own 'natural' territory, although organisational forms vary widely, as do the levels and ranges of activity. However, depending on the degree of control regional or local governments wish to exercise over the process, the most common organisational forms of organising co-operation are a council department or an agency.

According to their tasks one can distinguish three basic kinds of agency: (i) single-task management agencies; (ii) fund-raising and lobbying agencies; and (iii) general service providers, i.e. those that help other actors to succeed in their tasks. The question of control is here solved by establishing a forum, association or similar body consisting of representatives of the institutions which set up the agency, although the agency itself is run like a private company. The business community was in general pleased to respond to government requests for a stronger engagement in the public sphere. Closer public–private relations not only provided public actors with access to funds and advanced technologies available in the private sphere, but also provided the business community with opportunities for long-term, stable contractual relationships to avoid the second part of Thatcher's 'boom-and-bust' economics.

However, the new influence of private actors in matters of regional development did not permeate significantly into actual policy formation. Neither did any one private actor manage to gain overall influence across Wales. On the other hand, public and semi-public organisations which legally were endowed with decision-making powers for all Wales or, even if formally powerless in this sense, responded fast to the need for adjustment to the new situation, had no difficulties in building a reputation as being 'important' – i.e. practically capable of engaging in a meaningful process of regional mobilisation. The REGE panel was asked whom they regarded as important in that sense: the resulting 'league table' (see Table 4.2) seems quite remarkable.

TABLE 4.2
REGE PANEL* PERCEPTIONS OF RELATIVE OVERALL AND NETWORKING
IMPORTANCE OF ACTORS IN REGIONAL DEVELOPMENT IN WALES, 1996

Ranking	Organisation	Level of operation	Named as important by ... (%)	Contacts established by ... (%)
1.	WO Industry Department	UK	76.2	48.4
2.	Welsh MEPs	European	75.4	45.9
3.	County councils	Sub-regional	74.3	61.5
4.	Secretary of State for Wales	UK	73.8	32.8
5.	WDA board	Regional	73.8	45.9
6.	European Commission, DG XVI	European	70.5	23.8
7.	WEC	Regional	69.7	36.1
8.	Local TEC	Sub-regional	59.0	50.7
9.	District/City councils	Local	58.2	44.3
10.	House of Commons/Welsh MPs	UK	54.9	41.0
11.	WDA area divisions	Sub-regional	54.9	36.9
12.	WDA International Division	Regional	51.6	24.6
13.	DBRW	Regional	50.8	27.0
14.	UK Department of Trade and Industry	UK	50.7	27.0
	All others: under 50%			
18.	CBI Wales (highest-ranking private actor)	Regional	44.3	25.4
46.	South Wales Exporters Association (lowest-ranking private actor)	Sub-regional	18.9	9.0
53. (last)	House of Lords	UK	5.7	7.4

* 123 = 100%

Source: REGE Wales, 1996.

What is most striking with regard to the results in Table 4.2 is that not even the highest-ranking private actor, the CBI Wales, quite made it into the top flight of organisations as judged by all actors, being ranked eighteenth. It is also quite remarkable that even in the days before devolution the UK Department of Trade and Industry was ranked well below other government bodies which had a specific Welsh brief: the WO, the Secretary of State for Wales, and also the county and district councils. Since 1999, the vast majority of functions associated with economic development have been transferred to the WA and its associated offices. The WO has become the NAW's bureaucracy, and the NAW's First Secretary and Economic Development Secretary, along with its Economic Development Committee, have taken over the Secretary of State's economic development management roles – and enjoy a far greater political and financial[14] freedom of manœuvre than any Secretary of State for Wales ever had. Therefore it is reasonable to assume that nowadays these new actors would at least formally be able to claim a similar status to that accorded to their institutional predecessors in 1995. What is interesting, however, is that this status for the new actors would not be a product of devolution – with its supposed synergetic effects on Wales – but an organisational rearrangement of functional practice already previously established.

Although not all organisations who regard another organisation as important made the effort to get in contact with the latter, it is fairly safe to assume that the organisations in Table 4.2 are the ones who are in the best position to facilitate widespread liaising activities, and to become nuclei of deepened co-operation networks and long-term alliances, especially with regard to the crucial contacts between public and private actors. Nevertheless, at least private actors naturally exercise a high degree of selectivity with regard to choosing their potential partners, as 'useful' contacts for them are 'profitable' contacts – though not only in purely financial terms. So despite acknowledging other organisations as being 'important', contacts are likely to be established only with partners having a specific bearing on a private actor's field of activity. Since private actors are involved in development projects only in some specific, often only occasional ways, their individual network of contacts tends to remain smaller and more flexible, according to shifting interest constellations, as opposed to the networks of larger public and semi-public actors who carry an all-encompassing territorial and/or functional brief.

However, a more detailed analysis of the perceived influence of various actor categories in five crucial stages of running development projects reveals that private actors still have considerably less influence than virtually all public and semi-public actors, as shown in Table 4.3. Therefore, one can observe a direct interrelationship between a convergence of public and private interests on the one hand, and the size and stability of regional mobilisation networks involving private actors on the other hand.

TABLE 4.3
REGE PANEL* PERCEPTIONS OF RELATIVE INFLUENCE OF ACTORS ON VARIOUS
STAGES OF DEVELOPMENT PROJECTS IN WALES, 1996

Actor category	Degree of influence	Selection of eligible areas (%)	Planning (%)	Implemen- tation (%)	Monitoring (%)	Evaluation (%)
Local	High	21.2	31.7	58.9	23.3	17.5
authorities	Medium	38.8	40.4	31.0	52.3	46.5
	Low	40.0	22.5	9.2	24.4	36.0
WO and	High	67.9	63.1	45.8	54.9	53.7
WDA	Medium	23.8	32.1	36.1	31.7	35.3
	Low	8.3	4.8	18.1	13.4	11.0
UK	High	59.8	23.8	17.1	19.0	20.2
government	Medium	28.7	44.0	39.0	41.7	44.0
	Low	11.5	32.2	43.9	39.3	35.7
European	High	70.9	43.4	15.7	25.6	38.5
Commission	Medium	22.1	39.8	36.1	57.3	45.8
	Low	7.0	16.8	48.2	17.1	15.7
Private actors	High	2.4	1.3	7.5	1.3	1.3
in Wales	Medium	10.8	20.3	32.5	14.1	13.0
	Low	86.8	78.4	60.0	84.6	85.7

* 123 = 100%

Source: REGE Wales, 1996.

Despite considerable profit opportunities, the business community is very unlikely to engage in regional mobilisation efforts if it perceives that it is kept out of the loop of meaningful decision-making. Consultative bodies help little in that respect, as their elaborations lack the force of authority. Hence this concept never really took off in Wales. The REGE survey counted 34 consultative bodies, but only the Welsh Economic Council and the Welsh European Forum received predominantly positive verdicts from the business community. Most private actors preferred participation in advisory bodies run by individual actors, such as the WDA, the Association of Welsh County Councils, or even the CBI itself, but by far the most usual – and very cost-effective – way for private actors to have their say is still the use of traditional formal means. These include giving evidence in public hearings, informal private discussions, traditional lobbying, and at least three 'old boy networks' which can be observed in Wales today: one based on traditional industry and mining, and firmly associated with 'old Labour' in south Wales; another based on

'Welshness' and loosely associated with Plaid Cymru in north Wales and Anglesey; and a third based on private education as in the rest of the UK – though in Wales this is not necessarily the most influential.

In the end, the forms of new public–private relationships largely depend on the purpose of mobilisation. While widespread consultations as such are valuable, the ultimate criterion of success for co-operation is actually to get things done. Critics argue that the most important – and indeed only – purpose of co-operation is to obtain cash from Europe. It is true that many EU grants depend on the existence of regional networks capable of implementing the envisaged projects, and delivering the desired results. It is also true that mobilisation will only make sense if in the end it becomes relatively self-sufficient in financial terms and generates benefits (though not necessarily monetary ones) for those involved. But access to grants cannot and should not be the only rationale for establishing public–private relationships. A learning process is required on both the public and the private side if co-operation is to be established even in circumstances when there is no obvious convergence of interest between the two. Public actors need to understand that if they want private actors to get involved in public works – for example in the recently well-propagated private financing initiatives (PFIs) – and put up private money for public projects, businesses actually need to have a say in planning and decision-making procedures, to set realistic targets and ensure the feasibility of projects. The same goes for feasible bids for EU grants, an example being the large infrastructure projects where most of the Welsh ERDF money went during the early 1990s. The business community profited indirectly from these, too, with construction contracts straightaway, and better-served industrial estates later on. It is also noteworthy that an elaborate system of non-monetary support for businesses has been put in place in Wales. However, apart from large-scale prestigious actions such as attracting the Asian high-tech company LG to Gwent – since curbed considerably due to LG's own financial difficulties – and very small-scale STRIDE initiatives in north Wales, ERDF and ESF money going into human resource development took second stage during that period. Only very recently, after Labour took office, early signs for a shift of emphasis from infrastructure to human resource development can be observed.

On the other hand, the business community needs to understand more clearly that public (including EU) funds are not a cow to be milked to death for private gain – otherwise public actors will rightfully remain unwilling to let private actors in on decision-making processes. Business leaders, just as politicians, must come to realise that obtaining grants ought not to be an end in itself. High eligibility is not something to celebrate and relish, but – more often than not – an indication of previous failure to succeed.

The new Labour government has pledged to make use of Welsh private actors' willingness to become more closely involved in all aspects of the regional development process. Motivated – among other things – by the wish to provide room for more inclusive consultation, co-operation and decision-making among all actor categories, the changes that are now being implemented go beyond a change in 'policy styles' as described by Knodt (1998) for the Baden-Württemberg example.

The difference here is that in Wales constitutional changes were called for to bring about the desired shift in the ways and means of policy-making. The key element of the changes is the NAW. Even though powers of primary legislation and taxation are not devolved to the Assembly at the moment, three important considerations need to be taken into account: (i) the importance of secondary legislation and its impact on everyday life; (ii) the enhanced status in terms of legitimacy of an elected body for the sole purpose of looking after Welsh interests; and (iii) the obvious potential of the NAW to serve as a forum for political exchange (in Négrier's sense; see Négrier 1997, 1998), where all the distinct interest groups can mediate their different interests and search for a common 'Welsh voice' to be presented to the outside world. This is the theory, anyway, and whether this vision will stand the test of time will depend on how fast a new culture of enhanced public–private co-operation can be implemented, and how efficient the new arrangements, dependent as they are on the goodwill of present actors, are going to work. The key period in that respect will be 2000–07, when, probably for the last time, significant amounts of EU money (around £185 million per year on average) are available to west Wales and the Valleys.

Saxony: Regional Mobilisation 'from above'?

The Saxon government's general policy of non-interference with the private sector did not prevent the establishment of new public–private relations in areas where to do so was unavoidable or was deemed favourable. The question is, however, whether or not such co-operation amounted to the initiation of regional mobilisation activities.

As outlined above, at least during the first legislative period (1990–94) the key elements of industrial renewal were a federal rather than a *Land* responsibility in the East German *Länder*. The THA's relationship with the *Land* governments varied. In Saxony, two distinctive forms of co-operation between the THA and the government emerged, in particular involving the Ministry of Economic Affairs and Employment. The first was based on the 1992 ATLAS agreement between the THA and the *Länder*, encouraging the government to become a shareholder in some assets which could not be privatised immediately. In Saxony, the government took up that opportunity with some limited degree of enthusiasm, in particular in transport[15] and infrastructure-related companies, but always with a view to push through full privatisation as soon as the companies concerned started to show a profit.[16] However, as mentioned above, the manufacturing industry was largely precluded from such arrangements.

The second form of direct co-operation between the Saxon government and semi-public and private partners was the *Aufbauwerk in Sachsen*, founded in 1992, which was designed to serve as an umbrella partnership for a number of labour market policies. The centrepiece of the *Aufbauwerk* was the establishment of 11 sub-regional initiatives, which ran centres, similar to the British TECs. These initiatives served as a base for vocational training activities, and as managing agencies for both federal employment promotion schemes (*Arbeitsbeschaffungsmaßnahmen* – ABM) and similar regional and local efforts.[17] The *Aufbauwerk* was dismantled in 1996, when a number of federal ABM-funding arrangements were not renewed, and the Saxon government decided against the idea of providing further funds of their own to make up the shortfall. By then, however, the CDU had won the 1994 elections both nationally and in the region. However, after 1996, nine of the eleven centres continued their work on a much smaller scale under the management of the local authorities in their territories (Tooze and Nativel, 1998: 7).

The most important role the Saxon government defined for itself in creating new public–private relationships was to offer their good offices for all kinds of contact-making, mediating and negotiating services for the establishment partnerships among private partners both within Saxony, and across the Saxon borders. After all, the development of cross-border interregional co-operation is a *Staatsziel*, and one which the Biedenkopf government took very seriously indeed. This applies in particular to interregional relations with the Czech Republic and Poland, culminating in the establishment of three EUREGIOs along their borders.

One key focus in cross-border co-operation was the improvement of transport links. The governments concerned, the local public actors and the private sector – the latter at least on the implementation, i.e. construction side – ran these development initiatives as a truly joint task of public–private partnership. The large-scale projects of improving road and rail links would have been impossible to fund from private initiatives alone, while public actors needed technical expertise and implementation capabilities. The best-known example in this field was the creation of a new rail link between Dresden and Prague designed to transport lorries across the mountain ranges dividing Saxony and the Czech Republic, the *Erzgebirge* and the *Elbsandsteingebirge*, with their notoriously small and overcrowded pass roads.

The route has an additional importance as a transit link between central Germany and the countries of east-central Europe.

In general, however, Saxony's policy of improving cross-border relations, across an outer border of the EU, seem to have benefited the economies of the partner countries more than they have benefited the Saxon manufacturing industry. The emerging trade patterns (see Table 4.4) reveal that the Saxon export deficit with non-EU European partners, though becoming smaller while showing a significantly increased volume, has only recently become more than counterbalanced by an export surplus in trade with EU partners. The Russian figures are somewhat misleading: the large Saxon imports consist almost entirely of oil and gas. However, the Saxon export deficits in trade with its immediate neighbours[18] must be regarded as indicative of Saxony's commercial buyer's and individual consumer's desire to make the most of the comparatively low prices for goods and services across the border. Saxony's own industry, however, has so far failed to a large extent to establish new or regain old markets that were lost with the breakdown of the COMECON. Nevertheless, in buying from non-EU countries and selling to EU countries, the Saxon economy has indeed started to develop a kind of bridge function – though traffic across that bridge is not quite moving in the expected direction. Saxony's economy, in effect, behaves like an applicant country's economy – and to some extent rightly so. In terms of business patterns, legacies of the COMECON past are reinforced by new needs and desires for development – including getting a strong foothold in the common market.

TABLE 4.4
VOLUME OF SAXON FOREIGN TRADE WITH SELECTED COUNTRIES,
1995 AND 1999 (IN M DM)

Country	Exports 1995	Exports 1999	Imports 1995	Imports 1999
To/From Czech Republic	404.1	755.9	831.9	1375.8
To/From Poland	325.6	669.2	487.7	629.6
To/From Slovakia	85.1	184.1	301.7	201.0
To/From Russia	695.2	419.4	1,167.5	986.4
To/From the USA	261.0	1346.9	417.4	955.0
To/From EU countries	5,789.0	9105.4	3,042.6	3718.3
To/From European Non-EU countries	1,341.9	3552.1	4503.3	4690.2
Total (all countries)	8,901.9	16,033.0	10,752.1	12,556.3

Source: SLA, 1997: 385 (for 1995 figures); SLA 2000: 455 (for 1999 figures).

A relatively successful act of managing public–private co-operation was achieved by the Saxon government with regard to channelling ERDF and ESF funds into R&D being undertaken by private actors. The political responsibility lay with the Technology and Energy Division of the SMWA. For the purpose of handling applications and supervising projects a special semi-public actor, the *Projektträger Technologieförderung*, was set up in Dresden. Such a step was unusual, for in other fields, such as infrastructure-related measures, attracting inward investment, and general SME support (for example the *Mittelstandsförderungsprogramm*), the government normally left it to sub-regional and local public actors to set up or hire such agencies, for example the *Mittelständische Beteiligungs-gesellschaft Sachsen mbH* and the *Wirtschaftsförderung Sachsen GmbH*), if those sub-regional or local bodies chose to do so.[19]

At the sub-regional and local levels, hiring emerged as the standard solution, saving the city or *Regierungspräsidium* considerable planning effort. In most cases, relationships between the public actors and their private agency partners were amicable indeed. In Chemnitz, for instance, the *Regierungspräsidium* and the leading sub-regional development agency even share the same building. However, in other cities, e.g. Leipzig, this led to a significant amount of competition among a whole host of both larger (Saxony-wide) and smaller (local) private agencies for such contracts. Research and development policy matters, however, were not devolved to the sub-regional level. The brief of the *Projektträger Technologieförderung* encompassed all Saxony. According to the Operational Programme for Saxony 1994–1999 (SMWA, 1994a: 41–54), interested parties were eligible to submit applications for projects aimed at the development of new products and production procedures (either individual companies alone or in co-operation with other private and semi-public partners); for research projects run by private research institutes or those in the process of being privatised; for the establishment and running of technology centres (regardless of ownership); and for the hiring of qualified personnel by SMEs (maximum eligibility: two years' salary).

What has to be noted, however, is the fact that the Saxon way of managing regional development projects was, and still is, to establish or facilitate direct public–private co-operation as far as possible without resorting to using semi-public actors. The political rationale behind this principle is that the government retains a direct influence in the implementation of policies, while private actors are able to obtain and cultivate direct access to political decision-makers.[20] Here we are back at the beginning, though, with the government deciding who – in their opinion – is worthy of such access. Under these circumstances, the regional development effort in Saxony has turned into a management game for 'insiders' and specialists – i.e. away from the inclusiveness and joint pursuit of interests that is characteristic for a meaningful regional mobilisation effort. This is not to say that the Saxon solution has failed. Indeed, the structures developed in Saxony allowed a rapid and forceful decision-making process to develop, and on the whole larger private actors, capable of delivering resources of their own, have benefited from this system. For smaller private actors, and individuals, however, the answer was to fight for whatever benefits trickled down to them – be it particular jobs or sub-contracts, participation in ESF-funded human resource development initiatives, or free management advice under the *Mittelstandsförderungsprogramm*.

Popular involvement in the Saxon development project was firmly confined to the socio-cultural field. There, however, initiatives could be found in abundance, in addition to the government's aforementioned efforts to promote *Heimat* traditions and feelings. A typical example was a private initiative, called *Sachsen für Sachsen* (Saxons for Saxony). In 1999, this group sent a letter to each and every Saxon household promoting a competition asking people to complete the line 'I like Saxony because...'. To get potential respondents into the right mood, the letter stated:

> Our land is beautiful, we have splendid schools and higher education establishments, our infrastructure is new, and the most modern industries are coming to us. We did incur less debts than others, and we enjoy a high level of stability. However, the best argument for us [Saxons] is our proverbial diligence. This is the main reason why progress is being made here step by step year in year out.[21] (Winkler, 1999: 1)

The group describes itself as an initiative of citizens and private enterprises. Among the supporters are such ordinary citizens as athletics champions, football club chairmen, MdBs, MEPs, and regional party leaders from all parties except the PDS. The businesses represented are as diverse as Volkswagen AG and bruno banani Underwear GmbH. Regional mobilisation? If at all, and not just hype, this initiative too must be regarded as a top-down approach, designed less to 'promote Saxony in Germany and abroad', as the letter claimed; but more to instil the Saxon population with the belief that they are well off, rather than to motivate them to work more proactively in their own interest: leave that to *Landesvater* Biedenkopf and his government. In effect, this was regional *demobilisation*, but remarkably it was working quite well among large sections of the population – see the 1999 regional election results. Maybe this is no surprise among a population accustomed to – and apparently longing for – all-round social security, stability, and indeed tranquillity, after the upheavals of 1988–94. However, with the full introduction of the Euro in 2002, and the very likely end of Objective 1 funding after the forthcoming EU enlargements. The wisdom of such an approach must at least be questioned, despite its apparent success.

In short, the Saxon efforts at creating viable new forms of public–private interaction can be described as state-controlled task management. The utility of programmes and projects is to a large extent determined by the government, ostensibly judging by strict economic criteria but also incorporating social considerations if deemed politically expedient. The latter element mirrored the preparedness of Chancellor Kohl's federal government to interfere in socio-economic processes by short-term means to combat public unrest about perceived shortcomings. However, the Saxon government in general limited its involvement in public–private co-operation to cases where this was regarded as unavoidable, as in the case of handling the incoming EU funds. Beyond this, the government limited its role to one of indirect support for development tasks carried out by the private sector, and to political re-education of the population with a view to making them adapt more speedily and more willingly to the new socio-economic realities.

In sum, the issue of developing sustainable public–private relationships in order to promote the regional economy has been a major point of concern for both the Welsh and Saxon public actors in the 1990s. The most important feature of co-operation that is common to both regions was that these initiatives usually revolved around projects which were funded in part by ERDF, ESF and EAGGF programmes. Beyond this, however, the differences in the regional political environments have contributed to the development of quite different approaches towards the establishment of cross-sector actor coalitions in regional development policy.

Notable among these differences were the existence in Wales, and the virtual absence in Saxony, of networks of regional and local private and semi-public actors capable of instigating regional mobilisation efforts on their own. In Wales, such actor coalitions started to operate even before the changes to the political system that took place between 1995 and 1999. These initiatives ran mostly with the co-operation of the WO, but also, occasionally, in spite of its intentions and policies. In these processes, regional interests were expressed and pursued not only by regional and UK public actors, but also by local groupings and initiatives acting as surrogate in the absence of a strong regional leadership. Indeed, out of this situation the political demand for a strong(er) regional leadership emerged, and in the devolution process structures of authoritative decision-making have been created which are potentially capable of becoming a focus for an integrated approach to regional interest formation and interest representation – a system comprising public and private actors, and thus containing the capability to embark on a sustained regional mobilisation effort. This potential, however, has yet to be fulfilled, as so far not even the protagonists of devolution are quite sure how to proceed from here on.

In Saxony, on the other hand, the slow emergence of a viable scene – let alone networks – of private actors has played into the hands of a government eager to take on a dominating role in regional development management. While in Wales existing interest coalitions forced through a change in the structure of public actors, in Saxony public actors have had a considerable say in the creation of other types of actor. While this was to some extent a federal policy, as in the case of the THA, the Saxon government, too influenced the development of private actors by granting selective access to authoritative decision-making, and behaving equally selective in the use of semi-public actors. So, in both cases, though by reverse means, a system for public–private interaction emerged which utilises the principle of such interactions as and when common interests are at stake while falling short of politically proclaimed intentions of inclusiveness and transparency.

NOTES

1. Some environmentalist groups may disagree with this view, as far as some individual projects are concerned.
2. See, for instance, their criticism of the old Ministry of Public Works in the 1960s and 1970s, but this Ministry was already dissolved when Thatcher came to power.
3. Interestingly, in the 1998 budget Labour did exactly the same thing, so Council Tax payers found the same complaints by local councillors in the letters accompanying their 1998/99 Council Tax bills (see Bettinson, 1996, 1998).
4. At the time Chairman of CBI Scotland and later Deputy Leader of the Scottish Conservatives.
5. Rifkind was succeeded by Ian Lang as Secretary of State for Scotland when John Major became Prime Minister in November 1990, but later during the Major era Rifkind became Secretary of State for Defence and then Foreign Secretary until the Conservatives' 1997 election defeat. Rifkind also failed to win his personal seat in both the 1997 and 2001 general elections.
6. Personal communication to author by Professor Kevin Morgan, Department of City and Regional Planning, University of Wales, Cardiff.
7. The General Elections on 1 May and the Referendum for a Welsh Assembly on 18 September.
8. Except Housing Benefit and Council Tax Benefit, which are in the responsibility of local councils.
9. The point being that only those who are unemployed and are actively seeking work can claim – thus cutting official unemployment by about one-third virtually overnight.
10. Interview, SMWA, 1996.
11. The Saxon SPD did not realise this and campaigned vigorously for the Euro – with corresponding results in their own popularity status.
12. Most of these assets were in the construction sector and in handling various kinds of household and industrial waste.

13. I am referring here to a craftsman (not bureaucrat) in public employment.
14. On the financial side, this freedom is on the distribution of expenditure side only, and not on income generation side.
15. Excluding local government-owned businesses which remained outside the THA's brief and mostly remained in local public ownership.
16. Interview, SMWA, 1996.
17. Interview, SMWA, 1996.
18. The first year since 1990 that Saxony had a positive balance of payments with Poland was 1999.
19. Interview, *Wirtschaftsförderung Sachsen GmbH*, 1997.
20. Interview, SMWA, 1996.
21. Translation by author. Original text: 'Unser Land ist schön, wir haben hervorragende Schulen und Hochschulen, unsere Infrastruktur ist neu, und die modernsten Industrien kommen zu uns. Wir haben weniger Schulden als andere gemacht und genießen hohe Stabilität. Das beste Argument ist aber unsere sprichwörtliche Tüchtigkeit. Ihr ist es zu verdanken, daß es hier seit Jahren Schritt für Schritt aufwärtsgeht.'

5

Conclusions: What Makes a Modern Region?

ACTORS, INTERESTS AND THE CHANGING NATURE OF THE STATE

The empirical analysis in the previous two chapters has identified a series of patterns of actor behaviour in the 1990s which has altered the political landscape of both Wales and Saxony – if not beyond recognition, at least sufficient to postulate that a change in the nature of the two states concerned, the UK and Germany, has begun. This chapter discusses to what extent the hypotheses concerning this process, outlined in Chapter 1, hold some explanatory power, contributing to our understanding of these changes.

The first point to be considered deals with the development of a new actor landscape. Within the EU there are a number of public, semi-public and, in particular, private actors who regard it as being to their advantage to instigate a series of changes in the EU system of governance which would allow them a better or more efficient pursuit of their interests. This includes a growing number of regional actors. Since the mid-1980s, the EU system of governance has seen significant changes. Formally, most of these changes are embodied in the Single European Act, and the Treaties of Maastricht, Amsterdam and Nice. Key changes, such as the 'four freedoms of movement', the enhancement of the common market, and the introduction of the Euro, were designed to allow a better utilisation of capital throughout the EU, enhancing its competitiveness in an increasingly globalised economic system. Even the increased output of regulatory measures by EU institutions can be regarded as part of this drive: ensuring common high standards for the trademark 'Made in the EU'. To some extent, one could also argue that the EU just sanctioned already established practice among the more significant members the European business community, in order to re-gain political control over ongoing processes of co-operation and corporate accumulation of economic powers.

Richardson (1995, 1996), Cram (1996, 1997) and others have shown to what extent the exertion of influence by strong – and mostly internationally organised – private actor groupings has contributed to a process of turning the EU into a Mecca for big business. However, what we are concerned with here is another aspect of changing EU governance – the role of regions in these processes. Regions, too, have caught the attention of decision-makers on the European level, and have developed a role in European policy-making not only as recipients of some handouts in the name of creating that elusive 'ever closer union' in terms of socio-economic cohesion. Nowadays, an increasing number of regional actors pride themselves to be European decision-makers, travelling back and forth to Brussels, taking their seats in the CoR, and telling their constituents at home how successfully they represent the region's interests in the highest echelons of European governance.

What we have to ask, however, is to what extent the representatives of regions have really become a force in European governance, capable of influencing the rules by which Europe is governed, and thus able to become a significant player in multi-level governance. At this point it is worthwhile to follow Hrbek and Weyand's (1994) distinction of 'vertical' and 'horizontal' integration, since multi-level governance, going beyond mere government, comprises both these aspects. On the vertical side, the creation of the CoR and the introduction of the principle of partnership have gone a long way to secure some – previously virtually absent – direct influence by public and some semi-public regional actors in EU decision-making procedures. Credit is undoubtedly due to some forerunners in the campaign for such influence, in particular Catalonia, Scotland, Baden-Württemberg, and some French and Italian regions. One cannot fail to notice, however, that the regions in that group were either already strong in socio-economic terms, and were wishing to make the most of the new opportunities of the common market, or whose economy was not particularly well developed but which had a strong incentive to get involved, having the most to gain from support facilities offered under the terms of the reformed EU regional policies.

With regard to Wales and Saxony, it does not come as a surprise that both regions are not among those forerunners. When the process started in the 1980s, Saxony did not even exist as a territorial and political entity. Wales, existing territorially, and already part of the EU, had not yet been fully recognised as a political entity, lacking the political structure to act for itself on the European scene. So not to have been proactive from the very beginning is not a charge that could justifiably be levied against the two regions. Indeed, most European regions only caught the drift after 1988, as the reforms in EU regional policy began to take effect, making dealing with European matters a more worthwhile pursuit for many regional actors. In

Wales, consortia of local public actors, in co-operation with regional and local semi-public actors, instigated the process of involvement as soon as they could (around 1990), but for domestic reasons – Whitehall closely guarding its foreign policy monopoly and running Wales almost exclusively through the WO – these efforts were limited in both scope and force. Saxony, on the other hand, received its vertical influence on a silver plate in 1990. Upon its (re)creation as a territorial and political entity, becoming a *Land* of the FRG, immediately bestowed upon Saxon actors the possibility and the right to represent its interests not only within the German federal system, but also towards the EU. This was later reinforced by the introduction of the new Article 23 GG, sections 2–6 spelling out in detail on what occasions the *Länder* can influence Germany's official stance in negotiations and on the question of signing and ratifying EU treaties and agreements. These occasions include all those policy matters in which the *Länder* would have a say under existing domestic legislation, whether at the federal level or at the *Land* level itself. Thus, Article 23 GG guarantees the German *Länder*'s influence in European policy-making as an integral part of Germany's general influence.

However, with regard to formal means of vertical interest representation, what has been achieved so far by the EU's regions seems to be as far as they can go for the time being. Most national governments are not interested in granting the regions greater formal influence in EU policy-making and neither have the EU institutions expressed a particular interest in expanding such influence. It would be proper to reflect whether such an expansion would be worthwhile, even from the point of view of the regions themselves. The rules governing the activities of the CoR give regions a full say on any aspect of EU policy-making, not only in regional policy. Trying to have that say has stretched the CoR's capabilities to breaking point during the first mandate period; hence their decision to cut back and focus on issues clearly of interest and relevance to regions and local territorial units in the member states. Increasingly, regional representatives have direct or indirect access to the Council of Ministers' as part (or as observers) of their member state's delegations. The regions' offices in Brussels are now a well-established feature of the political culture of the EU. Regional public – and if need be semi-public and private – actors now have the right to influence EU-funded socio-economic development programmes in their regions routinely written into the appropriate planning and operational documents. To be sure, for some of the more radical regionalists and minority nationalists this is not enough, but for the vast majority of regions, Wales and Saxony among them, the task at hand is to utilise the now existing means of vertical interest representation in ways appropriate to foster their own specific set of interests. Given the diversity of these interests throughout the EU, shifting alliances and short-term co-operation are likely to characterise this process in the foreseeable future.

This situation also puts a new emphasis on horizontal co-operation, and its two main elements: bi- and multilateral co-operation agreements and initiatives, and interregional associations. While the former have become the main form of actor involvement in European matters, the latter have, for a while, been a valuable tool for joint interest representation among those regions where such joint interests really exist. However, apart from organisations designed to address very specific joint interests, for example the CMPR, interregional organisations such as the AER seem outdated now, the role of general joint interest representation having passed to the CoR. In theory, the CoR could evolve into a more efficient tool for both vertical and horizontal networking, although there is precious little evidence of this actually happening so far. The interregional associations, on the other hand, retain a valuable role as a forum for meeting potential partners from regions whose countries are not, or not yet, members of the EU.

Horizontal interest representation is also where semi-public and private actors really come into their own. The larger private actors, in particular the larger businesses, have held interests in various regions for some time now, at least as far back as the 1960s. Prior to regional policy becoming an EU issue, these larger actors just applied market criteria to determine their interests in regions and they continue to do so now, regardless of politicians' wishful thinking. What is new, however, is that smaller private actors, who previously lacked the resources to go down that route on their own, are now gaining politically facilitated access to business opportunities which were not available to them. However, an often forgotten precondition of such co-operation is the existence of demonstrable mutual benefits to the actors involved. A Greek sandwich-maker, for instance, would probably lose money trying to supply Saxon or Welsh schools. Non-perishable goods and services, though, can now be exchanged with less effort and red tape than ever before. To organise this has become a market in itself, giving a whole new meaning to the term 'business services', and public as well as private actors have taken on this role with a remarkable degree of enthusiasm. True, if the regional actor structures are not sufficiently compatible or complementary, political agreements negotiated between public actors are unlikely to be filled with day-to-day life in terms of actual co-operation measures. But as Eißel et al. (1999) demonstrated, co-operation initiatives between regions not located close to each other or sharing specific common interests are now starting to take off.

How, then, do the regional actors go about the business of using their new rights and opportunities? Our initial assumption was that given sufficiently similar interests held by regional actors, similar strategies of mobilisation and political exchange are employed even under apparently quite different political, social and cultural circumstances. The empirical evidence for Wales and Saxony suggests that the similarity of socio-economic problems encountered in the two regions, plus the similarities in opportunities for combating these problems, have led to some similar output in terms of regional development policy, and – most remarkably – to similar changes in the political system, altering the rules of governance within the region. The key differences, on the other hand, mostly derive from special country-wide or regional features of the policy environment, which cannot easily be replaced or circumvented, and from personal or ideological preferences of the regional leadership élites.

By the late 1980s, the economies of both Wales and Saxony were undoubtedly in severe crisis, mainly due to a breakdown of both regions' traditional economic system. By the late 1990s, in both regions a change of the political system had occurred, designed to alleviate the pressing socio-economic needs of the society. In both cases, measures of EU regional policy, in particular the availability of ERDF and ESF grants, have influenced both the economic transformation processes, and the political behaviour of regional élites in terms of regional development policy-making. So, at first glance, both cases seem to be full of striking similarities. A more detailed look, however, reveals considerable differences. In Wales, the changes to the political system appear as the product of adjusting to needs and desires – and hence interests – of regional development. In Saxony, the changes to the political system stand at the beginning of the transformation process, creating regional interests as this process went along and gathered momentum. Most certainly the developments in Saxony could not have occurred independent of the general changes to the system in Germany following the breakdown of the East German regime and German unification. It is also true that to a large extent the economic crisis in Saxony was due to failures associated with economic and political mismanagement that took place in the pre-unification era of a socialist command economy. However, as the Welsh example shows, systems of capitalist market economies may also fail, if not in general at least within smaller territorial units, due to economic mismanagement and/or deliberate political decision-making (see, for example, Thatcher's agenda). Therefore, economic reform is inseparably linked to political readjustment, whether in a more orderly evolutionary process, or in the more radical version of changing the entire regime.

Bearing this general principle in mind, it is worthwhile noting that regional public actors feel a duty to promote the socio-economic interests of the region to the best of their ability. The starting point for this process is usually the recognition that some features of socio-economic life are no longer viable or may be about to become unsustainable. This creates an interest in addressing this situation by embarking on a programme of development. While the general aim of this development programme is fairly straightforward, precise details of what is to be achieved are usually less clear: we are dealing with market economies, after all. Precise planning targets would force public actors to take on a very stringent and interventionist steering role which would be likely to be incompatible with the general economic environment, and indeed, given the factional nature of any political leadership, detrimental to vested rights of democratic participation. Given these constraints, it is a risky business for any political leadership to make a particular promise.[1] Therefore, it is not only advisable but even necessary that individual strategies and measures, as well as the degree of involvement of suitable non-public actors in socio-economic development processes, are open to debate within the society concerned.

This leads us directly to the interests to be considered. We have already established that there is no such thing as 'the regional interest'. Interest constellations in a region are determined by the interests held by individual actors who bring them into the regional policy arena, there to be accommodated or not in direct struggle with alternative interests brought by other actors. The prevalence or dominance of specific interests in a region depends on the resourcefulness, influence and formal political power of the interest holders. Such prevalence is therefore transitory, constellations of actors and their influence being subject to change over time. This is another clear indicator for the link between socio-economic and political developments within a territory. However, this situation leads to an important consequence. In an ideal meritocratic world, only the very best ideas and plans would convince most people, making it their interest to pursue them, and hence gathering the resources and momentum to become predominant. This, then, for as long as this uniting force of a common interest holds, should become the public interest, to be acted upon, and represented, by public actors. Market economies, however are not ideal meritocratic worlds. As Schumpeter (1970: 251) puts it, 'there is ... no such thing as a uniquely determined common good that all people could agree on or be made to agree on by the force of rational argument'. While the quality or popular appeal of a particular idea or strategy is in itself a resource, its chances of success also depend on other resources of the actor representing it. Parties or politicians, however well developed their programmes are, cannot hope to be elected if they are unable to fund their election campaign. Publicly owned companies, however socially conscious their contracts with the workforce are phrased, are unlikely to succeed in competition with the private sector if their ledgers do not, in the long run, show at least some profit.

Notwithstanding general declarations of intent, such as the listing of the *Staatsziele* in the Saxon constitution, the shaping of regional interests is a permanent balancing act among the significant regional actors – public, semi-public and private. As the outcome of this balancing act depends entirely on the resources of the actors involved, a red-carpet road to regional development success can be – and has been – envisaged by a number of regional actors, and academics. This vision, similar to Keating's (1995) 'virtuous model' of regional development, and Negrier's (1997) notion of 'political exchange', would comprise a close co-operation between regional actors. Rationalising that the pooling or sharing of resources in pursuit of a common goal makes more sense than struggling on alone, actors would engage in large-scale, sustained interaction and co-operation – in short, regional mobilisation – reaping mutual benefits for all concerned. This would not only be done on the internal, regional scene, but also in the European context, liaising and co-operating with partners beyond the borders of one's own region or state. 'Policy learning' from the best, associating with as many partners as possible, enhancing opportunities of trade, political discourse and cultural exchange – all this would create a synergy of resources which would not only be beneficial for the self-development of the actors concerned, but also secure the standing and acceptance of one's territory in the community of nations, regions, economies and peoples that make up the present EU.

Indeed, a remarkable amount of empirical evidence has been amassed by researchers on regionalism over the last few years, indicating that such a benign process of regional development is under way in a number of European regions; the best-known examples include Baden-Württemberg, Lombardy, Emilia-Romagna, Rhône-Alpes, Catalonia, the Basque Country, Galicia, Scotland, and Wales. It is undeniable that all these regions have come a long way in their socio-economic development over the last ten to twenty years. This can be regarded as an indicator that regional mobilisation may work, given the right conditions, at least within certain territorial limits over a certain period of time. However, it has to be asked why not all of these regions are now on top of the European rankings in terms of their state of development. The most frequently used answer to this question is a reference to the often very low starting level of development in these regions; however, the model also seems to work in better-developed regions (see, for example, Baden Württemberg).

Why, then, have more regions not yet successfully embarked on such a process of regional mobilisation? Is it just a matter of 'entrenched policy styles', as Knodt (1998) suspects in the case of Lower Saxony? Is it adverse regional actor structures, the potential participants being unwilling or unable to co-operate because some other consideration outweighs their preparedness to participate in regional mobilisation – as one could claim in the case of Northern Ireland? Are there better, more efficient models for regional development – as the Saxon government was trying to prove from their very first day in office? All of these suggestions hold considerable explanatory power in particular cases. In the end, though, the whole conundrum boils down to the question of convergence of vested interests by the actors concerned. These interests are factional in nature, due to the role of private actors in the socio-economic life of the society to which they belong. Any attempt to deny or ignore this fact would be incompatible with a market-based economic and political system. Regional mobilisation cannot overcome this ultimate obstacle. Therefore, provided that the aim of regional mobilisation is not to overthrow the entire market-based economic system, successful efforts mobilisation depend on a sufficient convergence of interests among the participants. Actor coalitions are likely to be formed and remain relatively stable as long as this commonality of interests remains intact. Either achieving common goals, or a perception by a sufficient number of participants that common goals are no longer adequate or achievable, stops the process immediately. This accounts for the limitations, both in space and in time, of regional mobilisation successes.

Where a commonality of interests exists, however, regional mobilisation can be a useful tool to promote these interests. This applies not only to internal mobilisation efforts, but also to measures of external mobilisation. European funds, however, are a somewhat special case in this respect. Their very nature as a resource lets obtaining them become an interest in itself. To become eligible, and, once eligible, to get the largest share possible of the forthcoming support measures for one's region is an interest which all actors in a region share until the funds actually are approved. At this point, though, competition breaks out for access to the funds. No matter how precisely spending plans and schedules have previously been drawn up, no matter how well regulated, monitored and audited the application process is, factional interests are bound to state their 'special' case as forcefully as possible. Here we are back at the root problem of regional mobilisation: ostensibly purely a meritocratic process, ultimately it is the resource 'access to decision-making' which decides whether a particular project is approved or rejected. A side-effect of this is that projects backed by that resource need not be particularly viable in order to be approved. One indicator for this is the project's self-sufficiency in the long run, an area where Saxony encountered a number of severe problems between 1993 and 1997. Another side-effect of this situation is that actors may perceive the obtaining of funds as a goal in itself, regardless of the actual use. The theory is that in order to be eligible, the region or particular actors in that region have to be in some sort of special need. To be needy, however, is essentially a bad thing, a situation to be rectified by utilising the helping hand stretched out by the EU. Rhodri Morgan AM, first Economic Development Secretary of the NAW and now First Secretary, holding both posts in the crucial period when the key decisions on Welsh Objective 1 funds utilisation for the period 2000–06 were made, has repeatedly subscribed to that theory both in Assembly sessions and in media interviews. However, a significant number of Welsh actors, including Plaid Cymru, has yet to be fully convinced about this line of thinking. In the early and mid-1990s similar problems have occurred among a number of sub-regional and local actors – public and private – in Saxony, too.[2]

It is also worthwhile noting that the decision-makers in EU institutions have to be regarded as the creators of this common interest in access to EU resources which in turn led to similar policy outcomes in regions with seemingly considerable socio-economic and political set-ups. Regional strategic planners not only look at how a particular project might serve the needs and desires of the region, but also at how to fit it into general regulations and schemes designed and funded by the EU. While the application of the principle of partnership has given those regional planners at least the chance to have some input concerning the shape of the specific regulations applicable to them, union-wide rules set by the Commission and the Council of Ministers must still be adhered to. This influence at the European level on the thinking of planners and decision-makers in the regions opens a back door to the openly stated political aim of cohesion within the EU. This is the main reason why seemingly different political systems produce similar regional development policy outputs in the EU's regions. 'Policy learning', on the other hand, often hailed in its own right as a success of horizontal networking, is not a reason but a means of similar policy output: more often than not the learning curriculum basically consists of finding and adapting ways and means of using the common rules to one's best advantage.

Despite the transitory nature of predominance of ideas and interests, and hence the uncertainty of a long-term outcome to strategies based on these ideas and interests, the process of balancing them out at any given moment needs to be organised politically. It is a function of the system of governance in the territory concerned to devise ways and means of managing this contest of concepts. From this follows that if the current system of governance is unable to conduct this function, the system itself needs to be adapted. The question is, however, how far these changes have to go in order to achieve the desired result. A change in the nature of the state only occurs if the political entities replacing the old rules and structures are not only in place but also capable of taking over. Following Marks' (1996) definition of the state as 'rules of authoritative decision making', a change in the nature of the state would basically consist of significant changes to these rules, qualitatively altering the system of governance, not only government.

Political demands of regional actors for decision-making procedures which would allow them a greater say in the running of their own affairs are often interpreted as a demand for multi-level governance. This is academic shorthand for a process which substantially alters the nature of the state as we have come to know it over the last 200 years or so: the nation-state. However, it does not necessarily imply that the regionalist demand-makers would have a clear-cut alternative concept of statehood in mind. What these actors, whether their motivation is purely socio-economic, (minority) nationalist, socio-culturalist, or a mixture of all these elements, really want, is access to the authoritative decision-making procedures in their polity. The key word here is 'authoritative': the access must be to the establishments of institutionalised decision-making which, under the prevalent system of governance, have the power to make binding decisions, safeguarded from undue interference by outside decision-makers, and have the authority to conduct and enforce policies derived from these decision-making procedures. This wish by regional actors to gain access to authoritative decision-making accounts for the varying nature and intensity of their demands. In the West European democracies, it is often not necessary to throw out the old rule-book altogether in order to secure desired access, although in difficult circum-stances quite drastic rule-changes may be necessary to accommodate the demands for access – see, for instance, the changes to the Spanish and Belgian constitutions since the 1980s, and the entirely new set of rules now applicable to Northern Ireland, requiring changes to the systems of governance of not only one but two countries, the UK and the Republic of Ireland.[3] Often, however, the degree of necessary changes is subject to political debate among actors.

Typical examples are usually nationalist parties whose desires go beyond mere changes to the existing rules, although a majority of the population is not – or not yet – convinced that to overthrow the existing system of governance would be appropriate at a particular point in time. The more extreme wings of both the SNP and Plaid Cymru have indicated this by their dissatisfaction with the UK devolution deals on offer in the late 1990s. The failure to succeed straightaway, encountered by the protagonists of more extreme demands, such as the SNP's secessionist 'Independence in Europe' strategy, or Plaid's 'self-government in Europe' ideas, indicates a basic problem inherent in regional mobilisation. The actor coalitions required for bringing about rule-changes stay intact only to the extent that is necessary to achieve a common goal. If the agreement on the envisaged changes does not include a reasonably well-defined alternative set of rules of authoritative decision-making, the likely outcome is a compromise, based on the lowest common denominator. So it was possible for the Welsh Labour Party, Plaid Cymru, and also the Welsh Liberals, to campaign jointly for a 'Yes' vote in the referendum on establishing a Welsh Assembly, with quite different views on its roles and powers in mind. With half the population not caring either way, and hence abstaining in the referendum, Welsh devolution must be regarded as a remarkable piece of political craftsmanship by a rather weak actor coalition, consisting of prospective regional development managers like Rhodri Morgan and Mike German,[4] 'old Labour' socialists dissatisfied with Blairite social democracy, and the nationalists, the latter sensing the unique opportunity to become, for the first time, a significant force in Welsh politics. Until late 2000, this weak interest coalition still held – not because of a joint sense of purpose, but rather out of a shared feeling that the whole exercise had failed. Therefore, 'our fragile young dragon needs care' (Michael, 1999). Behind the scenes, however, the underlying motives and interests which brought them all to join the devolution movement are still as diverse as ever. While Plaid has by no means given up on its 1997 and 1999 campaigns idea of a 'Powerhouse Parliament' as a first step to 'self-government in Europe', Alun Michael, at the time First Secretary of the NAW, warned in November 1999:

> I believe in a dynamic devolution but this devolution settlement is the preferred choice of the Welsh people themselves. ... We enjoy the benefits of the UK economy, which is stronger and more stable than it has been for decades with public spending far higher than we could possibly support from our own resources. To me, and I believe to the majority of the Welsh people, this is the best of all worlds. ... Let's not fool ourselves, self-government in Europe is not an option. The European Union is a union of member states. Our European partners do not want to see the Balkanisation of the United Kingdom. (Michael, 1999)

The fact that such a warning was regarded as timely by the leading representative of the most powerful Welsh public actor indicates that not all is well, yet; because, indeed, a change in the nature of the state only occurs if the political entities replacing the old rules and structures are not only in place but also capable of taking over. The UK devolution project has so far implemented the first of these two conditions: putting the new structures in place. The project also holds the promise – but by no means a guarantee – that a true, lasting change of the nature of UK governance is forthcoming, a change which satisfies the socio-economic, political and socio-cultural needs, ambitions and desires of the people in the constituent parts of the UK, enabling them to shape the lifestyle of their society as they see fit in the larger environment of the EU and beyond. To succeed in this, however, not only the 'young dragon' of welsh devolution but all the emerging new systems of governance throughout the UK, from the Council of the Isles to the Mayor of London, need care and support: meaningful, sustained regional mobilisation in the individual territories, and an open, honest application of multi-level governance throughout the UK. Whether the new structures now put in place or about to be put in place are really capable of taking over – and thus changing the nature of UK governance for good – remains to be seen.

In Saxony, on the other hand, a change in the nature of the state has not taken place. In the light of events leading up to German unification, this claim may seem somewhat surprising. Did not the East Germans throw out their old system of governance altogether? Did they not only change the nature of their state, but scrap that state itself? Isn't the regime change that has occurred the most radical form of changing the nature of the state that one could imagine? And were not the Saxons in the forefront of it all, with the city of Leipzig claiming to be the capital of the 'Peaceful Revolution'? This line of questioning, however, misses the key point: the attempted regime change before unification was abortive, as it had to be, because there were no alternative political entities replacing the old rules and structures. One cannot demand access to means of authoritative decision-making if such means are non-existent. The coalition of clergymen, artists, dissidents, ecologists and disenchanted young citizens which was the driving force for the removal of the old regime was bound together by a single joint interest: to get rid of the Honecker administration. Much has been written about the heroism in the face of adversity displayed by some of the members of this movement, and one should avoid any belittlement of their achievements; however, one cannot fail to notice that in their intense – and often dangerous – pursuit of their goal, only very few members took the time to consider options for the 'time after Honecker'. Astonished by their own seemingly smooth and quick success – the whole process lasted barely 18 months – over an adversary who after all was much weaker than anyone really suspected at the time, they found themselves in a political void, a void that was quickly filled with makeshift institutions of semi-authoritative decision-making such as the famous 'Round Tables' mushrooming everywhere. These newly established bodies were usually populated with representatives of likewise newly established interest groups who were not, and maybe could not be, certain where their own – let alone the public – interest lay in the changed circumstances. Just about the only point they could agree on was to rid themselves of representatives of the old regime wherever possible. The key force behind a speedy unification with the FRG was the lack of long-term alternatives to this course of action. This was supplemented by an awakening of the general public, who, having been mostly unaware of the ongoing 'revolution'[5] until after it succeeded, now determined to 'Test the West'[6] with their enthusiasm for unification after the opening of the border on 9 November 1989.

The FRG government at the time had been fully aware of the socio-economic crisis in East Germany;[7] however, the speed of the political developments was a surprise even to them. The *Mantel der Geschichte* ('Greatcoat of History'), Kohl's metaphorical call for 'unity and freedom' for *all* Germans (Article 146 GG), was once again highlighted, but became something of a constitutional straitjacket: the old Article 23 GG, which paid lip-service to similar sentiments when appropriate for over four decades, but all but forgotten in practice, clearly stated that East Germans had a right to be reunified with the FRG whenever they saw fit. So the FRG could not have not embarked upon a pro-unification course. On the other hand, any serious disruption to the lifestyle of the old FRG had to be avoided if at all possible, and the momentum had to be kept in order to fill the East German political void, of which an increasingly serious side-effect was the beginning of an economic meltdown. So, what was established in Saxony and elsewhere in the 'new' *Länder* was an old system of governance, supposedly tried and tested in the FRG, consisting of prefabricated old sets of rules of authoritative decision-making. Hence, despite unification Germany has not experienced a change in the nature of the state.

The task at hand in Saxony and the other east German *Länder*, therefore, has been to develop an actor structure to fit the imported set of rules of authoritative decision-making – not the other way round, as was the case in the UK and elsewhere in West European regions. It is not surprising that the largest, most resourceful, and most organised of these actors, from 'big business' to the CDU, encountered little resistance in establishing themselves as the new predominant actors in the region. Smaller or less resourceful actors, including newly founded small businesses, local government, the SPD, the trade unions, and the voluntary sector, found it much more difficult to establish themselves in the regional political arena – too late, in fact, to get their just emerging interests more fully vested in the Saxon constitutional, legal and administrative system. Nevertheless, general dissatisfaction with the current set of rules of authoritative decision-making is so limited that further changes are not seriously on the agenda at the moment. Not only is there no actor coalition in place which would be at the helm of such a movement; but for the time being most organisations and individuals are willing to give the present system a try, to steer the ship of state into less troubled waters after the storms of the 1990s. It helps that the German federal system is already very conducive to interest representation from the regions, both towards the federation and towards the EU. Apparently, the Germans have put a remarkable array of MLG-style decision-making structures and procedures into place, constitutionally vested, without explicitly saying so. Therefore, regional actors have already obtained what is a key demand among regionalists in most European regions: the right to influence decisions at the higher levels of government, insofar as those decisions have a bearing on the region. Within Germany, however, the Bavarian and Saxon governments are isolated in their requests for more action in that direction.

This is not to say that Saxony is now in for a prolonged period of tranquillity. While questions regarding the means of governance of the region are now settled for the time being, the task of regional development very much remains at the top of the regional agenda. To tackle this task successfully will be the proving ground for the new regime. A significant number of individuals and organisations have not yet found their home within the new system, indicated by considerable support for the PDS (seen by many as the only true opposition), by the rate of failures among new businesses, by the unemployment rate which still remains at around twice the federal average, and not least by the publicly stated disenchantment among many of the 1989 'revolutionaries'. It will be crucial to accommodate them all to a greater extent than the one offered now, by operating a more open, inclusive policy of regional management. Regional mobilisation run like an exclusive private members club ('movers and shakers only') may have made perfect sense in the start-up phase. In the long run, however, it is bound to lose momentum as a more diverse landscape of interest groups establishes itself and starts to represent their interests more forcefully. Then, though not before, will it be time to address the question of the nature of Saxon governance afresh.

CHANCES AND CONSTRAINTS OF REGIONAL DEVELOPMENT

Both Wales and Saxony can be regarded as fairly typical examples of the way to develop into a modern region. Saxony has in general just about completed a phase of quantitative infrastructure development, with some larger road links projects still under construction. The focus of development efforts has, since 1999, slowly shifted towards qualitative infrastructure development, with particular emphasis on the enhancement of human resources. However, the general pace of progress in various fields of development has slowed down considerably. The reason for this slacking of pace is the fact that because the progress rate was so enormous in the period 1990–96 it would have been impossible to carry on at that rate anyway. Two other key reasons are that potential investors have already begun to look further east, and that sufficient funding for the envisaged human resource development has not been secured at an adequate level. Thus, there are only small signs of an emerging modern company base, with some well-advanced, well-resourced – and well-publicised – show-pieces, amidst a landscape of smaller new enterprises struggling on shoestring budgets and extremely vulnerable to changing market conditions, tax laws and regulatory measures.

Wales has mostly completed an extensive phase of quantitative infrastructure development in the early 1990s, and has now also made some inroads into qualititative infrastructure development. However, Wales is proceeding at a slower pace than Saxony used to. Until about late 1994 it was reasonable to speculate that the two regions might be level in the not too distant future. However, in Saxony it has been noted with considerable relief by many public and semi-public actors that the region retained Objective 1 status after the end of the first Saxon Operational Programme in 1999 – but probably not forever. Progress in Wales, on the other hand, is currently being slowed down as the effects of devolution, of the 1995–96 local government reform, and not least the crisis in agriculture, mainly brought about by the BSE and foot and mouth desease outbreaks and their economic and political fallout, have to be digested. Medium- to long-term planning in most parts of Wales is faced with the task of utilising the current Objective 1 status (2000–06) for qualitative development, which will have to become self-sustainable by the end of that period, as an extension of EU support at a level anywhere near Objective 1 funding will not be forthcoming. So, for both Wales and Saxony the key criterion for their chances of becoming truly modern regions in Europe will be the degree of success in their qualitative infrastructure development until about 2010. The foundations for this success are now in place in both regions, but much work needs to be done by the public, semi-public and private actors.

An integrated approach to development is arguably the most important factor for a region's progress towards modernisation. To secure this progress, regional mobilisation efforts have to comprise a number of key elements, in particular economic steering through public–private co-operation, political interest representation, and socio-cultural generation of ideas, aims, means and popular support. In all three areas, actor competence – on both the public and the private side – is the key to success. Since the 1988 Structural Funds reforms, the EU has developed a well-endowed framework of support for regional actors in their actions to overcome specific regional problems. While this support was, and still is, certainly very welcome indeed at the regional level, it can only be a temporary means to facilitate long-term progress. A truly modern region does not need EU cash; as the political behaviour of stronger regions indicates, their main interests lie in influencing regulatory policies that have an impact on the socio-economic state of affairs in their territories. This is not to say that weaker regions would not have such an interest – Biedenkopf, for one, has made that clear repeatedly. The publicly stated key interests of virtually all Welsh actors, with the exception of Plaid Cymru, on the other hand, is mostly confined to access to funds, regardless of any strings attached to it.

However, for the present socio-economic and political regional development processes, and for the drive towards a meaningful regional involvement in multi-level governance, the prime initiative has to come from within the region, as has the political will to see these processes through. The desire for economic and social development can be regarded as the key driving force behind a region's development efforts. To get the regional economy into a healthy and sustainable state has clearly proved to be fundamental to any regional development efforts because here, to a very large extent, the resources are determined which a region can draw upon to conduct the tasks it wishes to conduct. The stronger the economic base, the better are the chances of making the most of non-financial assets. Therefore, theoretically, economic development can be regarded as an interest shared by all actors within a region. However, the precise ideas concerning how to pursue that theoretical goal may vary widely, with varying or even conflictual interests of different actors or groups of actors being put forward. There is no guarantee as to whether this leads to the formation of strong and sustained interest coalitions formed by these actors.

In the Welsh case, processes of regional mobilisation have begun to emerge since the early 1990s, and have been documented both in this investigation and elsewhere (Cooke et al., 1993; Price et al., 1994; Loughlin, 1997; Loughlin and Mathias, 1998, 1998a). However, actor coalitions in Wales so far have tended to be relatively informal, and with regard to private actor involvement relatively unstable. The engagement of a considerable number of public actors has been more sustained, but, up to 1999, has suffered from a limiting influence exercised by actors from outside Wales, in particular Westminster and Whitehall. It has to be noted that, apart from some initiatives of horizontal networking by semi-public and local public actors, virtually all the efforts of Welsh economic interest representation have evolved around the question of securing and then utilising funds from the EU. Despite the considerable size of the funds obtained by Welsh actors, this is a relatively small base for regional mobilisation, and the coalition of economic actors who did most of the work in that respect is unlikely to survive much beyond 2006 unless a wider approach to integrating Wales into the European and global economies is taken. There will be a political steering process required to bring about this shift in direction, and whether the NAW, at the moment already almost overburdened focusing on the issues dealing with Objective 1 status, will be up to the task remains to be seen.

In Saxony, economic development has been at the top of the agenda of all actors in the economic sphere, but actor coalitions capable of engaging in regional mobilisation efforts have not emerged. Two key reasons for this are the weakness of the regional actor structure, filled with inexperienced actors who frequently are in doubt as to their own interests, on the one hand, and an apparent lack among the political leadership, in particular the Saxon government, to engage in regional mobilisation in any meaningful way, on the other. Formally, actor coalitions are formed as and when required to secure and administer EU grants, but beyond these market forces and competition among – equally inexperienced – private actors dominate the Saxon economic landscape. Therefore, ten years after its creation in its present form, the Saxon scene presents an unstable picture, characterised by significant social hardship. While progress in regional development in Saxony has initially been faster than elsewhere in the territory of the former East Germany, only some parts of Saxony can be regarded as really on their way to becoming a modern region. While there are islands of significant success, in particular in and around the cities of Dresden and Leipzig, large parts of Saxony, including more or less the entire *Regierungsbezirk* Chemnitz, and the area along the Polish border, have become marginalised to an extent that securing what has been achieved so far will be a key task for the foreseeable future; sustainable growth is a long way off yet. Whether Saxony will continue to receive sufficient long-term outside support to address this problem by a series of small steps and local initiatives[8] must be open to doubt.

Therefore, at the moment, both regions are in a phase of restructuring their economy to adapt it to present and future challenges and demands. Despite much political rhetoric to the contrary, neither of the two has dared to veer off the standard model of development outlined in Chapter 1, mostly for reasons of a possible loss of EU funding. It is, in both cases, much too early to judge upon success or failure of this approach, but while key foundations for the success, such as a significant quantitative enhancement of the physical infrastructure, have been achieved, no clear strategies for the transition into and successful conduct of the next phase, qualitative infrastructure development, have emerged. To develop these is a key task of the regional actors at the present time.

At first glance, Saxony with its now strong and stable system of governance seems to be in a better position to do this, while the Welsh first need to come to terms with the new system of governance emerging from UK devolution – a process which itself is still in flux. Political cultures and administrative structures matter insofar as, whatever their shape and operational procedures, they must be able to deliver necessary feasible creative ideas and initiatives, as well as a suitable framework for effective action to steer and sustain the development process. This issue has two dimensions. First, the structures and procedures in place need to be capable of discharging regional 'domestic' duties and responsibilities effectively and efficiently. Secondly, a region aspiring to become modern is also required not only to define, but also to represent its own interests, in all their variety, to other regions as well as on the national and the European stages. As outside circumstances are subject to change, this creates the further necessity to develop a certain flexibility in the ways and means of policy development, project implementation and interest representation.

On the domestic side, the two systems in place in Wales and Saxony differ considerably. The newly emerged post-devolution structures in Wales constitute significant progress towards some form of political self-determination within Wales. While the formal powers and rights now enjoyed by the NAW fall short of those of a German *Land*, the key element of progress that has been made since 1998 is that the process of devolution took place at all. This is a major achievement in itself, given the fact that, judging by the results of the 1997 referendum, about half of the population does not care either way, and that of those who do care, roughly 50 per cent are actually against it. However, this may well be an indicator that regional mobilisation need not necessarily comprise an all-encompassing mass movement. While a greater direct involvement might be beneficial – see, for instance, the Scottish case (Lynch, 1996; Stolz, 1997; Lange, 1998) – a few determined 'insiders' seem to be all that is needed to get regional development strategies going, including political reform processes.

On the other hand, given the degree of scepticism surrounding the NAW's creation, it is not surprising that devolution protagonists were keen to promise an open, transparent, accessible, and inclusive system to be adopted by the new regional public actors. This has yet to emerge. While the Assembly is certainly physically more approachable than Westminster, its business has so far been dominated by making procedural arrangements – an unavoidable chore during the first ever legislative period – and two economic debates: managing the crisis in Welsh agriculture, and securing Objective 1 status for the period 2000–06. In both cases, the private actors concerned, the NFU and the FUW on the one hand, and the CBI Wales on the other, complained loudly that their interests were not taken seriously enough. In the first case, this led to a vote of no confidence against the then Agriculture Secretary of the Assembly, Christine Gwyther (in the event, it was toned down into a verbal admonition), and in the other case Plaid Cymru has managed to force First Secretary Alun Michael to resign by threatening a vote of no confidence for failing to secure more money from London (!) to match the forthcoming EU grants.

Certainly, the original model of two opposition parties tolerating a minority executive can be seen as a new departure in British politics,[9] overcoming the clear-cut confrontational style dominating the Westminster system. However, the model, created out of the mathematics of seat distribution rather than positive political choice, spectacularly failed in Wales too, within 15 months or so. Stormy debates over economic policy, the forced resignation of a First Secretary, and just a few too many votes of no confidence and motions of censure against a series of members of the Welsh Executive and not least a constant wrangling over competencies between the Executive and the Assembly's committees characterised this failure of the WA. On the other hand, the later solution of a coalition government based on a partnership agreement that details ways and means of handling policy matters within the coalition is looking quite promising. The period October 2000 to April 2003 saw NAW debates return to calmer waters, and an actual return to politics after the previous severe spell of nationalist posturing and procedural brinksmanship.

On the administrative side, the changeover from the WO's to the NAW's administration amounted to little more than a change of the sign at the front of the administration's building, from 'Welsh Office' to 'National Assembly for Wales'. There was a change of some senior personnel, but the vast majority of civil servants is sitting at the same desk, conducting the same business as before. This legacy is nevertheless beneficial, as some inexperience among the new political masters can be mitigated by the combined experience of the junior ranks of civil servants, and the old WO had already begun a policy of hiring young Welsh personnel,[10] not – or less – burdened by having served the previous Conservative administrations.

As far as local administration in Wales is concerned, the effects of the local government reform have still not been fully absorbed. Introduced by the Conservative government prior to devolution, it forced certain long-serving Labour councillors not only to redraw the maps of their fiefdoms,[11] but also to cut down the administrative infrastructure – in many cases, for example Powys, increasing the physical distance between the administrators and the citizens they serve. The 1999 local government elections yielded some unexpected results; Plaid Cymru doing exceptionally well, removing Labour's overall control in many councils, and actually winning control of two southern councils (Caerphilly and Rhondda-Cynon-Taff; Balsom, 2000: 420–558). In places where huge Labour majorities are still intact, for example in Cardiff, old social link between legislature and administration that have evolved around the local Labour leadership are still in business, but most people involved in these are now desperate to portray themselves as managers *extraordinaire* to justify the self-approved salaries that go with it.[12] To this end, these groups are not afraid to use the language of 'New Labour', but their ability to deliver the required capabilities to handle the local end of regional development must nevertheless be questioned.

The Saxon political and administrative structures have already shown quite forcefully that they are prepared to act. Helped by federal constitutional and legal provisions of empowerment, the political actors running the *Land* institutions showed no hesitation whatsoever in using these powers to further their own interests. This applies also to the external representation of Saxony's interests. In these processes, the government has kept a sufficient proportion of the Saxon population satisfied enough to get re-elected twice, thus establishing an element of stability in the government of Saxony.[13] While this is regarded as a positive development by many Saxons, it has also helped to establish a policy style based on Schumpeter's model of democracy: 'The democratic method is that institutional arrangement for arriving at political decisions in which individuals acquire the power to decide by means of a competitive struggle for the people's vote' (Schumpeter, 1970: 269). The role of the population in decision-making procedures is thus reduced to voting every so often in order to decide who should make all other political decisions for them[14] – a situation the CDU government seems to be very comfortable with. This concept also leaves no safeguarded room for interest representation by organisations and interest groups, other than through the individual votes of their members. Access to the decision-makers is either granted or denied on the sole discretion of the decision-makers themselves, again a role the Saxon government apparently feels very comfortable with – Saxony's *Staatsziele* proclamations notwithstanding. Therefore, the shaping and implementation of development strategies at the regional level in Saxony has become an 'insider business', even more so than in Wales.

General political involvement by the population is not really required, lest it might lead to confrontations and an open struggle for access to authoritative decision-making powers among the various interest groups. Helped by the weakness of meaningful political opposition, at times the

Saxon government has come very close to reducing public scrutiny to unacceptably low levels. The reduction of the *Landtag's* size,[15] the lengthening of its legislative period from four to five years, implemented in 1994, and the introduction of two-year Budgets in December 1998, i.e. the year before the 1999 regional elections, are but three examples. For obvious reasons, however, this cannot be stated publicly, so the government has introduced an element of populism and regionalism into their policy style, but in a cultural sense only. At the moment, this still works, but whether it will last much beyond the current legislative period.

The involvement of local government structures in regional develop-ment is less crucial than in Wales as the functions associated with this are mainly carried out by the intermediate sub-regional executive, the *Regierungsbezirke*. These offices are filled with senior and medium-rank civil servants, not elected officials. Their active engagement and managerial skill has been most crucial in conducting regional development affairs in Saxony so far; and it is probably their achievement more than anyone else's that some key projects at the sub-regional and local levels have been successful.[16] The possible lack of democratic control introduced by the fact that these are unelected officials has so far been outweighed by their remarkable approachability and preparedness to engage in various forms of public–private co-operation. While it is to be hoped that this momentum can be sustained, a generalisation in terms of applicability of this concept elsewhere is not (yet) in order, but clearly deserves further research.

Regional culture, heritage, and similar foci of regional identity can be powerful aides to the generation of ideas, to decision-making, and to rally popular support for proposed measures. However, the performance of such assets may be severely damaged by a lack of financial support – for example the limited availability of sponsors in Saxony – or the lack of political will to use them, as displayed by the Conservatives with regard to Welsh nationalism. Nevertheless, the absence or lack of influence of such regional culture can be overcome by increased political efforts. Regional cultures, heritage and widely accepted sets of belief and perception which constitute identity, whether or not they can be described as 'national', are important, because as constituent elements of regional identity they, in essence, make identity recognisable. This goes beyond 'image making'. A well-developed regional identity becomes an experience, both in the everyday life of the people at home and in the views of the outside world, to go alongside territorial definitions and shared economic lifestyle.[17]

The concept of Welshness, not only as opposed to Englishness, Irishness, etc., but also as opposed to Britishness, has been used repeatedly and forcefully by a number of regional and local public, semi-public and private actors over the last few years to stake a specific claim of recognition in higher levels of government, and to promote Welsh goods, services, and investment opportunities domestically and abroad. To do this can be regarded as standard behaviour in regional interest representation, and has been observed in many other European regions (Lynch, 1997; Kohler-Koch u.a., 1998).

However, what is particularly interesting, and much less common though by no means unique, concerning the Welsh case is that manifestations and images of cultural nationalism have been successfully employed by Welsh actors to promote political demands, leading into the devolution process, and contributing to sustaining the momentum of the steps to devolution. Undoubtedly such representations alone would have been unlikely to succeed had not outside circumstances created a political environment which proved to be very conducive of these demands. Among these outside circumstances one has in particular to take note of the devolution movement in Scotland, a UK government in power which was more sensitive to the problems in Wales than their predecessors, and a strengthened and well-funded EU regional policy. The creative idea put forward by Welsh activists was simply that because Wales is a nation it should have a National Assembly. Here, the protagonists of devolution were disadvantaged in comparison to their Scottish counterparts, as they could to some extent stake a claim for the re-establishment of previously existing structures, for example a Scottish Parliament. In Wales, such structures have never been in existence; the demands therefore had to promote entirely new structures, with no chances of showing any historical proof of their feasibility or utility.

To have an Assembly was in itself seen by many protagonists of devolution as an end in itself, enhancing the nation's status and prestige in the UK and abroad, regardless of the powers and responsibilities that were to come with it. A small group of individuals, mostly associated with Plaid Cymru and the Welsh Language Board, saw and still see devolution as a first step towards a – so far ill-defined – Welsh 'self-governance'. Prospective regional development managers saw the Assembly as a forum and tool for enhanced interest representation. This was enough to set up the new structure of government. However, it would be too early to certify that a new system of governance has already been established in Wales. The generation and processing of new, creative ideas has yet to emerge. Day-to-day policy discussions in the new structures have so far been limited to modifying old policies, such as how to distribute the annual block grant from London, how to draft the Objective 1 application – again a modification of the old Objective 2 and Objective 5b operational programmes for the parts of Wales that were concerned with these – and how to press the UK government for more money: old-style claim-staking at its very best. It can be argued that many detailed policies have to be continuances from pre-devolution days because the problems to be addressed are still the same, and solutions which were only partially implemented so far need to be seen through.

It may be that in the future the NAW will evolve into a body for generating and processing ideas and strategies which prove to be appropriate to Welsh problems, and to be more efficient and effective than pre-devolution institutions. Then, and only then will the NAW be able to become a true focus for national identity. However, it would probably be very important for the NAW to avoid an over-reliance on cultural distinctness, and images thereof, for they can neither be a substitute for sound economic planning, nor an acceptable reason for claiming preferential treatment within the new political system of the UK, and within a multi-level system of governance in the EU.

The situation in Saxony varies considerably from the Welsh situation in this respect. Three key differences can be observed. First, a sufficient number of Saxon regional actors – among them all public actors – have plenty of access to authoritative decision-making about matters concerning their region or area. In Wales the absence of such access was the main driving force for devolution among both nationalists and regionalists. The second difference, closely associated with the first, is that Saxony's recognition and legitimacy, both legally and morally, has never been questioned since its re-creation in 1990. So there was no supposed opponent[18] against whom a claim for recognition had to be continually asserted. Thirdly, in the Saxon case there is no 'national' dimension to the question of identity. Most Saxons feel rather at home within the German nation; and within Saxony the Sorbs have been accommodated to a more or less satisfactory degree.

Saxon regionalism, therefore, must to a very large extent be regarded as an exercise in political steering by the Saxon government; with the double aim of the usual economic place marketing within Germany and towards its immediate neighbours, and, probably even more important, creating a 'feel-good factor' among the Saxon population despite the significant socio-economic problems within the region. Indeed, a number of local cultural initiatives, in particular, businesses involved in buildings and artworks restoration, and people involved in the quite large folk music scene, have willingly jumped on the green-and-white bandwagon, but it is reasonable to assume that economic incentives, such as the availability of public funds for these activities have played a major role in their decision to emphasise their 'Saxonness'. As on the political side, the majority of the population is reduced to a rather passive role of consumer, spectator, and flag-waver (if and when required). The potential of a regionalist movement to develop creative ideas and to help implement them seems to be deliberately avoided in order to prevent wider access to authoritative decision-making procedures. The strict focus on cultural matters therefore has become a means to prevent – rather than encourage – popular involvement in other spheres of Saxon society. In Saxony, cultural regionalism has become a tool for regional demobilisation. However, as long as this seems to meet with the wishes of a large proportion of the population – and there is little if any evidence to the contrary – this situation is likely to prevail for the foreseeable future.

To sum up, Wales and Saxony are not modern regions yet, but they are both modernising. The regional economies are still in a period of reconstruction, after a severe decline in the 1980s and early 1990s. The regions are now embarked on various strategies and programmes of regional development. While some initial progress in this respect has already been achieved, both regions are still relying heavily on means of outside support, in particular on ERDF and ESF funds, but also on a number of means of assistance provided by the governments of their countries.

The political systems of Wales and Saxony also have recently undergone a programme of reconstruction, but the long-term outcome for these processes, in particular the capabilities and efficiency of the newly established structures are not yet fully proved, in particular in the Welsh case. This has a direct bearing on regional interest formation and interest representation, and it will be up to the regional actors – public and private – to overcome the significant shortcomings that can still be observed in both regions. In Wales, this mainly means making the new institutions work. In Saxony, the emphasis will have to be on actor development and accumulation of experience, both individually and within co-operation arrangements, utilising the existing structure of institutions.

In both regions, there is enormous potential for enhanced utilisation of human resources. This goes beyond the development of skills for new jobs, although that is a major task, too. However, the human potential lies also in people's capabilities as active citizens, politically and in the socio-cultural sphere. It will not be enough to bemoan an alleged *Politik-verdrossenheit* (disenchantment with politics in general). People will only return to the ballot boxes, to party meetings, to active membership in organisations representing the various interests in the society, and – if need be – to protest rallies in the market square if they are convinced that by doing so they can actually achieve something worthwhile.[19] They will also return to work, given the opportunity. EU grants and helping hands from other regions are important, but they are not long-term solutions. Given the present socio-economic conditions, there is little choice but to press ahead with the ongoing development initiatives, but there is no guarantee whatsoever of success along the lines of Baden-Württemberg or south-east England.

NOTES

1. Former Chancellor Kohl discovered this the hard way, having promised in 1996 that the German unemployment figure of 4 million would be halved by the end of his term in office. On election day in September 1998, the figure stood at 4.8 million.
2. Interview, *Sächsische Staatskanzlei*, 1996.
3. In the case of the Republic of Ireland, the change basically involved the removal of Articles 2 and 3 of the constitution, removing the Republic's territorial claim to the six northern counties.
4. Leader of the Welsh Liberals.
5. For a critical evaluation of the applicability of this term in the East German context see Thompson, 1999.
6. Cigarette advertisement at the time (in English in the original).
7. After all, it was the FRG's own lines of credit extended to the East German government which enabled the Honecker administration to hang on just a little while longer.
8. This is the current policy of many sub-regional and local actors in the areas concerned (interviews, *Regierungspräsidium* Chemnitz, 1996, and *Industrie- und Handelskammer Südwestsachsen*, 1996).
9. A similar attempt in Westminster, starting in March 1974, failed within a few months, leading to a general election in October 1974.
10. Since the introduction of the Welsh Language Act, 1993, it had become a job requirement to be able to speak Welsh, or at least to learn this language within a short period after taking up the appointment. This reduced the influx of applicants from England considerably (interview, WO, 1997).
11. In the view of the largely unconcerned Welsh Liberals, this was the not publicly admitted but nevertheless most important reason for the reform (Interview, Liberal Democrats Wales, 1995).
12. The members of Cardiff County Council are now the highest-paid local councillors in the UK (Gosling, 2000: 2).
13. Although some personnel has changed, Saxony's CDU government is the only *Land* government that has managed to keep in office from the first elections in 1990 to date (2003). While Brandenburg's *Ministerpräsident* Manfred Stolpe remained in office too, he was forced into different coalition governments during that time. Each of the three other *Länder* has had at least two different *Ministerpräsidenten* and/or coalitions running their government.
14. The colloquial German term for this role is *Stimmvieh*, meaning a docile flock of animals being herded to the ballot box.
15. However, with currently 120 seats (previously 160) it is still one of the larger German *Land* parliaments.
16. A possible exception to this is the city – though not the rest of the *Regierungsbezirk* – of Leipzig, where the local government exercised considerable leadership, often without the agreement of the *Land* government.
17. However, if ethnicity comes into the equation and therefore the question of the right of self-determination arises, the water can become quite muddy indeed (e.g. Basque

Country, Northern Ireland). So regional mobilisation cannot expect plain sailing throughout the EU.
18. As the UK government, and the seemingly overpowering English socio-economic strength, were in the view of the Welsh nationalists.
19. Remarkably, among the political parties, it seems to be Plaid Cymru and the PDS which have so far been closest to understanding and utilising this phenomenon.

Appendix A:
The REGE Wales Project

A1. THE INTERNATIONAL FRAMEWORK OF THE PROJECT, AND EUROPEAN COMPARISON

The *Regional Development and its European Dimension in Wales* (REGE Wales) research project, on which some of the empirical evidence on Wales in this study is based, was conducted by Professor John Loughlin and this author at the School of European Studies, University of Wales, Cardiff, between April 1995 and April 1997. This project was part of a larger international research project, *Regions as Political Actors in Europe*,[1] better known by its German acronym REGE, which was devised and co-ordinated by Professor Beate Kohler-Koch at the Mannheim Centre for European Social Research (MZES), University of Mannheim, Germany.

The members of the REGE team were:

Mannheimer Zentrum für Europäische Sozialforschung, University of Mannheim, Germany	Prof. Beate Kohler-Koch Dr Jürgen Grote Dr Michèle Knodt Dr Fabrice Larat Santo Umberti, MA
Laboratoire RIVES, Ecole Nationale des Travaux Publics, Lyon, France	Dr Bernard Jouve
Centre Comparatif d'Etudes des Politiques Publiques et des Espaces Locaux, University of Montpellier, France	Dr Emmanuel Négrier
Departament de Cienca Politica, Universitat Autonoma de Barcelona, Spain	Prof. Francesc Morata John Etherington, MA Neus Gomez-Mataran, MA

School of European Studies,   Prof. John Loughlin
University of Wales, Cardiff, UK   Dip.-Pol. Jörg Mathias

The REGE project compared nine EU regions: Baden-Württemberg (BW), Lower Saxony (LS), Rhône-Alpes (RA), Longuedoc-Roussillon (LR), Lombardy (LO), Sicily (SI), Catalonia (CA), Andalusia (AN) and Wales (WA).[2] The main part of this study was a questionnaire survey, where the same questions – adjusted to fit the functional actor structure in the region concerned – were asked in all the regions. A total of 1,250 actors participated in this study. (See Table A1.1.)

TABLE A 1.1
COMPOSITION OF THE EUROPEAN PANEL

Region	Number of returns (cases)	Real distribution of cases (%)	Optimum distribution of cases (%)	Over-representation (%)	Under-representation (%)
BW	219	17.63	11.09	6.27	
LS	156	12.48	11.09	1.39	
RA	144	11.52	11.09	0.43	
LR	124	9.92	11.09		1.17
LO	170	13.68	11.09	2.59	
SI	81	6.48	11.09		4.61
CA	62	4.96	11.09		6.13
AN	171	13.68	11.09	2.59	
WA	123	9.84	11.09		1.25
Total	**1250**	**100.00**	**100.00**	**+13.2**	**−13.2**

Source: REGE MZES, 1996.

For a full account of the REGE methodology see Knodt, 1998a. Key findings regarding the European comparison have already been published (Kohler-Koch u.a., 1998; Négrier and Jouve, 1998; and numerous individual publications by team members). Therefore, here it is appropriate only to provide a summary of the key comparative data (Tables A1.2–A1.9) developed by the REGE project which show the position of Wales in relation to the other eight regions and the European – i.e. the REGE regions' – average (EA). (Table headings refer to questions asked by the project.)

TABLE A1.2*
THE IMPORTANCE OF REGIONAL GOVERNMENT IN GENERAL, AND WITH REGARD
TO REGIONAL DEVELOPMENT POLICY AND R&D POLICY IN PARTICULAR
(QUESTIONS 1, 7, AND 17)[3]

Region	In general (%)	For RDP (%)	For R&D (%)
BW	76.2	94.9	79.5
LS	75.5	92.7	88.0
RA	83.2	90.7	84.2
LR	88.4	87.0	84.1
LO	93.4	91.2	90.8
SI	96.2	89.2	79.3
CA	100.0	100.0	87.0
AN	93.4	99.2	92.6
WA	88.0	95.7	68.6
EA	90.1	92.9	82.7

* The table gives the percentage of organisations which thought that regional government was important (including 'somewhat important' and 'most important').

Source: REGE MZES, 1996.

TABLE A1.3
SHOULD REGIONS HAVE A GREATER INFLUENCE WITHIN THE EU IN GENERAL
(QUESTION 2), AND SHOULD REGIONS HAVE MORE DIRECT SAY IN THE SHAPING
OF EU R&D POLICY (QUESTION 22)?

Region	For greater general influence (%)	For a more direct say in R&D policy (%)
BW	65.7	76.4
LS	72.8	69.1
RA	63.6	53.2
LR	67.8	62.9
LO	87.1	94.3
SI	79.0	88.2
CA	81.7	95.2
AN	75.0	92.3
WA	93.2	88.5
EA	75.1	77.5

Source: REGE MZES, 1996.

TABLE A1.4
EXPECTED FEATURES OF A 'EUROPE OF THE REGIONS' (QUESTION 3)

Region	Reduction of regional disparities	More gains by already strong regions	Counter-balance to centralisa-tion	More complex decision-making processes	More cultural pluralism	Closer attention to needs of individuals
	(% Yes)	*(% Yes)*	*(% Yes)*	*(% Yes)*	*(% Yes)*	*(% Yes)*
BW	56.9	76.7	83.3	70.0	87.8	55.6
LS	64.0	69.6	87.7	66.5	81.4	56.0
RA	26.9	88.0	82.4	71.1	75.2	50.0
LR	42.7	74.4	88.2	76.7	73.2	59.8
LO	40.6	74.1	89.1	65.0	89.1	69.3
SI	62.4	61.1	76.4	65.4	79.9	83.0
CA	41.7	74.5	93.1	52.5	100.0	85.3
AN	65.1	47.4	77.3	62.6	81.1	81.3
WA	51.3	66.8	69.8	61.3	58.9	44.0
EA	**51.0**	**69.6**	**81.7**	**66.6**	**77.8**	**64.7**

Source: REGE MZES, 1996.

TABLE A1.5
VIEWS ON THE ECONOMIC IMPACT OF ESTABLISHING THE SINGLE EUROPEAN MARKET, IN PARTICULAR WHETHER IT WOULD BE USEFUL TO FOLLOW THE MARKET-ORIENTED TREND WITHIN THE SINGLE MARKET (QUESTION 4), AND WHETHER EU COMPETITION REGULATIONS HAVE HARMFUL EFFECTS ON THE REGIONAL ECONOMY (QUESTION 5)

Region	Useful to follow market-orientation (% Yes)	Competition rules hinder regional economy (% Yes)
BW	88.0	62.1
LS	72.8	66.6
RA	93.0	58.4
LR	77.0	55.5
LO	92.1	18.6
SI	80.2	50.6
CA	93.5	68.5
AN	88.8	79.4
WA	77.1	41.3
EA	**85.4**	**55.7**

Source: REGE MZES, 1996.

TABLE A1.6
HOW ARE STRUCTURAL FUNDS FROM THE EU REACHING THE REGION
PERCEIVED BY THOSE WHOM THEY ARE DESTINED FOR (QUESTION 9)?

Region	Not enough	Not distributed fairly	Too much spatially concentrated	Too rigidly earmarked
	(% Yes)	(% Yes)	(% Yes)	(% Yes)
BW	59.3	28.2	33.8	34.1
LS	70.7	43.0	39.9	53.9
RA	43.4	37.8	31.8	57.4
LR	60.2	63.0	29.1	59.5
LO	59.7	50.0	29.4	59.5
SI	57.1	65.1	20.4	61.7
CA	83.3	37.7	43.5	55.0
AN	59.3	48.6	44.8	62.9
WA	64.0	29.5	47.3	43.1
EA	**59.4**	**44.0**	**36.1**	**52.6**

Source: REGE MZES, 1996.

TABLE A1.7
GENERAL PERCEPTIONS OF THE POLITICAL CLIMATE IN THE REGION
(QUESTION 36)

Region	Innovative	Controversial	Market-oriented	Focusing on issues rather than personal relations
	(% Yes)	(% Yes)	(% Yes)	(% Yes)
BW	61.8	32.9	86.3	66.4
LS	50.4	59.0	63.0	48.1
RA	52.1	28.2	70.8	43.1
LR	46.4	72.5	42.3	33.3
LO	27.2	52.0	49.0	28.4
SI	7.5	55.5	22.9	14.4
CA	50.0	43.4	56.3	42.6
AN	62.2	64.1	27.4	52.7
WA	35.5	37.3	47.2	56.0
EA	**46.7**	**46.0**	**55.9**	**45.0**

Source: REGE MZES, 1996.

TABLE A1.8

THE ROLE OF PUBLIC ACTORS IN PUBLIC–PRIVATE RELATIONSHIPS: DOES THE REGIONAL GOVERNMENT USUALLY SET THE RIGHT PRIORITIES (QUESTION 37)? IS THE REGIONAL GOVERNMENT THE PRIMARY SOURCE OF INITIATIVES (QUESTION 38A)? ARE PUBLIC SERVANTS USUALLY OPEN TO OUTSIDE SUGGESTIONS (QUESTION 38B)? ARE THE INTERESTS OF IMPORTANT GROUPS USUALLY DISREGARDED IN THE PROCESS OF PUBLIC POLICY-MAKING (QUESTION 38C)?

Region	Usually setting right priorities (% Yes)	Primary source of initiatives (% Yes)	Open to suggestions (% Yes)	Disregard of group interests (% Yes)
BW	74.1	42.1	71.3	34.0
LS	38.8	42.0	56.5	45.5
RA	86.4	69.4	77.1	48.5
LR	80.7	70.0	69.1	50.9
LO	44.4	55.1	54.0	63.3
SI	5.2	50.7	35.4	83.2
CA	80.0	53.8	81.9	58.2
AN	51.7	69.2	65.4	52.3
WA*	42.7	36.0	50.2	45.3
EA	**57.1**	**53.6**	**62.9**	**50.8**

* In the absence of a Welsh regional government at the time, the data refer to the WO.

Source: REGE MZES, 1996.

TABLE A1.9

WHICH CAMPAIGNING PRIVATE INTERESTS GROUPS SHOULD HAVE MORE INFLUENCE IN THE FUTURE (QUESTION 39)?

Region	Strengthening of market forces (% Yes)	Close public–private relations (% Yes)	Safeguarded trade* (% Yes)	Social cohesion (% Yes)	Sustainable growth (% Yes)
BW	84.0	88.7	26.0	70.7	85.5
LS	80.4	87.7	26.7	75.1	87.3
RA	55.9	96.0	7.8	87.5	86.9
LR	59.0	96.1	15.9	78.1	87.0
LO	77.2	92.0	48.0	82.2	89.1
SI	84.3	95.6	53.9	87.2	90.9
CA	71.0	87.8	74.5	87.7	96.4
AN	63.7	93.4	81.3	96.8	89.0
WA	46.3	83.1	56.7	85.5	91.8
EA	**71.2**	**88.3**	**41.8**	**85.4**	**89.9**

Source: REGE MZES, 1996.

A2. Return Ratios and Composition of the Welsh Panel of Respondents

The main part of this project consisted of a questionnaire survey of public, semi-public and private institutions and organisations in Wales, on various themes associated with the structure of the Welsh actor landscape, the nature of politics in Wales, the development of regional interests and means of interest representation, and the impact on ERDF and other EU funds received by Welsh actors. Particular reference was made to the processes of regional development and R&D policy. The data of the questionnaire survey were supplemented by the study of relevant policy documents published by Welsh actors, and a series of interviews[4] with some key representatives of Welsh organisations. (See Tables A2.1–A2.4.)

TABLE A2.1
QUESTIONNAIRES SENT OUT PER AREA AND ACTOR CATEGORY

County	Business interests	Chambers	Trade unions	Companies	Semi-public	Parties/ legislature	Executive	Total
Regional	12	1	12	5	15	14	11	70
Gwent	0	2	0	10	3	7	11	33
South Glamorgan*	1	1	0	32	4	8	5	51
Mid Glamorgan*	3	0	2	8	9	12	12	46
West Glamorgan*	0	2	3	10	6	9	7	37
Powys	3	0	0	1	2	6	6	18
Dyfed	1	0	1	3	8	13	14	40
Gwynedd	1	1	0	1	2	8	9	22
Clwyd	4	2	0	1	7	12	11	37
Total	25	9	18	71	56	89	86	354

* Excluding Cardiff-based regional offices which also serve as sub-regional offices. Those are to be found in the category 'regional'.

Source: REGE Wales, 1996.

TABLE A2.2
RETURNS PER AREA AND ACTOR CATEGORY

County	Un-known	Business interests	Cham-bers	Trade unions	Com-panies	Semi-public	Parties/legislature	Executive-	Total	%*
Regional	0	7	1	4	1	8	5	3	29	23.6
Gwent	0	0	1	0	3	1	1	4	10	8.1
South Glamorgan	0	0	0	0	8	1	1	2	12	9.8
Mid Glamorgan	0	1	0	0	5	3	3	6	18	14.6
West Glamorgan	0	0	0	2	3	2	3	5	15	12.2
Powys	0	1	0	0	0	1	1	2	5	4.1
Dyfed	0	0	0	0	2	6	4	4	16	13.0
Gwynedd	0	0	0	0	0	1	3	1	5	4.1
Clwyd	0	0	1	0	0	2	3	5	11	8.9
Unknown	2	–	–	–	–	–	–	–	2	1.6
Total	**2**	**9**	**3**	**6**	**22**	**25**	**24**	**32**	**123**	**100**
%	1.6	7.3	2.4	4.9	17.9	20.3	19.5	26.0	100	–

* of returns (i.e. 123 = 100%).

Source: REGE Wales, 1996.

TABLE A 2.3
RETURN RATIO PER AREA

County	Out	In	% in
Regional	70	29	41.9
Gwent	33	10	30.3
South Glamorgan	51	12	23.5
Mid Glamorgan	46	18	39.1
West Glamorgan	37	15	40.5
Powys	18	5	27.8
Dyfed	40	16	40.0
Gwynedd	23	5	21.7
Clwyd	37	11	29.7
Unknown	0	2	–
Total	356	123	34.5

Source: REGE Wales, 1996.

TABLE A 2.4
RETURN RATIO PER ACTOR CATEGORY

Actor category	Out	In	% in
Business interest organisations	25	9	36.0
Chambers	9	3	33.3
Trade unions	18	6	33.3
Private companies	71	22	30.9
Semi-public actors	56	25	44.6
Parties/legislative actors	89	24	27.0
Administrations	86	32	34.9
Unknown	0	2	–
Total	356	116	34.5

Source: REGE Wales, 1996.

A3. Text of the REGE Wales Questionnaire

Regions as Political Actors in European Integration (REGE)

Regional Development and its European Dimension in Wales

Definition of terms
For the purpose of this survey, we regard Wales as a **region**.

In our use, the term **Regional Development Policy** comprises the whole complex of supportive measures aimed at the different sectors of the economy, including measures aimed at infrastructure development, the labour market, securing inward investment, vocational training, etc.

The term **Research & Development Policy (R&D)** refers to supportive measures related to the development of innovative products, and the modernisation of production (e.g. by aiding the transfer of innovative technologies, etc.).

Guidelines for filling in this questionnaire
In most cases, you simply need to tick the box ($\Box$) which corresponds most closely to your opinion.

Example:

most certainly					not at all
1	2	3	4	5	6

In some cases you will have the opportunity to state your own answers. In these cases please use CAPITAL LETTERS.

Answer the questions in the order in which they appear and jump ahead only when asked to do so in the text: (Please continue with question No. ...)

If you wish to make comments on any of the questions, or wish to give a more detailed answer, please feel free to do so using a separate sheet (indicating to which question your statement relates).

Having completed the questionnaire, please return it to us in the SAE to:

Prof. John Loughlin
School of European Studies
University of Wales College of Cardiff
P.O. Box 908
Cardiff CF13 YQ ;
Tel: (01222) 874585;
Fax: (01222) 874946;
e-mail: loughlin@cardiff.ac.uk

Thank you very much for your time and effort, it is sincerely appreciated.

This research project is concerned with investigating the position of Wales in relation to the developing integration of the European Union. The questionnaire is designed to shed light on the view of your organisation on this topic.

In the first section, we would like to ask you some questions concerning your perception of the importance of the regional level of administration (Welsh Office), compared to the local, national and EU levels of governance.

1. The general conditions of life in Wales are, to a large degree, shaped by the political system. In this respect, how important are the following levels of governance **at the present time?**

(*Please tick one answer per row.*)

	not important					very important
	1	2	3	4	5	6
Local level	☐	☐	☐	☐	☐	☐
Regional level (Welsh Office)	☐	☐	☐	☐	☐	☐
National level (Westminster)	☐	☐	☐	☐	☐	☐
European level	☐	☐	☐	☐	☐	☐

2. What degree of influence within the EU should Wales and the other UK regions have **in the future?** (*Please tick one box only.*)

They should have:

☐   more influence

☐   same as now

☐   less influence

3. Do you think that a 'Europe of the Regions' will bring about:

	1 not at all	2	3	4	5	6 most certainly
a reduction of regional disparities	☐	☐	☐	☐	☐	☐
a strengthening of already competitive regions	☐	☐	☐	☐	☐	☐
a counterbalance to centralising tendencies	☐	☐	☐	☐	☐	☐
an increase in the complexity of the European decision-making process	☐	☐	☐	☐	☐	☐
more cultural pluralism	☐	☐	☐	☐	☐	☐
closer attention to the needs and desires of individuals	☐	☐	☐	☐	☐	☐

other features (*Please specify*):..

The following questions wish to assess the economic impact of the establishment of the Single European Market on your region.

4. European economic policy is very much market-oriented. To what extent is it useful for Wales to follow this trend?

not at all useful   ☐   ☐   ☐   ☐   ☐   ☐   very useful

5. National economic and industrial policy measures are subject to EU rules regulating competition. To what extent does this produce harmful effects in Wales?

not at all   ☐   ☐   ☐   ☐   ☐   ☐   to a large extent

In our analysis, we are focusing on two policy areas:

a) Regional Development Policy, and b) Research and Development Policy.

For this reason, we would like to ask you some questions about these two policy areas in general, and, more specifically, with regard to the EU.

A.) Regional Development Policy

6. Is your organisation concerned at all with Regional Development Policy (whether national or EU)?

☐   yes
☐   occasionally/to some extent
☐   no (*Please continue with question No. 16.*)

7. From the point of view of your organisation, how important are the following levels of governance for Regional Development Policy? (*Please tick one box per row.*)

	not important				very important	
	1	2	3	4	5	6
Local level	☐	☐	☐	☐	☐	☐
Regional level (Welsh Office)	☐	☐	☐	☐	☐	☐
National level (Westminster)	☐	☐	☐	☐	☐	☐
European level	☐	☐	☐	☐	☐	☐

---

8. In the last 5 years, has your organisation been actively involved in any EU Regional Development Policy measures?

☐   no

☐   yes;

in an Integrated Operational Programme within one of the following programmes:

☐   objective 2 priority

☐   objective 3 priority

☐   objective 4 priority

☐   objective 5b priority

other features (*Please specify*):..

in one of the following Structural Programmes:

☐   INTERREG

☐   RECHAR I/II

☐   RETEX

☐   LEADER

other features (*Please specify*):..

---

9. Critics complain about the small size of funds obtainable, and also the spatial allocation of EU Structural Funds.

---

a) Compared to other regions, does Wales receive:

☐   too little EU Structural Funds?

☐   a satisfactory amount of EU Structural Funds?

b) What do you think about the spatial distribution of these funds within Wales?

	1	2	3	4	5	6	
unfair	☐	☐	☐	☐	☐	☐	fair
☐ don't know							
widely distributed	☐	☐	☐	☐	☐	☐	highly concentrated
☐ don't know							
rigidly earmarked	☐	☐	☐	☐	☐	☐	flexible
☐ don't know							

10. To what extent are the following institutions helpful in assisting your participation in measures of Regional Development Policy? (*Please tick one box per row.*)

☐ Don't know, because my organisation has not yet participated in such measures.

	not helpful				very helpful	
Regional Level (Wales)	1	2	3	4	5	6
Regional Offices of the Chambers of Trade and Industry	☐	☐	☐	☐	☐	☐
Regional Offices of Industrial Organisations and Trade Unions	☐	☐	☐	☐	☐	☐
European Information Centres	☐	☐	☐	☐	☐	☐
Regional Development Agencies	☐	☐	☐	☐	☐	☐
The Welsh Office	☐	☐	☐	☐	☐	☐
Local Authorities and their Institutions	☐	☐	☐	☐	☐	☐
Private Consultants	☐	☐	☐	☐	☐	☐

others; (*Please specify*): ....

National level (UK)						
National Offices of the Chambers of Trade and Industry	☐	☐	☐	☐	☐	☐
National Offices of Industrial Organisations and Trade Unions	☐	☐	☐	☐	☐	☐
UK Government Departments (except Welsh Office)	☐	☐	☐	☐	☐	☐
European Commission in the UK	☐	☐	☐	☐	☐	☐
Welsh MPs and House of Commons Committees	☐	☐	☐	☐	☐	☐
Private Consultants	☐	☐	☐	☐	☐	☐

others; (*Please specify*): ....

European level						
International Business Associations	☐	☐	☐	☐	☐	☐
International Affiliations of UK Industrial Organisations and Trade Unions	☐	☐	☐	☐	☐	☐
Wales European Centre, Brussels	☐	☐	☐	☐	☐	☐
UK Embassy to the European Union	☐	☐	☐	☐	☐	☐
European Commission	☐	☐	☐	☐	☐	☐
Welsh MEPs and the European Parliament	☐	☐	☐	☐	☐	☐
Private Consultants	☐	☐	☐	☐	☐	☐

others; (*Please specify*): ....

☐   In general, none of the institutions mentioned above has been very helpful. Our organisation, therefore, has:

☐   teamed up with others facing similar problems

☐   participated in the measures without external help

☐   undertaken other activities; (*Please specify*): ....

---

11. From the point of view of your organisation, why is it worthwhile to participate in EU measures in the field of Regional Development policy, assuming that this is the case? (*Please tick up to three boxes.*)

☐   Access to additional sources of funding.

☐   Sharing of experience.

☐   Promoting cross-border co-operation between regions.

☐   Promoting cohesion within the region.

☐   Strengthening the position of our region compared to other regions.

☐   Strengthening the position of our own organisation within the region.

☐   Attractiveness of new forms of co-operation between public and private actors within the region, initiated by the European Commission.

☐   Other reasons; (*Please specify*): ....

☐   Participation is not worthwhile.

---

12. Experience suggests that it is not always easy to participate in programmes related to EU regional policy. In the experience of your organisation, which of the following are the most common obstacles preventing participation? (*Please tick up to three boxes.*)

☐   Too big an effort in terms of the paperwork and co-ordination is required.

☐   Essential information is not available or arrives too late.

☐   Bureaucratic obstacles at the national level.

☐   Bureaucratic obstacles at the regional level.

☐   The programmes are not in line with existing needs.

☐   Suitable partners are not available.

☐   Minimum eligibility criteria in terms of scope exceed the size that could be handled by my organisation.

☐   Other obstacles: (*Please specify*): ....

☐   There are no such obstacles.

☐   Because of the reasons indicated above my organisation has refrained from submitting an application.

13. EU Regional Development Policy was reformed in 1988, and again in 1993. Some of the reforms were aimed at introducing procedural changes. In the light of these reforms, how do you perceive the relative influence, either formal or informal, of Local Authorities, the Welsh Office, the Welsh Development Agency, the UK Government, the European Commission, and private actors with regard to the selection of eligible areas, the planning of programmes, the implementation of programmes, monitoring the programmes, and evaluation of the programmes? (*Please tick one box per column in each table.*)

Local Authorities

	Selection of Eligible Areas	Planning of Programmes	Implementation of Programmes	Monitoring of Programmes	Evaluation of Programmes
high influence	☐	☐	☐	☐	☐
intermediate influence	☐	☐	☐	☐	☐
low influence	☐	☐	☐	☐	☐

Welsh Office/Welsh Development Agency

	Selection of Eligible Areas	Planning of Programmes	Implementation of Programmes	Monitoring of Programmes	Evaluation of Programmes
high influence	☐	☐	☐	☐	☐
intermediate influence	☐	☐	☐	☐	☐
low influence	☐	☐	☐	☐	☐

UK Government

	Selection of Eligible Areas	Planning of Programmes	Implementation of Programmes	Monitoring of Programmes	Evaluation of Programmes
high influence	☐	☐	☐	☐	☐
intermediate influence	☐	☐	☐	☐	☐
low influence	☐	☐	☐	☐	☐

European Commission

	Selection of Eligible Areas	Planning of Programmes	Implementation of Programmes	Monitoring of Programmes	Evaluation of Programmes
high influence	☐	☐	☐	☐	☐
intermediate influence	☐	☐	☐	☐	☐
low influence	☐	☐	☐	☐	☐

(*To be continued on following page.*)

Private Actors in Wales

	Selection of Eligible Areas	Planning of Programmes	Implementation of Programmes	Monitoring of Programmes	Evaluation of Programmes
high influence	☐	☐	☐	☐	☐
intermediate influence	☐	☐	☐	☐	☐
low influence	☐	☐	☐	☐	☐

14.a) Is your organisation a member of a monitoring committee for evaluating the implementation of EU Structural Programmes?

☐ yes   ☐ no (*If no, please continue with question No. 15.*)

b) If yes, how would you describe the strength of your organisation's influence within the committee?

very low   ☐   ☐   ☐   ☐   ☐   ☐   very high

c) Is the position of your organisation usually in line with the decisions taken by the committee?

☐ always   ☐ sometimes   ☐ never

d) How would you describe the 'atmosphere' of the discussions within the committee?

quite conflictual   ☐   ☐   ☐   ☐   ☐   ☐   quite co-operative

---

15. Which of the following reforms of EU Structural Development Policy, related to procedural changes, would you prefer? (*Please tick one box only.*)

☐   The EU advertises availability and applicants submit their proposals directly.

☐   The regional, national and European levels of government agree upon the distribution of Structural Funds.

☐   The management of the programmes is the responsibility of national governments.

☐   The funds are distributed among the regions, whose responsibility it is to see to an efficient and appropriate use of the funds.

☐   The task of selecting and implementing the programmes is to be carried out on a sub-regional level.

☐   Other: (*Please specify*): ....

B.)   **Research and Development Policy**

Since the early 1980s, EU Research & Development Policy (R&D) has become more important. As participation by organisations of various kinds is seen by some as an important aspect of this policy, we would like to ask you some questions concerning your organisation in this policy area.

16. Is your organisation concerned at all with Research & Development Policy (R&D) (at national, regional or EU levels)?

☐ yes   ☐ occasionally/to some extent   ☐ no (*Please continue with question No. 23.*)

17. From the point of view of your organisation, how important are the following levels of government in the field of R&D?

	not important				very important	
	1	2	3	4	5	6
Local level	☐	☐	☐	☐	☐	☐
Regional level (Welsh Office)	☐	☐	☐	☐	☐	☐
National level (Westminster)	☐	☐	☐	☐	☐	☐
European level	☐	☐	☐	☐	☐	☐

18. In the last five years, have you been actively involved in any measures of EU R&D?

☐ no
☐ yes; in the EU Framework Programme(s):
☐ ESPRIT   ☐ BRITE/EURAM   ☐ RACE   ☐ STRIDE

☐   Other; (*Please specify*): ....

19. To what extent are the following institutions helpful in assisting your participation in measures of R & D Policy?

☐ Don't know, because my organisation has not yet participated in such measures.

	not helpful				very helpful	
Regional Level (Wales)	1	2	3	4	5	6
Regional Offices of the Chambers of Trade and Industry	☐	☐	☐	☐	☐	☐
Regional Offices of Industrial Organisations and Trade Unions	☐	☐	☐	☐	☐	☐

European Information Centres	☐	☐	☐	☐	☐	☐
Regional Development Agencies	☐	☐	☐	☐	☐	☐
The Welsh Office	☐	☐	☐	☐	☐	☐
Local Authorities and their Institutions	☐	☐	☐	☐	☐	☐
Private Consultants	☐	☐	☐	☐	☐	☐

Others; (*Please specify*): ....

National level (UK)

National Offices of the Chambers of Trade and Industry	☐	☐	☐	☐	☐	☐
National Offices of Industrial Organisations and Trade Unions	☐	☐	☐	☐	☐	☐
UK Government Departments (except Welsh Office)	☐	☐	☐	☐	☐	☐
European Commission in the UK	☐	☐	☐	☐	☐	☐
Welsh MPs and House of Commons Committees	☐	☐	☐	☐	☐	☐
Private Consultants	☐	☐	☐	☐	☐	☐

Others; (*Please specify*): ....

European level

International Business Associations	☐	☐	☐	☐	☐	☐
International Affiliations of UK Industrial Organisations and Trade Unions	☐	☐	☐	☐	☐	☐
Wales European Centre, Brussels	☐	☐	☐	☐	☐	☐
UK Embassy to the European Union	☐	☐	☐	☐	☐	☐
European Commission	☐	☐	☐	☐	☐	☐
Welsh MEPs and the European Parliament	☐	☐	☐	☐	☐	☐
Private Consultants	☐	☐	☐	☐	☐	☐

Others; (*Please specify*): ....

In general, none of the institutions mentioned above has been very helpful. Our organisation, therefore, has:

☐   teamed up with others facing similar problems
☐   participated in the measures without external help
☐   undertaken other activities; (*Please specify*): ....

20. From the point of view of your organisation, why is it worthwhile to participate in EU Research & Development Policy (R&D) measures? (*Please tick up to three boxes.*)

☐   Access to additional sources of funding.

☐   Sharing of experience.

☐   Additional innovative potential through European co-operation.

☐   The EU runs a promising strategy of promotion.

☐   Improvement of our own reputation.

☐   Other reasons; (*Please specify*): ....

☐   A participation is not worthwhile.

21. On the basis of your organisation's experience, which of the following are the most common obstacles preventing participation in programmes related to EU R&D Policy? (*Please tick up to three boxes.*)

☐   Too big an effort in terms of preparation work and co-ordination required.

☐   Essential information not available or available too late.

☐   The programmes are not in line with existing needs.

☐   The structure of the programmes is too complex for Small and Medium Enterprises.

☐   Applications have too slim a chance of acceptance.

☐   Suitable partners are not available.

☐   Minimum eligibility criteria exceed what could be handled by my organisation.

☐   Other obstacles; (*Please specify*): ....

☐   There are no obstacles.

☐   For the reasons indicated above my organisation has refrained from submitting an application.

22. EU Research & Development Policy has spatial implications. Do you therefore think that the Welsh Office and/or the Welsh Development Agency should have a direct say in the process of developing and shaping R&D programmes?

☐   yes

☐   no

Close co-operation (even if informal) between the various kinds of organisation is sometimes regarded as very important for economic development within a region. This goes not only for the economy, but also for politics. Therefore, we would now like to ask you some questions about organisations which operate in your region; and about the relations between these organisations.

23. We would like to know which of the following institutions you regard as important for the development of Wales.(Please indicate in the first column.) We would also like you to indicate (In the second box) with which of those institutions you have regular contacts. (*Please tick as many boxes as you like.*)

	Important Organisation	Regular Contacts
1. Commission, DG XII (Science, R&D)	☐	☐
2. Commission, DG XVI (Regional Policy; before '92: DG XXII)	☐	☐
3. Commission, DG VI (Agriculture)	☐	☐
4. Commission, other DGs	☐	☐
5. UK Embassy to the EU	☐	☐
6. International Affiliations of UK Industrial Organisations	☐	☐
7. International Affiliations of UK Trade Unions	☐	☐
8. Committee of the Regions	☐	☐
9. European Parliament Committees	☐	☐
10. Welsh European Centre, Brussels	☐	☐
11. Welsh MEPs	☐	☐
12. Cabinet Office	☐	☐
13. Department of the Environment	☐	☐
14. Department of Trade and Industry	☐	☐
15. Other UK Government Departments (except Welsh Office)	☐	☐
16. House of Lords	☐	☐
17. House of Commons/Welsh MPs	☐	☐
18. National Offices of Industrial Organisations	☐	☐
19. TUC and National Offices of Trade Unions	☐	☐
20. The Secretary of State for Wales	☐	☐
21. Welsh Office (WO) Industry Department	☐	☐
22. WO Agriculture Department	☐	☐
23. WO Economic Development & Training Group	☐	☐
24. WO Legal Group	☐	☐
25. WO Establishments Group	☐	☐
26. WO Finance Group	☐	☐
27. WO Transport, Planning and Environment Group	☐	☐
28. WO Local Government Reorganisation Group	☐	☐

(*To be continued on following page*)

	Important Organisation	Regular Contacts
29. Welsh Development Agency (WDA) Board	☐	☐
30. WDA International Division	☐	☐
31. WDA Area Divisions	☐	☐
32. Development Board for Rural Wales	☐	☐
33. Land Authority for Wales	☐	☐
34. County Councils	☐	☐
35. County Council Planning Departments	☐	☐
36. District/City Councils	☐	☐
37. District/City Council Planning Departments	☐	☐
38. Local Development Agencies	☐	☐
39. Confederation of British Industry Wales	☐	☐
40. Federation of Small Businesses	☐	☐
41. Wales Chamber of Commerce and Industry	☐	☐
42. Industrial Organisations (incl. NFU and FUW)	☐	☐
43. South Wales Exporters Association	☐	☐
44. Wales Trades Union Council	☐	☐
45. Transport and General Workers Union, Wales	☐	☐
46. UNISON Wales	☐	☐
47. Local TECs	☐	☐
48. Advanced Technology Centres	☐	☐
49. European Information Centres	☐	☐
50. Wales Quality Centre	☐	☐
51. R&D Units of Major Companies in Wales	☐	☐
52. Research Institutes of Welsh Universities	☐	☐
53. Regional/Local Organisations of Political Parties	☐	☐

54. Other important Organisations (*Please specify*):

....   ☐   ☐

....   ☐   ☐

....   ☐   ☐

....   ☐   ☐

....   ☐   ☐

24. Consultative measures involving public and private actors take place at various levels. At which level(s) is your organisation participating in such consultations? (*Please state which is, in your view, the most important consultative body for each level, and name the leading organisation in it.*)

☐ European level:..   Leading organisation:.....................................
☐ National level: ....   Leading organisation:.....................................
☐ Regional level: ....   Leading organisation:.....................................
☐ Local level: ....   Leading organisation:.....................................
☐ We do not participate at any level.

25. In your opinion, what is the most important reason for participating in such consultations? (*Please tick one box only.*)

☐ Obtaining information.
☐ Developing useful contacts.
☐ Involvement in important decision-making processes.
☐ To be where it is important to be and to be seen there.

☐ Other reasons (*Please specify*): ....

☐ It is useless to participate.

Recently, governments in several EU member states have started to set up joint consultative bodies involving a number of interested organisations (public, non-governmental, and private). These bodies have been created with the intention of discussing potential problems related to controversial issues.

26. Do you think that this might be a useful approach to problem-solving?

not useful   ☐   ☐   ☐   ☐   ☐   ☐   very useful

27. In your opinion, what would be the most important advantage of such consultative bodies? (*Please tick one box only.*)

☐ It is probably better to discuss issues there rather than in public.
☐ Utilising the expertise of a broad range of organisations and interest groups should lead to improved public policy-making.
☐ New concepts will be developed in these settings and the participants will share the responsibility for their implementation.

☐ Other (*Please specify*): ....

28. What, in your opinion, would be the most important disadvantage of such joint consultative bodies? (*Please tick one box only.*)

☐ It would be just another talking shop.
☐ No-one would be prepared to accept responsibility.
☐ Participation would be very time-consuming.

☐ Other (*Please specify*): ....

29. Are you aware of the existence of any such joint consultative bodies in Wales?

☐ yes   ☐ no (*please continue with question No. 36.*)

30. Does your organisation participate in such joint consultative bodies?

☐ yes   ☐ no

31. In general, is participation in these consultative bodies important for you?

not important   ☐   ☐   ☐   ☐   ☐   ☐   very important
☐ I just think it would be worthwhile to be informed about the proceedings.

32. In your opinion, which is the most important consultative body in Wales? (*Please state.*)

....

33. How easy was it for your organisation to become a member of such consultative bodies?

difficult   ☐   ☐   ☐   ☐   ☐   ☐   easy

34. How would you describe the relations among members of the consultative body?

hierarchical   ☐   ☐   ☐   ☐   ☐   ☐   egalitarian

35. In the long run, do you expect that these consultative bodies will:

☐ become rather institutionalised ☐ remain informal and spontaneous?

In this section, we would like to know how your organisation perceives the 'political climate' in Wales.

36. How would you characterise the nature of politics in Wales?

innovative	☐	☐	☐	☐	☐	☐	conservative
controversial	☐	☐	☐	☐	☐	☐	consensus-based
market-oriented	☐	☐	☐	☐	☐	☐	state interventionist
ideological/partisan	☐	☐	☐	☐	☐	☐	focusing on personal relations

37. In your opinion, do the following bodies usually set the right priorities for economic development in Wales?

a) The Welsh Office

☐ yes   ☐ no

b) The Welsh Development Agency?

☐ yes   ☐ no

38. How would you describe relations between the public sector and the economy in Wales?

a) Initiatives are primarily developed by the Welsh Office.

never   ☐ ☐ ☐ ☐ ☐ ☐   always

b) Politicians and civil servants are open to suggestions from the business community and the wider society.

never   ☐ ☐ ☐ ☐ ☐ ☐   always

c) In public policy-making, the interests of important economic and social groups will be disregarded.

never   ☐ ☐ ☐ ☐ ☐ ☐   always

39. From the point of view of your organisation, which of the following groups should have more influence?

Those campaigning for:

	agree wholeheartedly					don't agree at all
strengthening of market forces	☐	☐	☐	☐	☐	☐
close co-operation between state and economy	☐	☐	☐	☐	☐	☐
safeguarded trade	☐	☐	☐	☐	☐	☐
social cohesion	☐	☐	☐	☐	☐	☐
environmentally sustainable growth	☐	☐	☐	☐	☐	☐

other issues; (*Please specify*): ....

Now we would like to ask you some questions concerning the ways and means utilised by your organisation in dealing with the challenges emanating from the EU.

40. Which measures of internal reorganisation have been undertaken in order to accommodate those challenges?

☐ none (*Please continue with question No. 42.*)

My organisation has:

☐ created a department/desk dealing with EU matters

☐ broadened the scope of activity of existing departments/desks to take into account EU matters

☐ established an adequate co-ordinating procedure between the departments/desks concerned with EU matters

41.a) Since these arrangements have been introduced, how many of the employees of your organisation are now dealing with EU matters? (*Please state percentage of total workforce.*)

.... %.

b) Have they all previously dealt with EU matters?

☐ yes   ☐ no

42. There are a number of conceivable strategies which aim to enhance one's position in negotiations with the EU. Which of the following are, in your opinion, the most promising? (*Please tick up to three boxes.*)

☐ A broad coalition of forces at the regional level
☐ Close co-operation among those mainly concerned with EU matters
☐ Transnational co-operation with partners in other EU member states
☐ Securing and strengthening one's own position by using organisations and social scientists who are experts on the economy
☐ Exercising influence via informal channels
☐ Organising public pressure

☐ Other strategies (Please specify): ....

43. If you compare your strategy with regard to Europe with how you pursue your interests in your dealings with the UK government, do you think that it is:

☐ simply refurbishing the same old methods; or
☐ developing an innovative approach?

44. In general, at which level do you think that it has become easier to represent your interests?

Through:
☐ local channels
☐ regional channels
☐ national channels
☐ transnational European channels

45. Do you think that over the last few years relations between the public sector and the economy have changed because of the increasing importance of the EU?

☐ yes   ☐ no

If yes: Do you think this is ...

☐ good   ☐ not so good?

46. Our survey is dealing with 'Wales in Europe', and with forms of co-operation between public and private actors in Wales. Are there any other aspects in this field which in your opinion deserve our attention? (*Please state.*)

....

....

....

....

....

....

....

....

....

....

....

....

....

....

....

Again, thank you very much indeed for your time and co-operation. Now please return the questionnaire to us in the SAE provided.

NOTES

1   The German project title is *Regionales Regieren in Europa: Regionen als Handlungseinheiten in der europäischen Politik.*

2.   An enivisaged inclusion of a second UK region, the West Midlands, had to be cancelled due to lack of funding. To fill this gap, an additional study by John Loughlin, Jörg Mathias and Adrian Reilly has since been published (see Loughlin *et al.*, 1998a).

3.   For the text of these questions, see the questionnaire in Appendix A 3.

4.   These interviews are not identical with those listed in Appendix B 3.1., which gives the interviews held for this study. The REGE interviews referred to here followed the semi-structured approach common to REGE (see Knodt, 1998a), which differs from the structure used for this study (see Appendix B 2.).

Appendix B:
Overview of Interviews

B1. INTERVIEW METHODOLOGY

The interviews listed below were held between May 1995 and May 1999. In order to minimise the number of necessary interviews, the interview partners were selected according to two criteria: (i) their representativeness for a particular actor category, and (ii) their previously demonstrated knowledge of, and involvement in, measures of regional development. To secure comprehensive and frank responses, in each case it was agreed at the beginning of the interview that it would be held under strict assurances of confidentiality, commonly known as Chatham House Rules. For this reason, only the name of the institutions represented by those interviewed partners and the year of the interview can be published, and direct quotes have to be paraphrased. No tape recordings were made, but notes taken during the interview are on file along with the dates, and details of individual officers and employees concerned. I am very grateful to all those who were interviewed for their generous provision of information and research material, without which this study could not have been done.[1] However, the responsibility for any inaccuracies that may have occurred is mine alone.

The interviews in Wales were conducted in English, those in Saxony were conducted in German. In each case these were semi-structured interviews which to some extent – but not entirely – mirrored the lines of questioning in the REGE study. A greater emphasis than in the REGE study was placed on the performance of public actors, in particular public administrations. The precise phrasing of the questions varied according to the individual circumstances of the region and the institution or organisation interviewed. Both the Welsh and the Saxon interviews followed the basic standard structure outlined below, but in Wales, for which the REGE data were available, fewer background and explanatory questions needed to be asked. Therefore, the average interview duration in Wales was 45 minutes, in Saxony 80 minutes.[2]

B2. STANDARD INTERVIEW STRUCTURE

1. *The organisation interviewed and its role in the political and/or economic system of the region.*
- legal base and formal functions of the organisation as a whole;
- specific functions of the department/desk/section represented by the interviewee within that organisation.

2. *General perceptions of the organisation's political and economic environment.*
- the relative importance of the levels of government within the EU;
- the role of regions in the EU, and in the UK (Wales only) or Germany (Saxony only);
- advantages and disadvantages of the current economic situation.

3. *Participation of the organisation in regional development policy.*
- past and current projects;
- funding received (sources, programmes, approximate amounts);
- experiences concerning various aspects of conducting projects (planning, application procedures, financial management, external supervision, perceptions of success or failure).

4. *The performance of public actors.*[3]
- involvement in policy-making, project administration, and evaluation;
- involvement in interest representation, and mediation of conflicts of interest;
- involvement in regional and interregional network-building, and in public–private partnerships;
- perceptions of success and failure (why)?;
- ideas for performance improvement.

5. *The way forward for regional development.*
- economic, infrastructure, and human development tasks;
- changes to the political and administrative systems;
- future role(s) of the EU in regional development;
- visions (wish lists), and strategic planning of the organisation interviewed.

B3. Institutions Interview in Wales

Public Actors

Blaenau Gwent County Borough Council, Ebbw Vale	1997
Council, City and County of Cardiff	1998
Development Board for Rural Wales, Newtown	1996
Employment Service Wales, Cardiff	1997
HM Customs and Excise, Private Office, Cardiff	1996
Merthyr Tydfil County Borough Council, Merthyr Tydfil	1997
Mid Glamorgan County Council, Cardiff	1996
Neath and Port Talbot County Borough Council, Neath	1997
Rhondda Cynon Taff County Borough Council, Mountain Ash	1996
South Pembrokeshire District Council, Pembroke	1997
Welsh Office, Business Services Division, Cardiff	1997

Semi-Public and Private Actors

Community Development Foundation Wales, Neath	1995
The Export Association, Welshpool	1996
John Lane Business Consulting Ltd., Swansea	1996
Liberal Democrats Wales, Cardiff	1995
National Rivers Authority, Cardiff	1996
Newport Development Board, Newport	1997
South Glamorgan TEC, Cardiff	1996
Wales Chamber of Commerce and Industry, Cardiff	1995
Wales Council for Voluntary Action, Welshpool	1996
Welsh European Forum, Cardiff	1995
Wales Labour Party, EU Expert, Cardiff	1995
Wales Labour Party, Domestic Politics Expert, Cardiff	1996
	and 1999
Welsh Development Agency, International Division, Cardiff	1996

B4. Institutions Interviewed in Saxony

Public Actors

Arbeitsamt Leipzig	1997
Oberbergamt Freiberg	1997
Regierungspräsidium Chemnitz	1996
Regierungspräsidium Dresden	1996
Regierungspräsidium Leipzig	1997

Sächsische Landeszentrale für Politische Bildung	1997
Sächsische Staatskanzlei, Büro des Beauftragten für Bundes- und Europaangelegenheiten, Dresden	1996
Sächsisches Staatsministerium für Landwirtschaft, Ernährung und Forsten, Dresden	1996
Sächsisches Staatsministerium für Wirtschaft und Arbeit, Dresden	1996
Sächsisches Staatsministerium für Umwelt und Landesentwicklung, Dresden	1996
Staatliches Amt für Ländliche Neuordnung, Oberlungwitz	1997
Stadt Dresden, Amt für Wirtschaftsförderung	1996
Stadt Leipzig, Amt für Wirtschaftsförderung	1996
Stadt Merseburg⁴, Amt für Wirtschaftsförderung	1996
Statistisches Landesamt des Freistaates Sachsen, Kamenz	1998

Semi-Public and Private Actors

AGIL Agentur für Innovationsförderung und Technologietransfer GmbH, Leipzig	1997
Beratungsgesellschaft für Technologietransfer und Innovationstechnik mbH, Dresden	1997
CDU Sachsen, Landtagsfraktion	1996
CDU, Leipzig	1998
Europa-Haus Leipzig, EU-Informationsstelle	1996
FDP, Leipzig	1997
Flughafen Leipzig-Halle GmbH	1998
Industrie-und Handelskammer Südwestsachsen, Chemnitz	1996
Industrie- und Handelskammer zu Leipzig	1997
Landesverband der Sächsischen Industrie e.V., Dresden	1997
Mittelständische Beteiligungsgesellschaft Sachsen mbH, Dresden	1997
Neues Forum, Leipzig	1996
PDS, Leipzig	1998
RC Innovation Relay Center, Leipzig	1998
SPD Sachsen, AG Europa	1996
SPD Sachsen, Landesvorstand	1996
SPD Sachsen, Landtagsfraktion	1996
Wirtschaftsagentur Halle/Leipzig GmbH	1997
Wirtschaftsförderung Sachsen GmbH, Dresden	1997

NOTES

1. Payment for verbal information was neither offered nor requested. However, payment for printed material designed for public sale, and for photocopying and postage fees (excluding REGE-related expenses) was made in a total of 48 instances, in the UK totalling £108.50, and in Germany DM 244.90.
2. I am particularly grateful to those interviewed in the Saxon institutions and organisations who gave their time so generously. Although the interviews were scheduled to last one hour, most interviews lasted way beyond 60 minutes.
3. Public actors of the same category and level in the same region (e.g. two Saxon State Ministries or two *Regierungspräsidien*) were not asked to comment upon each other, in order keep those interviewed at ease. Some of these actors, however, volunteered such comments without prompting.
4. Although Merseburg is located in Saxony-Anhalt, it is part of the RTP region which straddles the border between Saxony and Saxony-Anhalt.

Bibliography

Anderson, J. J., 1990, 'Sceptical Reflections on a Europe of the Regions: Britain, Germany, and the ERDF', *Journal of Public Policy*, 10, 4, pp. 417–47.

Anderson, J. J., 1995, 'Regional Policy and Politics in a United Germany', *Regional & Federal Studies*, 5, 1, pp. 28–44.

Angst, D., 1993, 'Ausbau und Struktur der Umweltverwaltung in den neuen Bundesländern am Beispiel des Freistaates Sachsen', in W. Seibel et al., *Verwaltungsreform und Verwaltungspolitik im Prozeß der deutschen Einigung* (Baden-Baden: Nomos), pp. 421–7.

Armstrong, H., 1995, 'The Role and Evolution of European Community Regional Policy', in M. Keating and B. Jones (eds), *The European Union and the Regions* (Oxford: Clarendon Press), pp. 23–62.

Ast, S., 1998, 'Institutionelle Anpassungsreaktionen im Europäischen Mehrebenensystem?', *Die Öffentliche Verwaltung*, 13 (July 1998), pp. 535–43.

Aurig, R., S. Herzog and S. Lässig (eds), 1997, *Landesgeschichte in Sachsen: Tradition und Innovation* (Dresden: Sächsische Landeszentrale für politische Bildung).

Balsom, D., 2000, *Wales Yearbook 2000* (Cardiff: HTV Wales).

Bannister, N., 1998, 'Watchdogs held at bay', *Guardian*, 5 February, p. 19.

Benz, A., 1993, 'Reformbedarf und Reformchancen des kooperativen Föderalismus nach der Vereinigung Deutschlands', in W. Seibel et al., *Verwaltungsreform und Verwaltungspolitik im Prozeszelt der deutschen Einigung* (Baden-Baden: Nomos Verlagsgesellschaft) pp. 454–73.

Bettinson, C., 1996, 'Editorial', *Council News* 1996, [Cardiff Council explanatory leaflet accompanying the annual Council Tax Bill] (Cardiff: City and County of Cardiff) p. 1.

Bettinson, C., 1998, 'Editorial', *Council News* 1998 (Cardiff: City and County of Cardiff), p. 1.

Bettinson, C., 1999, 'Editorial', *Council News* 1999 (Cardiff: City and County of Cardiff), p. 1.

Biedenkopf, K., 1998, 'Besuch in Niesky', *Neue Bundesländer Illustrierte*, 27/98, Special Issue for the 1998 general elections, sponsored by the CDU, pp. 24–5.

Biedenkopf, K., 1998a, *Wir sind nicht der Osten, wir sind Sachsen*, 1999/2000 Budget Speech (Dresden: Sächsische Staatskanzlei).

Blackaby, D., 1994, 'Wales: An Economic Survey', *Contemporary Wales*, 7, pp. 173–259.

Bramke, W. and U. Heß, 1998, *Wirtschaft und Gesellschaft in Sachsen im 20. Jahrhundert* (Leipzig: Leipziger Universitätsverlag).

Bullmann, U. (ed.), 1994, *Die Politik der dritten Ebene* (Baden-Baden: Nomos Verlagsgesellschaft).

Bundesrat, 1995, *Forderungen der Länder zur Regierungskonferenz 1996*, Drucksache 667/95.

Bundesverband der Katholischen Arbeitnehmerbewegung (KAB; eds), 1975, *Texte zur Katholischen Soziallehre* (Kevelaer: Verlag Butzon & Bercker).

Bundeszentrale für Politische Bildung (ed.), 1990, *Verträge zur deutschen Einheit* (Bonn: BZfPB).

Bundeszentrale für Politische Bildung (ed.), 1994, *Grundgesetz für die Bundesrepublik Deutschland*, 1994 edn (Bonn: BZfPB).

Carter, H., and H. M. Griffiths (eds), 1987, *National Atlas of Wales* (Cardiff: University of Wales Press).

Chapman, L., 1978, *Your Disobedient Servant. The Continuing Story of Whitehall Overspending* (London: Penguin Books).

Christiansen, T., 1995, 'Second Thoughts – The Committee of the Regions after its First Year', in R. Dehousse and T. Christiansen (eds), *What Model for the Committee of the Regions? Past Experiences and Future Perspectives*, EUI Working Paper No. EUF 95/2 (Florence: European University Institute), pp. 34–64.

Christiansen, T., 1997, 'The Committee of the Regions and the 1996 IGC Conference: Institutional Reform', *Regional and Federal Studies*, 7, 1, pp. 50–69.

City of Leipzig, Economic Development Office (ed.), 1996, *Wirtschaftsraum Leipzig*, Investors' Prospectus, 2nd edn (Leipzig: City of Leipzig).

Confederation of British Industry (CBI) (eds) *The Single Market and the Future Development of the European Union. Survey Results* (London: CBI).

Conzelmann, T., 1995, ' Networking and the Politics of EU Regional Policy: Lessons from North Rhine-Westphalia, Nord-Pas de Calais and North West England', *Regional and Federal Studies*, 5, 2, pp. 134–72.

Cooke, P., 1992, 'Regional Innovation Systems: Competitive Regulation in the New Europe', *Geoforum*, 23, 3, pp. 365–82.

Cooke, P., and K. Morgan, 1998, *The Associational Economy* (Oxford: Oxford University Press).

Cooke, P. K. Morgan and A. Price 1993, 'Regulating Regional Economies: Wales and Baden-Württemberg in Transition', in M. Rhodes (ed.), *The Regions and the New Europe* (Manchester: Manchester University Press).

Cram, L., 1996, 'Integration theory and the study of the European Policy process', in J. Richardson (ed.), *European Union: Power and policy-making* (London and New York: Routledge), pp. 40–58.

Cram, L., 1997, *Policy-making in the European Union. Conceptual lenses and the integration process* (London: Routledge).

Davies, P., 1996, 'No fanfare for miners' event of the year', *The Western Mail* (4 July), p. 4.

Day, G. and G. Rees, 1991, *Regions, Nations and European Integration. Remaking the Celtic Periphery* (Cardiff: University of Wales Press).

Development Board for Rural Wales (eds), 1997, *Rural Wales 1996/97: Challenge, Change and Achievement* (Newtown: DBRW).

Drehwald, S. and C. Jestaedt, 1998, *Sachsen als Verfassungsstaat* (Dresden: Sächsische Landeszentrale für politische Bildung).

Eißel, D., A. Grasse, B. Paeschke and R. Sänger, 1999, *Interregionale Zusammenarbeit in der EU. Analysen zur Partnerschaft zwischen Hessen, der Eimilia-Romagna und der Aquitaine* (Opladen: Leske + Budrich).

Elcock, H., 1997, 'The North of England and The Europe of the Regions, or, when is a Region not a Region?', in M. Keating and J. Loughlin (eds), *The Political Economy of Regionalism* (London: Frank Cass).

Europäische Kommission, 1994, *Sammlung der Gemeinschaftsbestimmungen über die soziale Sicherheit*, 4th edn (Luxemburg: Amt für Amtliche Vetröffentlichungen).

Europäische Komission, Vertretung in der Bundesrepublik Deutschland, 1995, *Sachsen in der Europäischen Union* (Luxemburg: Amt für Amtliche Veröffentlichungen).

European Commission, 1994, *EC Structural Funds: Rural Wales – Objective 5b Single Planning Document 1994–1999* (Luxembourg: Office for Official Publications).

European Commission, DG for Regional Policy and Cohesion, 1995, 'The structural funds and the reconversion of regions affected by industrial decline in the United Kingdom, 1994–1996', CX–89–95–688–EN–C, *inforegio* (May) EN.

European Commission in the UK (eds), 1995, *Wales in the European Union* (London: HMSO).

Evans, C. and E. George, 1999, *Swings and Roundabouts: What really happened on May 6?* (Cardiff: Welsh Labour Action, 1999).

Evans, J., 1998, *'The Committee of the Regions'*, Conference Paper, given at the ECPR Standing Group on Regionalism Conference 'Culture, Nation and Region in Europe', Cardiff, 10–12 September.

Evans, N. (ed.), 1989, *National Identities in the British Isles*, Coleg Harlech Occasional Papers in Welsh Studies, No. 3 (Harlech: Coleg Harlech).

Falkner, G. and M. Nentwich, 1995, *European Union: Democratic Perspectives after 1996* (Vienna: Service Fachverlag).

Farrows, M., and R. McCarthy, 1997, 'Opinion formulation and Impact in the Committee of the Regions', *Regional and Federal Studies*, 7, 1, pp. 23–49.

Federation of Small Businesses (eds), 1994, *Agenda for Enterprise. FSB Policy Guide* (London: FSB).

Fischer, T. and S. Frech (eds), 2001, *Baden-Württemberg und seine Partnerregionen* (Stuttgart: W. Kohlhammer Verlag).

Foulkes, D., J. B. Jones and R. A. Wilford (eds), 1983, *The Welsh Veto* (Cardiff: University of Wales Press).

Fraser, M. (ed.), 1998, *Britain in Europe: The Next Phase* (London: Stratagems Publishing).

Gensior, W. and V. Krieg, 1994, *Wahlrechtsfibel: Wahlrecht und Wahlverfahren in der Bundesrepublik Deutschland und im Freistaat Sachsen* (Darmstadt: NDV).

Gosling, N., 2000, 'Russel should give up Payrise', *The Welsh Mirror* (22 January), p. 2.

Grote, J., 1983, 'Regionale Vernetzung: Interorganisatorische Strukturdifferenzen regionaler Politikgestaltung', in B. Kohler Koch u.a., *Interaktive Politik in Europa: Regionen im Netzwerk der Integration* (Opladen: Leske+Budrich), pp. 62–74.

Haas, E., 1958, *The Uniting of Europe: Political, Social and Economic Forces, 1950–1957* (Stanford, CA: Stanford University Press).

Haas, E., 1964, *Beyond the Nation-State: Functionalism and International Organisation* (Stanford, CA: Stanford University Press).

Haas, E., 1970, 'The Study of Regional Integration: Reflections on the Joys and Anguish of Pretheorizing', *International Organisation*, 24, 4, pp. 607–46.

Hertle, H.-H., M. Junkernheinrich, W. Koch and G. Nooke (eds) 1998, *Vom Ende der DDR-Wirtschaft zum Neubeginn in den ostdeutschen Bundesländern* (Hannover: Niedersächsische Landeszentrale für politische Bildung).

Hill, S. and J. Keegan, 1993, *Made in Wales: An Analysis of Welsh Manufacturing Performance* (Cardiff: CBI Wales).

Hooghe, L., 1995, *Subnational Mobilisation in the European Union*, EUI Working Paper No. RSC 95/6 (Florence: European University Institute).

Hooghe, L., and G. Marks, 1995, 'Channels of Subnational Interest Representation in the European Union', in R. Dehousse and T. Christiansen (eds), *What Model for the Committee of the Regions? Past*

Experiences and Future Perspectives, EUI Working Paper No. EUF 95/2 (Florence: European University Institute), pp. 6–33.

Home Office (eds), 1999, *European Parliament Elections: How the new voting system works*, [Information leaflet for voters] (London: Home Office Communication Directorate).

House of Commons, *Regional Policy*, Fourth Report, Trade and Industry Committee, 1994/95, HC Paper 356–I, London: HMSO.

House of Commons, *Wales in Europe*, Fourth Report, Welsh Affairs Committee, HoC Paper 393–I (Report) and 393–II (Minutes of Evidence and Appendices) (London: HMSO, 1995a).

House of Commons, 1997, *A Voice for Wales. The Government's proposals for a Welsh Assembly*, Cmnd 3781 (London: HMSO).

Hrbek, R. and S. Weyand, 1994, *betrifft: Das Europa der Regionen*, (München: Verlag C. H. Beck).

Ihlau, O. and D. Pieper, 1996, 'Ein Stück Karl May ist mit drin', Interview with the Saxon Prime Minister K. Biedenkopf, *Der Spiegel*, 32/96 (8 August), pp. 34–8.

Jeffery, C., 1996, *The Regional Dimension of the European Union. Toward a 'Third Level' in Europe?* (London: Frank Cass).

Jeffery, C., 1996a, 'Conclusions: Sub-National Authorities and "European Domestic Policy"', *Regional and Federal Studies*, 6, 2, pp. 204–19.

Jeffery, C., 1996b, 'Regional Information Offices in Brussels and Multilevel Governance in the EU: A UK-German Comparison', *Regional and Federal Studies*, 6, 2, pp. 183–203.

Jessop, B. et al., 1988, *Thatcherism: A Tale of Two Nations* (Cambridge: Polity Press).

Jones, B. and R. A. Wilford, 1983, 'Implications: Two Salient Issues', in D. Foulkes, B. Jones and R. A. Wilford (eds), *The Welsh Veto* (Cardiff: University of Wales Press), pp. 216–30.

Junkernheinrich, M., 1998, 'Die Revitalisierung der ostdeutschen Wirtschaft: Anmerkungen zur ökonomischen Integration der neuen Bundesländer', in H.-H., Hertle, et al., *Vom Ende der DDR-Wirtschaft zum Neubeginn in den ostdeutschen Bundesländern* (Hannover: Niedersächsische Landeszentrale für politische Bildung).

Keating, M., 1992, 'Regional Autonomy in the Changing State Order: A Framework of Analysis', *Regional Politics and Policy*, 2, 3, pp. 45–61.

Keating, M., 1995, 'Europeanism and Regionalism', in B. Jones and M. Keating (eds), *The European Union and the Regions* (Oxford: Clarendon Press), pp. 1–22.

Keating, M., 1997, 'The Political Economy of Regionalism', in M. Keating and J. Loughlin (eds), *The Political Economy of Regionalism* (London: Frank Cass), pp. 19–43.

Keating, M., 1998, 'What's Wrong with Asymmetrical Government?', *Regional and Federal Studies*, 8, 1, pp. 195–218.

Keating, M., and J. Loughlin, 1997, 'Introduction', in M. Keating and J. Loughlin (eds), *The Political Economy of Regionalism* (London: Frank Cass), pp. 5–17.

Keating, M., A. Midwinter and J. Mitchell, 1991, *Politics and Public Policy in Scotland* (London: Macmillan).

Keller, B. and F. Henneberger, 1993, 'Beschäftigung und Arbeits-beziehungen im öffentlichen Dienst der neuen Bündesländer', in W. Seibel et al., *Verwaltungsreform und Verwaltungspolitik im Prozeszelt der deutschen Einigung* (Baden-Baden: Nomos Verlagsgesellschaft, 1993), pp. 177–207.

Kilian, M., 1997, *Staatsziele in den Verfassungen der neuen Bundesländer* (Magdeburg: Landeszentrale für Politische Bildung des Landes Sachsen-Anhalt).

Kleinknecht, T., K. Meyer and L. Meyer-Großner, 1991, *Strafprozeßordnung*, Beck'sche Kurz-Kommentare, Vol. 6, 40th edn (München: C. H. Beck'sche Verlagsbuchhandlung).

Knodt, M., 1998, *Tiefenwirkung Europäischer Politik* (Baden-Baden: Nomos Verlagsgesellschaft).

Knodt, M., 1998a, 'Methodik der Erhebung', in B. Kohler Koch u.a., *Interaktive Politik in Europa: Regionen im Netzwerk der Integration* (Opladen: Leske+Budrich), pp. 279–83.

Kohler-Koch, B., 1995, *Regions as Political Actors in the Process of European Integration*, Mannheim Centre for European Social Research Working Paper AB III/No. 9 (Mannheim: MZES).

Kohler-Koch, B., 1996, 'Regionen als Handlungseinheiten in der europäischen Politik', *WeltTrends*, 11, pp. 7–35.

Kohler-Koch, B., 1997, *The European Union Facing Enlargement: Still a System sui generis?*, Mannheim Centre for European Social Research Working Paper AB III/No. 20 (Mannheim: MZES).

Kohler-Koch, B., 1998, 'Europäisierung der Regionen: Institutioneller Wandel als sozialer Prozeß', in B. Kohler Koch u.a., *Interaktive Politik in Europa: Regionen im Netzwerk der Integration* (Opladen: Leske+Budrich), pp. 13–31.

Kohler-Koch, B. u.a., 1998, *Interaktive Politik in Europa: Regionen im Netzwerk der Integration* (Opladen: Leske+Budrich).

Kommision der Europäischen Gemeinschaften (eds), 1991, *Gemeinschaftliches Förderkonzept 1991– 1993 für die Gebiete Ost-Berlin, Mecklenburg-Vorpommern, Brandenburg, Sachsen-Anhalt, Thüringen und Sachsen – Bundesrepublik Deutschland*, Kat.-Nr. CM 70–91–411–DE–C (Luxemburg: Amt für Amtliche Veröffentlichungen).

Krämer, R., 1995, *Im Netzwerk der Integration: Brandenburg und seine auswärtigen Beziehungen* (Potsdam: Brandenburgische Landeszentrale für Politische Bildung).

Krehl, C., 1996, 'VW-Subventionen – Sachsen Kontra Europa?', *Sachsen-Euro-Info*, September 1996, p. 1.

Krehl, C. and A. Freytag, 1996, 'Föderdermöglichkeiten der Europäischen Union', *Thema Europa* [Journal of the SPD's MEPs], May 1996, pp. 5–34.

Kurth, J., 1997, 'Droht der Absturz Ost?', *Stern*, 29/97, pp. 114–16.

Lane, J. E., 1987, 'Introduction: The Concept of Bureaucracy', in J. E. Lane (ed.), *Bureaucracy and Public Choice* (London: Sage), pp. 1–31.

Lange, N., 1998, *Zwischen Regionalismus und Europäischer Integration: Wirtschaftsinteressen in regionalistischen Konflikten* (Baden-Baden: Nomos Verlagsgesellschaft).

Leicht, R., 1995, 'Eine Partei, deren Zeit vorüber ist', *Die Zeit* (2 May 95), p. 1.

Leipzig Business News (LBN), 1998, 'A Vision Becomes Reality: Leipzig on the way to becoming a Media Centre, *LBN*, 3/1998, pp. 1–3

Leipziger Volkszeitung (LVZ), (eds, 1998), 'Parteien im Osten offen für frühere SED-Mitglieder', LVZ, 14 October, p. 2

Lorenz, S. and K. Wegrich, 1998, 'Lokale Ebene im Umbruch: Aufbau und Modernisierung der Kommunalverwaltung in Ostdeutschland', *Aus Politik und Zeitgeschichte*, B 5/98 (23 January), pp. 29–38.

Loughlin, J., 1994, 'Nation, State and Region in Western Europe', in L. Bekemans (ed.), *Culture: Building Stone for Europe 2002. Reflections and Perspectives* (Brussels: European Interuniversity Press), pp. 229–47.

Loughlin, J., 1996, ' "Europe of the Regions" and the Federalization of Europe', *Publius: The Journal of Federalism*, 26, 2, pp. 141–62.

Loughlin, J., 1996a, 'Nationalism, Regionalisation and Regionalism in Ireland', in G. Färber and M. Forsyth (eds), *The Regions – Factors of Integration and Disintegration in Europe?* (Baden-Baden: Nomos Verlagsgesellschaft), pp. 79–90.

Loughlin, J. [with the assistance of J. Mathias], 1997, *Wales in Europe: Welsh Regional Actors and European Integration*, Papers in Planning Research, No. 164 (Cardiff: University of Wales Department of City and Regional Planning).

Loughlin, J., 1998, 'Nations and Regions in the European Union: Recent Paradigm Shifts', Conference Paper, given at the ECPR Standing Group on Regionalism Conference 'Culture, Nation and Region in Europe', Cardiff, 10–12 September 1998.

Loughlin, J., 2000, *Subnational Democracy in the European Union. Challenges and Opportunities* (Oxford: Oxford University Press).

Loughlin, J. and J. Mathias, 1996, 'Mobilisations et coopérations régionales au Royaume-Uni', in R. Balme (ed.), *Les Politiques du Néo-Régionalisme* (Paris: Economica), pp. 169–205.

Loughlin, J. and J. Mathias, 1996a, 'Die Regionale Frage im Vereinigten Königreich: Das Beispiel Wales', *WeltTrends*, 11 (July), pp. 52–68.

Loughlin, J. and B. G. Peters, 1997, 'State Traditions, Administrative Reform and Regionalization', in M. Keating and J. Loughlin (eds), *The Political Economy of Regionalism* (London: Frank Cass), pp. 44–64.

Loughlin, J., J. Mathias, F. Morata, J. Etherington and N. Gómez Matarán, 1998, 'Regionale Mobilisierung in Wales und Katalonien: Eine Vergleichende Analyse', in B. Kohler-Koch (ed.), *Interaktive Politik in Europa: Regionen im Netzwerk der Integration* (Opladen: Leske+Budrich), pp. 182–228.

Loughlin, J., J. Mathias and A. Reilly, 1998a, 'Mobilisation régionale et échange politique aux Pas-de-Galles et dans les West Midlands', in B. Jouve and E. Negrier (eds), *Que gouvernent les régions?* (Paris: L'Harmattan), pp. 135–59.

Lovering, J., 1996, 'New Myths of the Welsh Economy', *Planet*, 116 (April/May), pp. 6–16.

Luyken, R., 1998, 'Wiederbelebung am Hafen', *Die Zeit* (10 June), p. 55.

Lynch, P., 1996, *Minority Nationalism and European Integration* (Cardiff: University of Wales Press).

McAleavey, P., 1994, *The Political Logic of the European Community Structural Funds Budget: Lobbying Efforts by Declining Inustrial Regions*, Robert Schuman Centre Working Papers, May 1994 (Florence: European University Institute).

Majone, G., (ed.), 1990, *Deregulation or Re-regulation? Regulatory Reform in Europe and the United States* (London and New York: Pinter/St Martin's Press).

Majone, G., 1996, 'Regulation and its Modes', in: G. Majone (ed.), *Regulating Europe* (London and New York: Routledge), pp. 9–27.

Marks, G., 1993, 'Structural Policy and Multilevel Governance in the E.C.', in A. G. Cafruny and G. G. Rosenthal (eds), *The State of the European Community*, Vol. 2 (Boulder, CO and London: Longman), pp. 391–410.

Marks, G., 1996, 'An Actor-Centred Approach to Multilevel Governance', *Regional and Federal Studies*, 6, 2, pp. 20–38.

Marx, K., 1987, *Das Kapital. Kritik der Politischen Ökonomie*, Vol. 1, 31st edn, (Berlin: Dietz Verlag).

Mathias, J., 1996, 'Documentation Report: "Wales in Europe" and "Regional Policy"', *Regional and Federal Studies*, 6, 1, pp. 78–80.

Mathias, J., 1998, 'Structural Change, Political Re-alignment and Shifting Identities: the Emergence of Wales and Saxony as Modern Regions in

Europe', in F. Engelstad et al. (eds), *Regional Cultures*, Comparative Social Research Yearbook, Vol. 17 (Stamford, CT and London: JAI Press), pp. 65–103.

Mathias, J., 2000, 'Wales als assoziiertes Mitglied der "Vier Motoren"', in T. Fischer and S. Frech (eds), *Baden-Württemberg und seine Partnerregionen* (Stuttgart: W. Kohlhammer Verlag), pp. 214–38.

Mazey, S., 1996, 'The development of the European idea', in J. Richardson (ed.) *European Union: Power and Policy-Making* (London and New York: Routledge), pp. 27–39.

Michael, A., 1999, 'Our fragile young dragon needs care', *The Welsh Mirror* (23 November) p. 9.

Milward, A., 1992, *The European Rescue of the Nation-State* (London: Routledge).

Mitchell, J., 1997, 'Scotland, the Union State and the International Environment', in M. Keating and J. Loughlin (eds), *The Political Economy of Regionalism* (London: Frank Cass).

Morata, F., 1996, 'Regions in the European Community: A Comparative Analysis of Four Spanish Regions', in R. Leonardi (ed.), *The Regions and the European Community: The Regional Response to the Single Market in Underdeveloped Areas* (London: Frank Cass).

Moravcsik, A., 1991, 'Negotiating the Single European Act: national interests and conventional statecraft in the European Community', *International Organization*, 45, 1, pp. 9–56.

Moravcsik, A., 1993, 'Preferences and Power in the European Community: A Liberal Intergovernmentalist Approach', *Journal of Common Market Studies*, 31, 4, pp. 473–524.

Moravcsik, A., 1995, 'Liberal Intergovernmentalism and Integration: A Rejoinder', *Journal of Common Market Studies*, 33, 4, pp. 611–28.

Morgan, K., 1995, *The Learning Region. Institutions, Innovation and Regional Renewal*, Papers in Planning Research No. 157 (Cardiff: University of Wales Press).

Morgan, K. and E. Roberts, 1993, *The Democratic Deficit: A Guide to Quangoland*, Papers in Planning Research No. 144 (Cardiff: University of Wales Press).

Morgan, K. O., 1971, 'Welsh Nationalism: The Historical Background', *The Journal of Contemporary History*, 6, 1, pp. 153–72.

Morgan, K. O., 1982, *Rebirth of a Nation: Wales 1880–1980* (Oxford: Oxford University Press).

Morris, J. and S. Hill, 1991, *Wales in the 1990s. A European Investment Region*, Special Report No. 2143 (London: The Economist Intelligence Unit).

Morris, J. and B. Wilkinson, 1989, *Divided Wales*, Report commissioned by HTV Wales (Cardiff: University of Wales, Cardiff Business School).

Nagel, K.-J., 1994, 'Das Beispiel Katalonien. Europäische Zusammenarbeit als Bestandteil spanischer Innenpolitik', in U. Bullmann (ed.), *Die Politik der dritten Ebene* (Baden-Baden: Nomos Verlagsgesellschaft).

Negrier, E., 1997, *Territorialized Political Exchange and European Integration*, Paper presented at the 5th Biennial International Conference of the [American] European Community Studies Association, Seattle, WA, 29 May–1 June.

Negrier, E., 1998, 'Que Gouvernent les Régions d'Europe? Échange politique territorialisé et mobilisations régionales', in E. Negrier and B. Jouve (eds), *Que Gouvernent les Régions d'Europe?* (Paris l'Harmattan), pp. 11–31.

Newport Development Board (eds), 1998, *Strategic Themes and Priorities* (Newport: Newport County Borough Council).

Nooke, G., 1998, 'Nation und Identität – 7 Jahre nach dem 3. Oktober 1990', in H.-H. Hertle, et al., *Vom Ende der DDR-Wirtschaft zum Neubeginn in den ostdeutschen Bundesländern* (Hannover: Niedersächsische Landeszentrale für politische Bildung).

Osmond, J., 1989, 'The Modernisation of Wales', in Evans (ed.), *National Identities in the British Isles*, 1989, Coleg Harlech Occasional Papers in Welsh Studies, No. 3 (Harlech: Coleg Harlech).

Osmond, J., 1995, *Welsh Europeans* (Bridgend: seren).

Parliament for Wales Campaign, 1997, *Power to the People of Wales. Government of Wales Bill 1997* [draft proposal] (Cardiff: Parliament for Wales Campaign).

Piehl, E. (ed.), 1995, *Erster "EURO-RUNDER-TISCH" für Sachsen in Dresden am 8.–9. Juni 1995* (Berlin: Europäisches Parlament, Informationsbüro für Deutschland).

Poirier, J., 2001, *The Functions of Intergovernmental Agreements: Post-Devolution Concordats in a Comparative Perspective* (London, The Constitution Unit, University College London).

Price, A., K. Morgan and P. Cooke 1994, *The Welsh Rennaisance: Inward Investment and Industrial Innovation*, Regional Industrial Research Centre for Advanced Studies, Report No. 14 (Cardiff: University of Wales, 1994).

Randlesome, C., 1993, 'The Business Culture in Germany. Part II: East Germany', in C. Randlesome and W. Brierley (eds), *Business Cultures in Europe*, 2nd edn (Oxford: Butterworth-Heinemann, 1993).

Rat und Komission der Europäischen Gemeinschaften (eds), 1992, *Vertrag über die Europäische Union* [Maastricht Treaty] (Luxemburg: Amt für Amtliche Veröffentlichungen).

Regierungspräsidium Chemnitz (ed.), 1995, *Südwestsachsen. Eine Region im Wandel* (Chemnitz: Regierungspräsidium Chemnitz).

Regierungspräsidium Chemnitz (ed.), 1996, *Fördermaßnahmen 1996 im Rahmen der Europäischen Union, der Gemeinschaftsinitiative "Verbesserung der regionalen Wirtschaftsstruktur", [und] der Landesförderung des Freistaates Sachsen* (Chemnitz: Regierungspräsidium Chemnitz).

Regierungspräsidium Chemnitz (ed.), 1997, *made in. Der Regierungsbezirk Chemnitz im Spiegel von Wirtschaft, Architektur und Handel* (Merseburg: Gehrig Verlag).

Rhodes, M. (ed.), 1993, *The Regions and the New Europe* (Manchester: Manchester University Press).

Richardson, J., 1994, 'Doing Less by Doing More: British Government 1979-1993', *West European Politics*, 17, 3, pp. 178–97.

Richardson, J., 1995, 'The Market for Political Activism: Interest Groups as a Challenge To Political Parties', *West European Politics*, 18, 1, pp. 116–39.

Richardson, J., 1996, 'Policy-making in the EU: Interests, ideas and garbage cans of primeval soup', in J. Richardson (ed.), *European Union: Power and Policy-Making* (London and New York: Routledge), pp. 3–23.

Rose, R., 1982, *Understanding the United Kingdom* (London: Longman).

Sächsische Landeszentrale für Politische Bildung (eds), 1999, *Verfassung des Freistaates Sachsen* (Dresden: Sächsische Landeszentrale für Politische Bildung).

Sächsischer Landtag, 1991, 'Polizeigesetz des Freistaates Sachsen', *Sächsisches Gesetz-und Verordnungsblatt*, 20/1991, pp. 291–300.

Sächsischer Landtag, 1993, 'Gemeindeordnung für den Freistaat Sachsen', *Sächsisches Gesetz-und Verordnungsblatt*, 25/1993, pp. 301–56.

Sächsischer Landtag, 1994, 'Gesetz zur Änderung des Polizeigesetzes', *Sächsisches Gesetz-und Verordnungsblatt*, 30/1994, pp. 929–34.

Sächsischer Landtag, 1995, *Position des Sächsischen Landtags zur Regierungskonferenz 1996/97*, Antrag der CDU-Fraktion und Debatte, 2. Legislaturperiode, Drucksache 2/4050 (Dresden: Sächsischer Landtag).

Sächsischer Rechnungshof (ed.), 1997, *Jahresprüfungsbericht 1996*, Dresden: Freistaat Sachsen.

Sächsische Staatskanzlei (ed.), 1998, *Bürgerbuch Sachsen*, Dresden: Freistaat Sachsen.

Sächsisches Staatsministerium für Landwirtschaft, Ernährung und Forsten (ed.), 1994, *Operationelles Programm für die Gemeinschaftsaufgabe LEADER II 1994–1999* (Dresden: Freistaat Sachsen).

Sächsisches Staatsministerium für Soziales, Gesundheit und Familie (ed.), 1995, *Euroregion. Drei Regionen – Ein Thema*, Vol. 3: Soziale Sicherheit, (Dresden: Freistaat Sachsen).

Sächsisches Staatsministerium für Wirtschaft und Arbeit (ed.), 1994, *EFRE-dominiertes Operationelles Programm Sachsen 1994–1999* (Dresden: Freistaat Sachsen).

Sächsisches Staatsministerium für Wirtschaft und Arbeit (ed.), 1994a, *Operationelles Programm für die Gemeinschaftsaufgabe RECHAR II* (Dresden: Freistaat Sachsen).

Sächsisches Staatsministerium für Wirtschaft und Arbeit (ed.), 1995, *Der Europäische Sozialfonds im Freistaat Sachsen* (Dresden: Freistaat Sachsen).

Sächsisches Staatsministerium für Wirtschaft und Arbeit (ed.), 1998, *Förderfibel Sachsen 1998* (Dresden: Freistaat Sachsen).

Sächsischer Verfassungsgerichtshof, 1996, 'Urteil vom 14.5.1996 in der Sache Vf. 44–II–94', *Sächsische Verwaltungsblätter*, 4, 7/8, pp. 160–89.

Sagurna, M. and H. Müller (eds), 1996, *Wie lieb ich Dich, mein Sachsenland*, 2nd edn (Dresden: Sächsische Staatskanzlei).

Sandford, M. and P. McQuail, 2001, *Unexplored Territory: Elected Regional Assemblies in England* (London: The Constitution Unit, University College London).

Sandholz, W., 1994, 'Choosing Union: Monetary Politics and Maastricht', in B. F. Nelsen and A. C.-G. Stubb (eds), *Choosing union: monetary politics and Maastricht* (Houndmills and London: Macmillan), pp. 257–90. Reprinted from *International Organization*, 47, 1, pp. 1–39.

Sandholz, W. and J. Zysman, 1989, '1992: Recasting the European Bargain', *World Politics*, 42, 1, pp. 96–128.

Schmeitzner, M., 1997, 'Georg Gnadauer und die Begründung des Freistaates Sachsen 1918–1920', in R. Aurig, S. Herzog and S. Lässig (eds), *Landesgeschichte in Sachsen: Tradition und Innovation* (Dresden: Sächsische Landeszentrale für Politische Bildung).

Schröder, G., 1998, *Regierungserklärung vom 10. November 1998* (Berlin: BDA, 1998).

Schumpeter, J. A., 1970, *Capitalism, Socialism and Democracy*, 4th edn (London: Unwin University Books).

Schwaiger, P., 1997, 'The European Union's Committee of the Regions: A Progress Report', *Regional and Federal Studies*, 7, 1, pp. 11–22.

Scottish Office, 1997, *Scotland's Parliament*, Cmnd 3658 (London: HMSO).

Seibel, W., 1993, 'Lernen unter Unsicherheit. Hypothesen zur Entwicklung der Treuhandanstalt und der Staat-Wirtschaft-Beziehungen in den neuen Bundesländern', in W. Seibel, A. Benz and H. Mäding, *Verwaltungsreform und Verwaltungspolitik im Prozeß der deutschen Einigung* (Baden-Baden: Nomos Verlagsgesellschaft), pp. 359–70.

Seibel, W., 1993a, 'Zur Situation der öffentlichen Verwaltung in den neuen Bundesländern. Ein vorläufiges Resümee', in W. Seibel, *Verwaltungsreform und Verwaltungspolitik im Prozeszess der deutschen Einigung* (Baden-Baden: Nomos Verlagsgesellschaft) pp. 474–98.

Statistisches Landesamt des Freistaates Sachsen (SLA), 1997, Statistisches

Jahrbuch Sachsen, Vol. 6 (Kamenz: Statistisches Landesamt des Freistaates Sachsen).

Statistisches Landesamt des Freistaates Sachsen (SLA), 2000, *Statistiches Jahrbuch Sachsen*, Vol. 9 (2000), Kamenz: Satistiches Landesamt des Freistaates Sachsen.

Stolz, K., 1997, *Schottland in der Europäischen Union. Integration und Autonomie einer staatenlosen Nation* (Bochum: Brockmeyer).

Sturm, R., 1998, 'Multi-level Politics of Regional Development in Germany', *European Planning Studies*, 6, 5, pp. 525–36.

Thomas, D., 1987, 'United Kingdom', in H. Clout (ed.), *Regional Development in Western Europe*, 3rd edn (London: David Fulton Publishers), pp. 241–64.

Thompson, M. R., 1999, 'Die "Wende" in der DDR als demokratische Revolution', *Aus Politik und Zeitgeschichte*, B 45/99 (5 November, pp. 15–23).

Tocqueville, A. de, 1990, *Über die Demokratie in Amerika* (Stuttgart: Reclam).

Tooze, H. and C. Nativel, 1998, 'The significance of the region in East German restructuring', Conference Paper, Conference on East Germany: Continuity and Change 1945–1998, University of Birmingham Institute of German Studies, 9 May.

Trömmel, I., 1992, 'System-Entwicklung und Politikgestaltung in der Europäischen Gemeinschaft am Beispiel der Regionalpolitik', *Politische Vierteljahresschrift*, 33, 23, pp. 185–208.

Voigt, R., 1998, 'Ende der Innenpolitik? Politik und Recht im Zeichen der Globalisierung', *Aus Politik und Zeitgeschichte*, B 29–30/98 (10 July), pp. 3–8.

Wales European Centre (eds), 1994, *Wales in Europe* (Brussels: Wales European Centre).

Wales Labour Party (eds), 1994, *Wales and Europe: Setting the Democratic Agenda* (Pontypridd: Wales Labour Party).

Weir, S. and W. Hall, 1995, *Behind Closed Doors: Advisory Quangos in the Corridors of Power* (London and Colchester: Channel 4 Television and University of Essex Human Rights Centre).

Welsh Development Agency (eds), 1993, *Urban Development Wales 1993–94 Programme* (Cardiff: WDA).

Welsh Development Agency (eds), 1994, *Report and Accounts 1993–94* (Cardiff: WDA).

Welsh Development Agency (eds), 1995, *Working for Wales* (Cardiff: WDA).

Welsh Development Agency (eds), 1996, *EUROLINK: A fast track into Europe*, Information Pack prepared for the Wales European Business Fair 1996 (Cardiff: WDA).

Welsh Local Government Association (eds), 1996, *A New Opportunity for Wales* (Cardiff: WLGA).

Welsh Office, 1992, *Industrial South Wales Operational Programme 1991–92, Objective 2 Area* (London: HMSO).

Welsh Office, 1993, *Local Government in Wales – A Charter for the Future,* Cmnd 2155 (London: HMSO).

Welsh Office, 1994, *Digest of Welsh Statistics* (Cardiff: Welsh Office).

Welsh Office, 1994a, *The Government's Expenditure Plans 1994–95 to 1996–97,* Cmnd 2515 (London: HMSO).

Weyand, S., 1996, 'Inter-Regional Associations and the European Integration Process', *Regional and Federal Studies,* 6, 2, pp. 166–82.

Wild, T., 1992, 'From Division to Unification: Regional Dimensions of Economic Change in Germany', *Geography,* 77, Pt. 2, pp. 244–60.

Williams, C. H., 1994, 'Development, Dependency and the Democratic Deficit', *Journal of Multilingual and Multicultural Development,* 15, 2 & 3, pp. 101–12.

Williams, C. H., 1995, 'Questions Concerning the Development of Bilingual Wales', in B. M. Jones and P. A. S. Ghuman (eds), *Bilingualism, Education and Identity* (Cardiff: University of Wales Press), pp. 47–78.

Wilson, W., 1908, *Constitutional Government in the United States* (New York), quoted from A. M. Schlesinger, *The Imperial Presidency* (Boston: Houghton Mifflin, 1989), pp. viii and 501.

Wincott, D., 1995, 'Institutional Interaction and European Integration: Towards an Everyday Critique of Liberal Intergovernmentalism', *Journal of Common Market Studies,* 33, 4, pp. 597–609.

Winkler, V., 1999, *Brief an alle sächsischen Haushalte* (Dresden: Initiative 'Sachsen für Sachsen').

Wollmann, H., 1998, 'Um- und Neubau der politischen und administrativen Landesstrukturen in Ostdeutschland', *Aus Politik und Zreitgeschichte,* B 5/98 (23 January), pp. 18–28.

Yuill, D., K. Allen, B. Bachtler, K. Clement and F. Wishlade 1994, *European Regional Incentives,* 14th edn (London, Melbourne, Munich: Bowker Saur).

Young, H., 1989, *One of Us* (Houndmills and London: Macmillan).

Index

Please note that references to footnotes are denoted by the letter 'n' and number of note appearing after the page number.
References to figures or tables are in italic print.

Aberconwy, *55*
Aberconwy and Colwyn, *55*
ABM (*Arbeitsbeschaffungsmaßnahmen*), 129
actors *see* regional actors
Acts of Union (1536 and 1548), 30
ADC (Association of District Councils), 92
AEBR (Association of European Border Regions), 93
AER (Assembly of European Regions), 93, 139
A55, 38
Agriculture, Food and Forestry, State Ministry for, 45, 101
Alyn and Deeside, *55*
AMD, 45, 119
Amsterdam, Treaty of, 8, 136
Andalusia, 164, *164, 165, 166, 167, 168*
Anderson, J.J., 47
Angleichung der Lebensverhältnisse, 6
Angles, 34
Anglesey, 38, 43, *55*, 127
Anglicans, 76n5
A9 motorway, 45
Arbeitsbeschaffungsmaßnahmen (ABM), 129
Arbeitsgruppe Europa, 105
Arbeitslosenverband, 69
Arfon, *55*
Ashdown, Paddy, 63
Assembly of European Regions (AER), 93, 129
Association of British Chambers of Commerce, 60
Association of District Councils (ADC), 92
Association of European Border Regions (AEBR), 93
Association of European Regions of Industrial Technology (RETI), 93

Association of Welsh Counties (AWC), 88, 92, 93, 94, 126
ATLAS agreement, 128
Aufbauwerk in Sachsen, 129
Austria, 8
AWC (Association of Welsh Counties), 88, 92, 93, 94, 126

Baden-Württemberg, 22, 42, 91, 97, 128, 137, 142, 160, 164, *164, 165, 166, 167, 168*
Bank of Scotland, 39
Bank of Wales, 39
Barcelona, xv
Basque Country, 142
Bavaria, 65, 97, 103, 149
Belgium, 118, 145
Benefits Agency, 115–16
Benz, Arthur, 96, 99
Berlin, East, 102, *102*
'Best Value' slogan, 122
Bezirke, 34, 96
BGB (*Bürgerliches Gesetzbuch*), 67
Biedenkopf, Kurt, 97, 103, 104, 107, 109n30 and n31, 120, 132, 151, 156, 160–61n16;
government, 99, 129, 155
Bismarck, Otto von, 34
Blaenau Gwent, 43, *55*
Blair, Tony, 54, 62, 106; government, 89–90, 122
Bonn, 47, 102
Brandenburg, 35, 71, *102*, 160n13
Brecknock, *55*
Brecon Beacons, 38
Bremen, 53
BRIDGE, 41
Bridgend, *55*
Britain *see* UK/Britain
BRITE/EURAM, 41
British Exporters Association, 60

bruno banani Underwear GmbH, 132
Brussels, 6, 54, 58, 93, 102, 103, 104, 137, 138
Bundesgerichtshof (Federal Supreme Court), 45
Bundesrat, 65, 103–4
Bundestag, 51, 65
Bundesverwaltungsgericht (Federal Administration Court), 45
'*Bündnis für Arbeit*', 106
Bündis 90 *see* Greens
Bürgerliches Gesetzbuch (BGB), 67
Business Services Division (of Welsh Office), 87

Cabinet, 52, 54, 89, 114; Committee on Constitutional Reform, 63
Cabinet Office *see Staatskanzlei*
Caernarfonshire and Merionethshire, *55*
Caerphilly, 43, *55*, 155
Canada, 17
Cardiff, 32, 37, 40, 43, 51, *55*, 56, 58, 60, 155; University of Wales, xv, 163
Cardiff Bay Development Corporation, 59, 88
Cardiganshire, *55*
Carmarthen, *55*
Carmarthenshire, *55*
Catalonia, 8, 22, 25, 42, 91, 137, 142, 164, *164*, *165*, *166*, *167*, *168*
CBI/CBI Wales (Confederation of British Industry), 32, 60, 115, *124*, 125, 126, 154
CCT (compulsory competitive tendering), 40, 56, 59, 121–3
CDU (*Christlich-Demokratische Union*), 69, 70, *70*, 72, 97, 98, 103, 104, 105, 106, 129, 148
CEDRE (European Centre for Regional Development), 93
Ceredigion, *55*
Chapman, L., 19
Chemnitz, 34, 44, 45, 66, 70, 76n10, 99, 131, 152
Chepstow, 37
Child Support Agency, 115
Christian Democrats *see* CDU
Christianity, 30
Christiansen, Thomas, 14
Christlich-Demokratische Union see CDU
Church of England, 76n5

City Council (*Stadtverordnetenversammlung*), 67
Clwyd, 38, *55*, *169*, *170*
Cold War, 43
Colwyn, *55*
COMECON, 118, 130
Committee of the Regions of the European Union *see* CoR
Commons, House of *see* House of Commons; House of Commons Select Committee on Welsh Affairs
Comptroller and Auditor General, 58
compulsory competitive tendering *see* CCT
Confederation of British Industry *see* CBI/CBI Wales
Conference of Peripheral Maritime Regions (CPMR), 93, 139
Congress, 4
Conservatives/Tories, 33, 40, 52, 54, 56, 57, *62*, 62, 63, 64–5, 82, 87, 91, 92, 93, 94, 95, 112, 113, 114, 116, 122, 154, 156
control, 111–21
co-operation and mobilization, 121–33
CoR (Committee of the Regions of the European Union), 1, 6, 7, 8, 54, 94–5, 137, 138, 139
Council of Ministers, 3, 7, 54, 64, 86, 87, 89, 138, 144
Council Tax, 122, 134n3
CPMR (Conference of Peripheral Maritime Regions), 93, 139
Cram, Laura, 3, 15, 136–7
CSU, 97, 103
Cynon Valley, *55*
Czech Republic, 45, 50, 129, *130*; border, 45

David, Wayne, 88, 92
Davies, Ron, 89–90
DBRW (Development Board for Rural Wales), 52, 59, 88, 94, 115, *124*
Defence, Ministry of (UK), 43, 52
Delyn, *55*
Demokratische Bauernpartei Deutschlands (DPI), 69
Denbighshire, *55*
Department of Trade and Industry (DTI), 41, 52, 89, *124*, 125; Export Organisation, 60

Deutsche Bahn AG, 50
development *see* regional development
Development Board for Rural Wales
  see DBRW
Dinefwr, *55*
district government offices *see*
  Regierungspräsidien
district legislative assemblies *see*
  Kreistage
Domowina, 35, 76n13
DPD (Demokratische Bauernpartei
  Deutschlands), 69
Dresden, 36, 44, 45, 66, 70, 99, 119, 129,
  131, 152; Airport, 45
Druids, 30
DTI *see* Department of Trade and
  Industry
Dwyfor, *55*
Dyfed, *55*, 93, *169*, *170*

EAGGF (European Agricultural
  Guidance and Guarantee Fund), *49*,
  101, 102, *102*, 133
East Berlin, 102, *102*
east/East Germany, 6, 35, 36, 44, 47,
  48, 50, 67, 68, 69, 71, 73, 74, 80, 97,
  98, 99, 102, 103, 104, 106–7, 118, 119,
  128, 140, 147, 148, 152
EC, 82
economic and social features, 37–51
Economic Development Committee (of
  Welsh Assembly), 125
Economic Development Secretary, 125;
  Rhodri Morgan as, 144
Economics and Employment, State
  Ministry for *see* State Ministry for
  Economics and Employment
EEC (European Economic
  Community), 4, 6
Eggert, Heinz, 99
Einigungsvertrag see Treaties: German
  Unification
Eißel, Dieter, 139
Eisteddfods, 31
Elbsandsteingebirge, 129
Electors, 34
Emilia-Romagna, 142
England, 18, 31, 51, 94; south-east,
  160
EP (European Parliament), 3, 11, 63,
  78n52; Members of (MEPs), 51, 53,
  85, 88, 92, 93, 94, 105, *124*

ERDF (European Research and
  Development Fund), xiv, 1, 6, 40, 48,
  48, *49*, 87, 97, 101, *102*, 115, 120, 127,
  131, 133, 140, 159
Ermisch, 104
Erzgebirge (Ore Mountains), 44–5, 129
ESF (European Social Fund), 41, 48, *49*,
  86, 87, 97, 101, *102*, 115, 120, 127,
  131, 132, 133, 140, 159
ESPRIT, 41
Etherington, John, 163
EU *see* European Union
EUREGIOs, 129
Euro, 120, 133, 136
Euro-constituencies, 53
EUROLINK programme, 91
European Agricultural Guidance and
  Guarantee Fund *see* EAGGF
European Centre for Regional
  Development (CEDRE), 93
European Coal and Steel Community,
  2
European Commission, 104, *124*, *126*,
  144
European Court of Justice, 7
European Division (of Welsh Office), 87
European Economic Community
  (EEC), 4, 6
European Parliament *see* EP
European Research and Development
  Fund *see* ERDF
European Social Charter, 11
European Social Fund *see* ESF
European Union (EU), xiii–xiv, xv, 38,
  40, 42, 44, 46, 48, 51, 54, 56, 85, 86,
  87, 89, 90, 91, 92, 93, 94, 101, 102,
  103, 104, 105, 106, 107, 111, 114–15,
  120, 127, 128, 130, 133, 136, 137, 138,
  139, 140, 142, 144, 146, 147, 149, 150,
  151, 152, 154, 157, 158,
160; regions and regional development
  in competitive environment of, 1–29;
  see also
REGE; REGE Wales project; names of
  EU groups and funds
'Europe of the Regions' versus
  globalisation, 7–12
Evans, John, 95
Executive Quangos *see*
  quangos/managing bodies

Farmers' Party (DPD), 69

Farmers' Union of Wales (FUW), 61, 154
FDGB (Freier Deutscher Gewerkschaftsbund), 68
FDP (Freie Demokratische Partei), *70*, 70–71
Federal Administration Court (*Bundesverwaltungsgericht*), 45
Federal Cabinet, 106, 107
federal constitution *see* GG (*Grundgesetz*)
Federal Republic of Germany *see* FRG
Federal Supreme Court (*Bundesgerichtshof*), 45
Federation of Small Businesses (FSB), 60
First-Past-the-Post system, 53
First Secretary, 54, 62, 125; Alun Michael as, 90, 146, 154; Rhodri Morgan as, 144
Flint, 38
Flintshire, *55*
Foreign Office, 89
Forestry Commission / Forestry Enterprise, 57
'Four Motors', 86, 91, 93
France, 6, 118, 137
Franks, 34
Freie Demokratische Partei *see* FDP
Freier Deutscher Gewerkschaftsbund (FDGB), 68
Freistaaten (Free States), 65
FRG (Federal Republic of Germany), 65, 69, 76n14, 80, 96, 99, 138, 148 *see also* Germany
FSB (Federation of Small Businesses), 60
FUW (Farmers' Union of Wales), 61, 154

GA *see Gemeinschaftsaufgabe*
Galicia, 142
GDR (German Democratic Republic), 34, 35, 36, 44, 45, 50, 66, 67, 68, 69, 72, 73, 75, 96, 98, 99, 100, 102, 118, 119 *see also* Germany
Gemeinden, 66–7
Gemeinderat (Legislative Council), 66–7
Gemeinschaftliches Förderkonzept, 102, 103
Gemeinschaftsaufgabe (GA), 46–7, 102, 106

Gemeinschaftswerk 'Aufschwung Ost' Joint Initiative 'Boom East'), 47
General Federation of Trade Unions, 61
German, Mike, 146
German Democratic Republic *see* GDR
Germany, 6, 8, 16, 18, 20, 27, 34, 36–7, 38, 44, 46, 47, 50, 53, 54, 68–9, 73, 75, 80, 96, 106–7, 111, 120, 136, 138, 140, 147, 148, 149, 158 *see also* FRG; GDR
GG (*Grundgesetz*) (federal constitution), 65, 73, 79, 80, 148
Glamorgan, 88 *see also* Mid Glamorgan; South Glamorgan; Vale of Glamorgan; West Glamorgan
globalisation, 9–10, 12
Glyndwr, *55*
Gomez-Mataran, Neus, 163
governmental districts *see Regierungsbezirke*
Government of the Free State of Saxony (*Regierung des Freistaates Sachsen*), 65
Greens (Bündnis 90 / Die Grünen), *70*, 72–3
Grote, Jürgen, 163
Grundgesetz (federal constitution) *see* GG
Grünen, Die *see* Greens
Gwent, *55*, 88, 127, *169*, *170*
Gwynedd, 38, *55*, *169*, *170*

Haas, Ernst B., 2, 16
Hague, William, 64, 89, 90, 108n8
Hain, Peter, 90
Halbleiterwerk Dresden, 119
Halle-Merseburg, 71, 105
Handwerkskammern, 68
Health and Safety Executive, 123
Heimat, 34–5, 36, 37, 104, 132
Herefordshire, 31
heritage, regional, 27, 30–37
Holyhead, 38
Honecker administration, 147, 160n7
Hooghe, Lisbet, 12, 14
House of Commons, *94*, *124 see also* House of Commons Select Committee on Welsh Affairs
House of Commons Select Committee on Welsh Affairs, 51; Report (*Wales in Europe*), 85–7, 91
House of Lords, 82, *124*

Hoyerswerda, 35
Hrbek, Rudolf, 14, 89, 137
Hughes, Bill, 115

IGC (Intergovernmental Conference, 1996), 10, 11
infrastructure development, 23–5
Institute of Directors, 60
Institute of Export, 60
Institute of Management, 60
integration, theories of, 1–15
Intergovernmental Conference (IGC, 1996), 10, 11
intergovernmentalism, 2, 3–5, 5–6, 7
International Division (of WDA), 87
interviews, 191–5
Ireland, 18, 30; Northern, 31, 51, 143, 145; Republic of, 145, 160n3
Iron Curtain, 35
Islwyn, *55*
Italy, 6, 118, 137

Jeffery, Charlie, 14
Jessop, Bob, 114, 118, 120
Jobseekers' Allowance, 115
Joint Initiative 'Boom East' (*Gemeinschaftswerk 'Aufschwung Ost'*), 47
Jouve, Bernard, 163

Kanzlerrunde, 47, 106
Keating, Michael, 16, 17, 23, 142
Kilian, Michael, 80
Kinnock, Glennys, 92
Kinnock, Neil, 51, 92
Knauer, Chief Whip, 71
Knights of Malta Ambulance Service, 69
Knodt, Michèle, 128, 142, 163
Kohl, Chancellor Helmut, 50, 106, 109n30, 118, 133, 148, 160n1
Kohler-Koch, Beate, xv, 14, 163
KPD (*Kommunistische Partei Deutschlands*), 71
Krehl, Konstanze, 105
Kreistage (district legislative assemblies), 66, 67

Labour Party, 32, 33, 52, 53, 54, 61–2, *62*, 63, 64, 65, 74, 76n4, 82, 85, 90, 92–3, 94–5, 108n7, 112, 114, 115, 122, 126, 127, 128, 134n3, 154, 155
Land Authority for Wales, 52, 59, 115

Länder, 6, 8, 16, 18, 36, 46, 47, 48, 53, 65, 71, 73, 74, 76n14, 80, 96–7, 97–8, 99, 100, 102, *102*, 103, 105, 106, 107, 118, 119, 120, 128, 138, 148, 155, 160n13
Ländereinführungsgesetz (*Länder* Re-establishment Act, 1990), 34, 96
Länderfinanzausgleich, 6, 97, 106
Landkreise, 66, 67
Landrat, 66, 67
Landratsamt (Local Government District Office), 66
Landtag (Regional Parliament), 51, 53, 65, 72, 73, 98, 103, 104, 105, 106, 156
Lane, Jan-Erik, 19
Lang, Ian, 134n5
Larat, Fabrice, 163
Lausitz, 50
LEADER, 48
Legislative Council (*Gemeinderat*), 66–7
Leipzig, 34, 44, 45–6, 66, 71, 72, 73, 99, 102, 105, 131, 147, 152, 161n17
LG, 127
Liberal Democratic Party/Liberals, *62*, 62–3, 64
Liberal-Demokratische Partei Deutschlands (LPDP), 70
liberal intergovernmentalism, 2, 3–5, 5–6, 7
Liberals: Germany, 70–71; UK, *62*, 62–3, 64
LINK, 41
Liverpool, 75
Llanelli, *55*
Lliw Valley, *55*
Local Development Agencies, 59
Local Government District Office (*Landsratsamt*), 66
Local Government Reform (1968/69), 33
Local Government Self-Administration Act (1990), 96
Local Government (Wales) Act (1993), 56
Lombardy, 91, 142, 164, *164*, *165*, *166*, *167*, *168*
London, 33, 48, 52, 64, 122, 154
Longuedoc-Rousillon, 164, *164*, *165*, *166*, *167*, *168*
Lords, House of, 82, *124*
Loughlin, John, xiv, 5, 16, 163, 164
Lower Saxony, 34, 142, 164, *164*, *165*, *166*, *167*, *168*

LPDP (Liberal-Demokratische Partei Deutschlands), 70
Ludlow, 30
Lynch, Peter, 8
Lyon, xv

Maastricht, Treaty of, 136
Majone, Giaccomo, 112
Major, John, 90, 112, 113, 134n5; government, 116, 121
managing bodies/quangos, 58–61, 114–17 *see also* names of agencies
Manchester, 75
Mannheim Centre for European Social Research, University of Mannheim, xv, 163
Mantel der Geschichte, 148
Marches, the, 31
Marks, Gary, 12, 13, 14, 79, 145
Marx, Karl, 10
Mathias, Jörg, 164
Mayor, 67
MdBs (*Mitglied des Bundestags*), 65
Mecklenburg-West Pomerania, 71–2, 98, *102*
Meirionydd, *55*
Members of the European Parliament (MEPs), 51, 53, 85, 88, 92, 93, 94, 105, *124*
Members of Parliament (MPs), 51, 94, *124*
Merseyside, 38
Merthyr Tydfil, 43, *55*, 94
M4 motorway, 37
Michael, Alun, 90, 146, 154
Mid Glamorgan, *55*, 88, 94, *169*, *170*
Milan Chamber of Commerce, 91
Milford Haven, 43
Milton Keynes, 6
Ministerium für Staatssicherheit (GDR Secret Service), 98
Ministry for Agriculture, Food and Forestry *see* State Ministry for Agriculture, Food and Forestry
Ministry of Defence (UK), 43, 52
Ministry for Economics and Employment *see* State Ministry for Economics and Employment
Mitglied des Bundestags (MdBs), 65
Mittelständische Beteiligungsgesellschaft Sachsen mbH, 131
Mittelstandsförderungsprogramm, 131, 132

MLG (multi-level governance), 12–15, 18, 83, 149
mobilization, 121–33
Monmouth, *55*
Monmouthshire, *55*
Monopolies and Mergers Commission, 57
Montgomeryshire, *55*
Montpellier, xv
Morata, Francesc, 163
Moravcsik, Andrew, 4
Morgan, K. O., 33
Morgan, Rhodri, 144, 146
Mosel, 105
MPs (Members of Parliament), 51, 94, *124*
multi-level governance (MLG), 12–15, 18, 83, 149

National Assembly for Wales (NAW), 20, 32, 33, 42, 44, 52–3, 54–5, 62, 63, 64, 65, 74, 75, 78n52, 82, 84, 88–9, 90, 92, 93, 95, 103, 125, 128, 144, 146, 152, 153–4, 157–8
National Audit Commission, 114
National Audit Office, 52, 58
National-Demokratische Partei Deutschlands (NDPD), 70
National Farmers' Union (NFU), 61, 154
National Health Service (NHS), 59; Trusts, 115
National Parks, 38
NAW *see* National Assembly for Wales
Nazi regime, 71
Neath, *55*
Neath and Port Talbot, *55*
Négrier, Emmanuel, 111, 128, 142, 163
neofunctionalism, 2–3, 5, 6–7
'Neo-Liberal Accumulation strategy', 114
Neues Forum (NF), 73, 99–100
Newport, 32, 37, 43, *55*; County Borough Council, 88
Newport & Gwent chamber of commerce, 60
Newport Development Board, 88
NF (Neues Forum), 73, 99–100
NFU (National Farmers' Union), 61, 154
NHS (National Health Service), 59; Trusts, 115

Nooke, Günter, 50
Northern Ireland, 31, 51, 143, 145;
  Assembly, 53
North Wales Chamber of Commerce,
  60
NPDP (National-Demokratische Partei
  Deutschlands), 70

Objective 1, 40, 43, 48, 103, 133, 144,
  150, 152, 154, 158
Objective 2, 40, 87, 88, 90, 93, 94, 158;
  Monitoring Committee, 92
Objective 5b, 40, 158
Office of Fair Trading, 57
Offices of Economic Development, 49
Ogwr, *55*
Operational Programme, 48, 131, 150
Ore Mountains *see Erzgebirge*
organisational structure, 51–73

Parliament, 51, 52, 54, 81–2, 114 *see also*
  Westminster
Partei des Demokratischen
  Sozialismus *see* PDS
Partnership Council, 92
Party of Wales *see* Plaid Cymru/Party
  of Wales
PDS (Partei des Demokratischen
  Sozialismus), 51, *70*, 72, 73, 98, 105,
  132, 149, 161n20
Pembroke, 39, 43
Pembrokeshire, 38, *55*, 64; Preseli, *55*;
  South, *55*, 56
'Perlenkette entlang der Neiße', 50
PFIs (private financing initiatives), 127
Plaid Cymru/Party of Wales, 32, 33,
  53, *62*, 62, 63–4, 65, 76n9, 78n52, 94,
  95, 108n7,
  127, 144, 145, 146, 151, 154, 155, 157,
  161n20
Poland, 34, 35, 50, 129, *130*; border, 45,
  66, 152
Port Talbot, *55*
'Powerhouse Parliament' campaign,
  63, 146
Powys, *55*, 155, *169*, *170*; Kingdom of,
  30–31, 76n2
Prague, 129
Preseli Pembrokeshire, *55*
private financing initiatives (PFIs),
  127
problem recognition, 22–3

Projektträger Technologieförderung, 131
Public Accounts Committee, 58, 114
public-private interactions, 110–35

qualitative infrastructure
  development, 24–5
quality of life enhancement, 25
'Quangoland Wales', 74, 114
quangos/managing bodies, 58–61,
  114–17 *see also* names of agencies
quantitative infrastructure
  development, 23–4

Radnorshire, *55*
RECHAR, 48
Rechsstaat, 48
Red Cross, 68
Redwood, John, 64, 89, 90, 108n8
REGE (*Regionales Regieren in Europa*),
  xv, 18, 163–8 *see also* REGE Wales
  project
REGE Wales project (Regional
  Development and its European
  Dimension in Wales
project), xiv–xv, 83–5, 87, 89, 90–91, 92,
  93–4, 95, *124*, 124–5, *126*, 126,
  163–90, 191
Regierung des Freistaates Sachsen
  (Government of the Free State of
  Saxony), 65
Regierungsbezirke (governmental
  districts), 23, 49, 65–6, 156
Regierungserklärung, 106
Regierungspräsidenten, 66
Regierungspräsidien (district
  government offices), 45, 49, 66,
  99–100, 101, 131
region, definition of, 16–18
regional actors: concluding discussion
  about, 136–41; definition of, 18–20;
  and MLG, 13–14; organisational
  structure, 51–73, 73–4; public actors
  in regional development, 79–109
regional development: chances and
  constraints, 149–59; in competitive
  environment of
EU, 1–29; model of, 22–6; and public
  actors, 79–109; research project *see*
  REGE Wales project
Regional Development Agencies, 59
Regional Development and its
  European Dimension in Wales

research project *see* REGE Wales
    project
Regionales Regieren in Europa (REGE),
    xv, 18, 163–8 *see also* REGE Wales
    project
regional heritage, 27, 30–37
regional mobilization, 121–33
Regional Parliament *see Landtag*
Regional Technology Plan (RTP), 24,
    105
regulatory bodies, 57–8
Republic of Ireland, 145, 160n3
RETI (Association of European
    Regions of Industrial Technology),
    93
Rhondda, *55*, 56
Rhondda-Cynon-Taff, 43, *55*, 94, 155
Rhône-Alpes, 86, 91, 142, 164, *164*, *165*,
    166, *167*, *168*
Rhuddlan, *55*
Rhymney Valley, *55*
Richardson, Jeremy J., 3, 14, 15, 136–7
Rifkind, Malcolm, 115, 134n5
Romania, 34
Romans, 30
Rome, Treaties of, 11
'Round Tables', 147–8
Royal Air Force, 38
RTP (Regional Technology Plan), 24,
    105
Russia, 118, 130, *130*

Sachsen für Sachsen (Saxons for
    Saxony) initiative, 132
Sächsische Gemeindeordnung (Saxon
    Local Government Charter), 66
Sächsischer Rechnungshof (Saxon Audit
    Commission), 50
Sächsischer Verfassungsgerichtshof
    (Saxon Constitutional Court), 99
St David's, See of, 30
St John Ambulance Association, 69
Sandholz, W., 2, 5
Saxon Audit Commission (*Sächsischer
    Rechnungshof*), 50
Saxon Constitution, 65, 79–81, 142
Saxon Constitutional Court (*Sächsischer
    Verfassungsgerichtshof*), 99
Saxon *Landtag* (Regional Parliament),
    51, 65, 72, 98, 103, 104, 105, 106, 156
Saxon Local Government Charter
    (*Sächsische Gemeindeordnung*), 66

'Saxonness', 159
Saxon Police Act, 99
Saxons, 34, 37, 104
Saxons for Saxony (*Sachsen für
    Sachsen*) initiative, 132
Saxony: concluding discussion about,
    137, 138, 140, 142, 143, 147, 148–9,
    149–50, 152, 153, 155–6, 158–9;
    economic and social features, 44–51,
    75; interviews in 191; 193–4;
    organizational structure of regional
    actors, 65–73, 74; public actors and
    regional development, 79–81,
    96–107; public-private interaction,
    117–21, 128–33, 134; regional
    heritage, 34–7; brief mentions, xiv,
    xv, 18, 20, 23, 25, 26, 27, 30
Saxony, Kingdom of, 34
Saxony-Anhalt, 71, 72, 98, *102*, 105
School of European Studies,
    University of Wales, Cardiff, xiv, 163
Schröder, Chancellor, 106
Schumpeter, J.A., 141, 155
Schwanitz, Rolf, 107
Scotland, 22, 30, 31, 39, 51, 56, 61,
    76n4, 82, 94, 114–15, 137, 142, 157
Scottish Development Agency (SDA),
    114
Scottish Enterprise, 114–15
Scottish National Party (SNP), 33, 63,
    76n4, 145
Scottish Office (SO), 115
Scottish Parliament (SP), 53, 63, 82, 157
Scottish Trade International, 115
Scottish Unionists, 54
SDA (Scottish Development Agency),
    114
SEA (Single European Act), 2, 5, 11, 136
Secretary of State for Wales, 52, 54, 64,
    89–90, 94, 115, *124*, 125
SED (Sozialistische Einheitspartei
    Deutschlands), 71, 73, 78n62
Seibel, W., 66
Shropshire, 31
Sicily, 164, *164*, *165*, *166*, *167*, *168*
Single European Act (SEA), 2, 5, 11,
    136
Single Planning Document, 40
Slavic people, 35 *see also* Sorbs
Slovakia, *130*
small and medium-sized enterprises
    see SMEs

SMART, 41
SMEs (small and medium-sized enterprises), 38, 41–2, 45, 46, 114, 131
SMWA *see* State Ministry for Economics and Employment
Snowdonia, 38
SNP (Scottish National Party), 33, 63, 76n4, 145
SO (Scottish Office), 115
social and economic features, 37–51
Social Democrats *see* SDP
Sonderstruktur-programm (*'Perlenkette entlang der Neiße'*), 50
Sorabia, 35, 45
Sorb language, 35
Sorbs, 35, 37, 104, 158
South Glamorgan, *55*, *169*, *170*
South Pembrokeshire, *55*, 56
South Wales Exporters Association, 60, *124*
South Wales Objective 2 area, 93
Soviet Zone of Occupation, 71
Sozialdemokratische Partei Deutschland *see* SPD
Sozialistische Einheitspartei Deutschland *see* SED
SP (Scottish Parliament), 53, 63, 82, 157
Spain, 17, 145
SPD (Sozialdemokratische Partei Deutschlands), *70*, 71–2, 78n61, 98, 104–5, 106, 109n47, 134n11, 148
Special Air Service, 38
Special Select Committee, 57
Spiegel, Der, 104
SPUR, 41
Staatskanzlei (Cabinet Office), 49, 97, 99, 100, 104
Staatsministerium (State Ministry), 49, 65 *see also* State Ministry for Agriculture, Food and Forestry; State Ministry for Economics and Employment
Staatsziele, 79–80, 101, 117, 129, 142, 155
Stadtverordnetenversammlung (City Council), 67
Stalinisation, 71
'Standard Region' system, 18
State Ministry *(Staatsministerium)*, 49, 65 *see also* names of ministries
State Ministry for Agriculture, Food and Forestry, 45, 101

State Ministry for Economics and Employment (SMWA), 101, 119, 128; Technology and Energy Division, 131
STRIDE, 127
Structural Funds, 6, 7, 23, 24, 40, 42, 151
Swansea, 32, 37, *55*

Taff-Ely, *55*
Technology and Energy Division (of SMWA), 131
TECs (Training and Education Councils), 60, *124*
TEU (Treaty on European Union), 1, 2, 6, 8, 15, 94
THA (*Treuhandanstalt*), 67–8, 69, 117, 118, 119–20, 128, 134
Thatcher, Margaret, 32, 90, 112, 113, 115, 124, 140; government, 84, 112, 114, 121; *see also* Thatcherism/Thatcherite policies
Thatcherism/Thatcherite policies, 6, 32, 33, 40, 58, 84, 111, 112, 113, 114
theories of integration, 1–15
Thuringia, 65, *102*
Tocqueville, Alexis de, 9, 10
Torfaen, *55*
Tories *see* Conservatives/Tories
Trade and Industry, Department of *see* Department of Trade and Industry
Trades Union Congress (TUC), 61
Training and Education Councils (TECs), 60, *124*
Transport and General Workers' Union, 61
Treasury, 113, 114
Treaties: Amsterdam, 8, 136; European Union (TEU), 1, 2, 6, 8, 15, 94; German Unification (*Einigungsvertrag*), 67–8, 96–7; Maastricht, 136; Rome, 11
Treuhandanstalt see THA
TUC (Trades Union Congress), 61

UK/Britain, 6, 8, 16, 17, 18, 27, 33, 34, 36, 39, 51, 52, 53, 54, 75, 82, 86, 87, 89, 93, 112–13, 114, 115, 117, 123, *126*, 136, 145, 146–7, 153, 154, 157, 158
Umberti, Santo, 163
Unemployment Benefit, 115
UNISON, 61

United Kingdom *see* UK/Britain
United Nations, 11
United States (US), 4–5, 118, *130*
University: of Mannheim, xv, 163; of
    Wales, xiv, 163

Vale of Glamorgan, *55*
Valleys, the, 32, 37, 42, 63, 88, 94, 128
Valleys Initiative, The, 59
Volkskammer, 34, 35, 76n13, 96
Volkswagen AG, 104–5, 120, 132

Wales: concluding discussion about,
    137, 138, 140, 142, 149, 150, 151–2,
    153–5, 156, 157–8, 159; economic and
    social features, 37–44, 75; interviews
    in, 191, 193; organizational structure
    of regional actors, 51–65, 73–4, 74–5;
    public actors and regional
    development, 81–3, 83–95, 107;
    public–private interaction, 111–17,
    121–8, 133–4; regional heritage,
    30–34; brief mentions, 8, 18, 20, 23,
    25, 26, 27, 36, 103; *see also* REGE
    Wales project
Wales Chamber of Commerce and
    Industry, 60
Wales European Centre (WEC), 54, 58,
    85, 89, 93, *124*
Wales in Europe see House of Commons
    Select Committee on Welsh Affairs:
    Report
Walker, Peter, 115
WDA *see* Welsh Development Agency
WEC *see* Wales European Centre
Weimar Republic, 65, 71
Weir, Stuart, 116
Welsh Assembly (WA) *see* National
    Assembly for Wales (NAW)
Welsh Civil Service, 53, 54
Welsh Conservative Party, 64–5
Welsh Development Agency (WDA),
    42, 52, 58–9, 84, 85, 87, 88, 90, 91–2,
    94, 114, 115,
124, *126*, 126; International Division,
    87
Welsh Economic Council, 126
Welsh European Forum, 126

Welsh Executive, 54, 154
Welsh Labour Action, 53
Welsh Labour Party, 53, 61–2, 85, 146
Welsh language, 33, 75, 76n7
Welsh Language Act (1993), 51, 76n8,
    160n10
Welsh Language Board, 157
Welsh Language in Education Act
    (1991), 51, 76n8
Welsh Liberals/Liberal Democratic
    Party, 63, 94, 146
Welsh Local Government Association
    (WLGA), 88, 92, 93, 94
Welshness, concept of, 157
Welsh Office (WO), 33, 42, 51, 52, 53,
    54, 74, 84, 85, 86, 87, 88, 89, 90–91,
    92, 93, 94, 95, 107, 108n15, 115, 117,
    124, 125, *126*, 133, 138, 154; Business
    Services Division, 87;
    Establishments Group, 59; European
    Division, 87
Welsh Unionists, 54
west/West Germany, 6, 35, 36, 47, 68,
    69, 73, 74, 97, 98, 100, 120 *see also*
    Germany
West Glamorgan, *55*, *169*, *170*
Westminster, 31, 51, 53, 54, *62*, 63,
    81–2, 85, 107, 117, 151, 154
West Wales chamber of commerce, 60
Weyand, Sabine, 14, 89, 137
Whitehall, 18, 52, 86, 112, 117, 121, 138,
    151
Wilson, Harold, 6
Wilson, Woodrow, 5
Wirtschaftsförderung Sachsen GmbH, 131
Wirtschaftswunder (economic miracle),
    36, 97
WLGA (Welsh Local Government
    Association), 88, 92, 93, 94
WO *see* Welsh Office
Worcestershire, 31
Wrexham, *55*, 60
Wrexham Maelor, *55*

Ynys Mon, *55*

Zwickau, 105
Zysman, J., 2